Explore
Good English Grammar
Master the Structure of the Language

Mark Slim

A.D. R.(London) Limited England

18.50

Dedication

In memory of my English language teachers who taught me diligently

ADR's Publishing Motto

'A person who searches for knowledge is a student'

British Library Cataloguing in Publication Data

A catalogue record for this book is available from the British Library

ISBN 190 1197 204 First published by ADR in UK 2004

Warning and Disclaimer

Every effort has been made to make this book as complete and as accurate as possible, but no warranty or fitness is implied. Names of terms, interpretation of rules of grammar and their application is not universally the same. Sometimes there are disagreements. Language and opinions change all the time. The information given in this book is on an "as is" basis. This book is sold, therefore, on the condition that the author and the publisher shall have neither liability nor responsibility to any person or entity with respect to any misunderstanding, consequences of any error or the omission there may be, loss or damages arising from the use of the information contained in this book.

Direct Order

In case of difficulty, you can obtain a copy from the publisher:

A.D.R.(London) Limited
24 St. Alban Road
Bridlington
YO16 7SS
England

Tel: 01262 605538/400323
Fax: 01262 400323
E-Mail: sales@ adrlonodon.ltd.uk
Web Site: http:// www.adrlondon.ltd.uk

Printed in Great Britain

Contents

****

Chapter 4 Verbs(1)

Contents   V

****

Chapter 5 Verbs(2)

Chapter 6 Adjectives

Chapter 7 Adverbs

VI   **Contents**

****

Chapter 8 Prepositions

Chapter 9 Determiners & Interjections

Chapter 10 Conjunctions

Chapter 11 Phrases

Chapter 12 Clauses

****

Chapter 13 Sentences

Chapter 14 Punctuation

Introduction   **1**

****

Introduction

What is grammar? *Grammar* is an umbrella term. In essence, it is concerned with the words of a language and the mechanism, or rules of combining, or joining them together in meaningful phrases, clauses and sentences. It can also mean a person's knowledge and use of a language. For our purpose, the word *rule* means a recognised standard way of constructing structures. Therefore, the rules of grammar are principles for both spoken and written language. Grammar is for anyone who is interested in the English language and wants to master the structure of the language.

Whether you are a native speaker or a student of the English language, you must learn *English grammar* in order:

- to be able to put words into recognised structures, namely phrases, clauses, sentences and paragraphs

- to identify grammatical structures, e.g. sentences, etc.

- to understand the meaning associated with these structures

- to analyse these structures in order to explain them to others, if there is a need for it

- to apply the language with confidence and to enjoy doing so

In this age of the World Wide Web, the use of English is expanding exponentially through the Internet, and the correct use of English and its grammar is becoming increasingly desirable. Boldly speaking, it can be said that you are only as good as your grammar.

The English language is widely used in the world and therefore it has many different forms. I am concerned with the contemporary English in use in Britain. Despite the fact that there are many regional variations, there is *standard English*. Standard English is the form of the language that is nationally

2 **Introduction**

****

used in Britain. It is the medium of communication at the national level. It is used by institutions including educational bodies, text books, newspapers, broadcasting services, government agencies, etc. Standard English is socially accepted as the most correct form of the English language. Speakers of other languages also learn standard English.

The *linguistic* aspects of English grammar are beyond the scope of this book. In passing, the *linguistics* is the scientific study of language. Linguistic is connected with linguistics. A *linguist* studies languages and works in the linguistic field, mainly in the academic world. In this book, uncommon words, such as *discourse* (for combining sentences) and *lexis* (the words of a language) i.e. linguistic terminology used by linguists, are not included.

The *prescriptive method* of grammar explanation is applied in this book. This approach is concerned with prescribing what is correct. It means discussing how the language should be used.

The prime aim of this book is to describe and explain with the aid of numerous helpful examples, those aspects of English which are essential for both written and spoken standard English. The general objective of this book is to enable readers to improve their knowledge and skills in using the language with confidence. If you are an intermediate or advanced learner of English, or anyone interested in the English language, or a teacher of English, you will find this book invaluable. This book is equally suitable as a course text or a self-instruction text.

How to use this book – It is most likely that you have picked up this book from a shelf or acquired it from another source because you are seriously interested in English and striving to master the structure of the language. Your needs may not be the same as those of many equally enthusiastic learners and teachers of the English language. For this reason, it is perceived that not all readers will read this book from the beginning to the end consecutively. This book can also be used for reference purposes. For this purpose, a glossary of terms and a detailed index are provided.

At the end of each chapter, some *exercises* are included and their solutions are given towards the end of the book. It is recommended that self-learners and students work the exercises out for themselves first and then compare them with the solutions provided. In fact, the answers will give you some more new information and this activity will enhance your confidence in applying the language with increased self-reliance and satisfaction.

Chapter 1
Word Classes

• Introduction

A word is a single and independent unit of vocabulary.

It can be recognised in both speech and writing (or print). Many words have several meanings. A recognised word has the following features:

- it has a distinct sound, which can be a combination of sounds

- it has a meaning, i.e. definition

- a written word is recognisable by its structure, i.e. the number of letters in it and the combination pattern

Yes, you can have words consisting of not only alphabetic letters but also other elements such as recognised symbols, e.g. £ sign.

For instance, the word **CHAIR** consists of five alphabetic letters. To speakers of English, it is recognisable as a combination of five letters when arranged in this given order. Therefore, when this word is used in **speech**, a speaker of the English language knows it by its distinct sound. When the same word is written, a reader of the English language identifies it by the pattern of letters put together side by side to structure it.

We know that a chair is a piece of furniture with a seat, a back and four legs. A person can sit on it **(meaning/definition)**. When it is a part of a sentence, we are interested in understanding what role**(function)** it plays in the sentence. You know many such words, and most likely you consider them as the building blocks of the English language. Now consider the following sentence: **She is singing a song.**

This text has spaces between the words which makes it easy to identify and count the words used there. It has five words. Normally, in English writing, there are spaces between words, but there are occasions when word identification as a single independent unit is not so easy. For example, when two or more words make a single unit:

. **newly-married** $\Rightarrow$ compound word $\Rightarrow$ word class $\Rightarrow$**adjective**

For instance, as a compound word:

> . A newly-married couple arrived last night.
> --------------------

used here as an adjective ↵ - before the noun $\Rightarrow$**couple**

. On the other hand, you can also write the above hyphenated
  compound word as two words side by side:

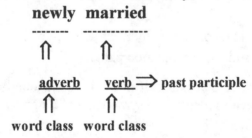

Here, these are two single words side by side and each is clearly placed in its word class. Here is an example:

. **John and Jane are newly married.**

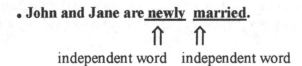

Word Classes   **5**

****

Words in the English language vocabulary are classified in accordance with **word classes** or **parts of speech**. The idea of classification of words is a well-known fact, but some words can be put into more than one class. Sometimes in a phrase or an expression the **lexical meaning** of a word, that is what it means in the English language, is not meant but its **metaphorical** usage, that is an imaginative meaning, is conveyed instead.

For instance, **hold your horses** is an English **idiomatic expression** which is well understood through the common usage over a long period of time. In this expression each word does not render its lexical meaning because the expression means **wait a moment**. This is an imaginative way of asking you to stop or wait for a while. Let's attempt to classify each word in this expression as follows:

<u>**Hold**</u> <u>**your**</u> <u>**horses**</u>.
  ⇑   ⇑   ⇑
  1   **2**   **3**

1 ⇒ verb ⇒ idiomatic use here
2 ⇒ possessive determiner – also called 'possessive adjective'
     it is also considered as: dependent form of the
     possessive pronoun
3 ⇒ noun - idiomatic use here

In this idiomatic expression, words cannot be readily classified because each word does not render its true lexical meaning. Indeed, in isolation you can recognise these words and place each of them in its appropriate part of speech. These examples illustrate that it is vitally important to comprehend word classes in order to understand and appreciate the use and role play by words in correct writing and speaking the English language.

. <u>Word classes</u>

In this book word classes are divided into **major** and **minor** classes. These are shown in Diagram 1.

. <u>Word classes at first glance</u>

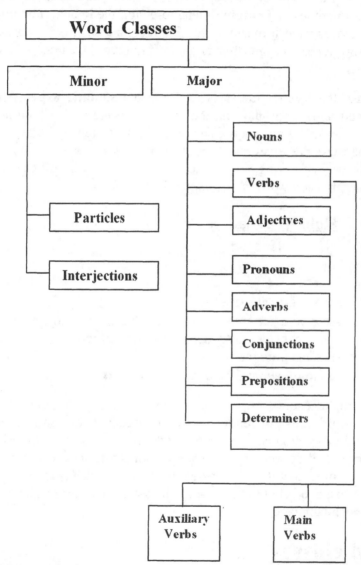

<u>Diagram 1</u>

You may find that word classes or parts of speech are not always discussed under these classes. Some books may classify words into eight
classes and some other books may have more than eight parts of
speech. It is a matter of preference. If you come across some other
ways of classifying words, you have to decide for yourself which classification appeals to you most for your specific requirements. Word
classes and parts of speech mean the same and thus I have used these
terms interchangeably.

Among the major word classes, pronouns are somewhat a source of
confusion when placing some words in this class. Both minor classes
are comparatively much smaller classes. These are outlined now.

.Particles class

Many writers do not discuss particles class as a word class in its own
right, because there are a few words in it. Particles are used with verbs
to make phrasal verbs (e.g., multi-word verb). For instance:

   . Andrew look out! A motorcycle is coming fast.

                         look out $\Rightarrow$ phrasal verb

   . He tore up the contract.   **tore up $\Rightarrow$ phrasal verb**

   . She fell off the stairs in a shop.   **fell off $\Rightarrow$ phrasal verb**

   . Our washing machine broke down. **broke down $\Rightarrow$ phrasal verb**

In these sentences, **out, up, off** and **down** are particles. In fact, **out,
up, off** and **down** words can be placed in more than one class. However, when you use them with verbs to make phrasal verbs such as
look out, tear up, fall off and **break down**, they are classed as adverbial particles or just particles (for the sake of simplicity). The negative
particle is **not**. The word **to** is a also particle. It is used to make the infinitive verb. See $\Rightarrow$Phrasal Verbs in Chapter 4.
For instance:

8

Word Classes

****

- **Richard asked Rebecca to marry him.**
  ----

  to infinitive form of the verb⤶ - see verb

. <u>Interjections class</u>

These are exclamations. Interjections are useful for expressing feelings such as excitement, surprise, etc. They are not essential for the construction of sentences. Some interjections are listed below:

> Aha! Alas! Damn! Gosh! Hey! Ooh! Ouch! Phew! Ugh! Wow! Yuck!

Here are some examples:

- **Oh!** How is he now?

Here it is used to show someone's reaction to something that has been said. It also indicates that one did not know it before.

- **Phew**, it is stuffy in here.

It shows disapproval as the place is warm in an unpleasant way and without enough fresh air.

- His appointment as head of security – **alas**! – has been blocked by an unexpected damaging report.

Alas means sad or sorry. Sometimes **alas** is used in a sentence in order to indicate sad or sorry feelings. This use of **alas** is similar to the use of parenthesis **(parenthesis)**. This is illustrated by the above examples. Of course, you can simply say or write **Alas!**

- Some of the most commonly used exclamatory phrases of the present day are as follows:

  - Good heavens!
  - Oh dear!
  - Marvellous!
  - Great!
  - Splendid!
  - What nonsense!

- You can see from the above examples that some interjections are made from other words. Similarly, there are some interjections in which verb forms are used. For instance:

  - Watch out!
  - Cheers!
  - Look out!
  - Shut up!
  - How warm it is today!
  - Thanks a lot! ⇐ sarcastic remark

An exclamation mark(!) is also discussed under punctuation.

Each major class has its own chapter. These word classes are discussed next.

****

Over to you

1. Explain to a friend with the help of an example how a word can be recognised.

2. Identify particles/ adverbial particles in the following sentences:

- Our trip to France has eaten up my salary for this month.
- How did it come about?
- You must go ahead.
- His shoes are worn off. Can't he afford another pair?
- We will touch down at Heathrow Airport at 18.00 hours.
- I came away with the impression that he was sad and lonely.
- I will stand in for my manager during his trip to China.
- John and I go back thirty years.
- I wanted to stop over in India on my way to Singapore.
- I hardly go out during weekdays.
- James' story did not hang together.
- Hold on! This isn't our aim.
- After ten years, their marriage fell apart.
- We are too busy to sit around here.
- Carl came forward with information.
- Drop by sometime for a nice cup of tea.
- He's fallen behind with the completion date.

Chapter 2

Nouns

• Introduction

The word **noun** is derived from the Latin word *nomen*. In Latin, it means *name*. Therefore, when a word is used as a name, it is called a **noun**. Nouns make up the biggest category of word classes. Every thing in our world has a name – noun. For example:

- **People** - James, Brown, Clinton, Henderson, Mary

- **Places** - London, Paris, Delhi, Singapore, Edinburgh

- **Objects** - radio, chair, magazine, pencil, computer, car

- **Creatures** – bird, fish, cow, horse

- **Nature** - star, earth, moon, sea, sky, flower, tree

- **Abstract** – love, happiness, communism, capitalism, truth, beauty

Nouns are at the heart of our language as they are frequently used in speech and writing. For instance, in the following simple sentences:

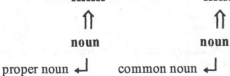

- Silvia will bake a cake.

    noun   noun

proper noun ↵   common noun ↵

****

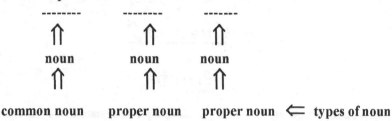

. <u>Types of nouns</u>

The above two examples illustrate that there are two types of nouns, **proper nouns** and **common nouns**. Silvia, France and Paris are proper nouns for the following reasons:

- the words **Mary White** refer to ⇒ someone **unique**

<u>It is true to say that more than one person can be called **Mary White**, but still that particular person *Mary White* is unique.</u>

- the word **Silvia** refers to ⇒ a specific person

- the word **France** refers to ⇒ a particular country in Europe

- the word **Paris** refers to ⇒ a particular city in France

- Cake and capital are **common nouns** as they are descriptive words. Some other examples are woman, town, tree , cow.

. <u>Why is it so?</u>

- the word **cake** by itself does not refer to any unique cake

- the word **capital** by itself does not refer to a particular capital city of the world

There are many different types of cakes and a large number of capital cities in the world.

A guide to proper and common nouns

Proper Noun	Common Noun

. begins with a capital letter, **e.g.**
 	
    London
    John
    France
    Monday
    Richard Burton
    Manchester
    Ford
    Buckingham Palace
    Christmas
 	
. refers to specific or unique names as listed above
 	
. **Exception to the above rules:**
 	
Seasons : *spring, summer, autumn and winter* begin with a capital letter, when they start a sentence, **e.g.**
 	
. <u>Winter</u> has started here.
  ⇑
  Begins with a capital W
 	
. In <u>winter</u>, I read a lot.
  ⇑
Begins with a small **w**
	. initial capital letter is not essential, **e.g.**
	
	    bus
	    dream
	    city
	    apple
	    idea
	    tea
	    singer
	    meat
	    innovation
	
	. refers to a member of a group or the whole group
	For instance:
	
	. a musician is a member of a group of people who perform music.
	musicians ⇒ a whole group
	
	. refers to things, ideas or concepts which are descriptive, **e,g.**
	
	. an **innovation** means a new idea or a new way of doing something
	innovation⇒ <u>descriptive name</u>
	      ⇑
	  it is describing something

Table 1

- **How can you know whether a word is a proper noun or a common noun?** The above guide will help you to decide whether a noun is a proper noun or a common noun.

• Concrete and abstract common nouns

Common nouns may be classified as concrete and abstract. This classification is based on the idea of tangible and intangible. One can see and touch **tangible** things. Such things may be concrete nouns.

On the other hand, there are **intangible** things, which cannot be seen or touched, but they exist as ideas, concepts and qualities. Such non-material things may be abstract nouns . The following list shows some nouns of both types.

Some concrete and abstract nouns

Concrete Nouns	Abstract Nouns
garden	dictatorship
donkey	liberty
nail	communism
quilt	impression
bush	autonomy
clerk	reality
man	capitalism
magazine	assertion
central heating	common sense

Table 2

. Noun gender

Another feature of common and proper nouns is that they have gender.
In the English language, gender classification is based on a man and
woman as natural creation. In accordance with this idea, a **woman** is
classified as **feminine** and a **man** as **masculine.** The third gender class
neuter covers inanimate objects and things which are neither feminine
or masculine. For instance, **computer** is a neuter noun.

Some examples of proper nouns and their genders

Masculine	Feminine	Neuter
James	Cherie	India
John	Rachel	Boing 707
Adam	Anne	Orient Express
Daniel	Petra	Africa
George	Jane	England

Table 3

Some examples of common nouns and their genders

Masculine	Feminine	Neuter
prince	princess	table
boy	girl	book
horse	lioness	banana
conductor	conductress (on a bus collects money)	post
dog	bitch	cinema
bull	cow	Show

Table 4

****

English nouns are not masculine, feminine or neuter in the
way that nouns in some other languages are.

● **Are there any nouns which do not fall into any of these gender groups?**

A few nouns have their own gender class known as **dual gender**.
Here are some examples:

- **teacher** man or woman   ⇐ dual gender

- **singer**   man or woman   ⇐ dual gender

- **adult**   man or woman   ⇐ dual gender

- **player**   man or woman   ⇐ dual gender

- **student** man or woman   ⇐ dual gender

- ***manager** man or woman   ⇐ dual gender*

- **sales representative** man or woman ⇐ dual gender

* manageress (female) becoming old-fashioned

● Compound nouns

A compound word is formed by joining two or more different words
together. Here are some examples:

- **weekend** ⇒ **week + end** - it is a compound noun

- **milkman** ⇒ **milk + man** - it is a compound noun

- **headache** ⇒ **head + ache** - it is a compound noun

- **postman** ⇒ **post + man** - it is a compound noun

- **armchair** ⇒ **arm + chair** - it is a compound noun

- **brainwashing** ⇒ **brain + washing**- it is a compound noun

Brainwashing – it means an alteration to someone's way of thinking, faith or belief in order to make one accept your ways or ideas.

- **international** $\Rightarrow$ **inter** + **national** - it is a compound noun

- **miniskirt** $\Rightarrow$ **mini** + **skirt** - it is a compound noun

- **mother-in-law** $\Rightarrow$ **mother** + **in**+ **law** - it is a compound noun

- **next of kin** $\Rightarrow$ **next** + **of**+ **kin** - it is a compound noun

Some compound nouns

Single Word	Hyphenated Word	A pair of Words
superstore	father-in-law	free will
superwoman	mock-up	melting pot
handbag	make-up	dance floor
housewife	run-up (e.g. an increase in spending in the run-up to Christmas)	blind spot
lookout (e.g. lookout tower)	waste-bin	health food
shoreline	warm-up	wine bar
doorstep	free-for-all	magic carpet
ladybird	lady-in-waiting (e.g. a lady who helps a queen/princess)	death blow (e.g. it can deal a death blow to our reputation)
teapot	travel-sickness	business hours
countryside	top-up (e.g. top-up money)	bus stop

Table 5

● **Some compound words are written as hyphenated words**

There are no exact rules about whether two or more specific nouns or words should be hyphenated or not. A compound noun can be written as a single word, a hyphenated word or as a pair of words. Some compound nouns are shown in Table 5 above.

● **Some hyphenated compound nouns are formed with**

   (a) ● **noun + gerund:**

        ● standing room ⟹ it is a compound noun
         ----

      gerund ↵ - space for people to stand in a theatre
             or similar places (see gerund)

        ● swimming pool ⟹ it is a compound noun
         ----

      gerund ↵ (see gerund)

   (b) ● **verb + adverb**

        ● take-**off** ⟹ it is a compound noun
      adverb↵ (see adverbs)

        ● stand-**out** ⟹ it is a compound noun
      adverb↵ (see adverbs)

● **Sometimes words have prefixes such as non, pre, anti, self, semi and ultra.**

Here are some examples:

- anticlockwise $\Rightarrow$ anti + clockwise = a compound noun

- antisocial $\Rightarrow$ anti + social = a compound noun

- non- cooperation $\Rightarrow$ non + cooperation = a compound noun

- non-violence $\Rightarrow$ non + violence = a compound noun

- prerequisite* $\Rightarrow$ pre + requisite = a compound noun

  * it is used as an adjective before a noun, i.e. prerequisite skill

- pre-school* $\Rightarrow$ pre + school = a compound noun

  * it is used as an adjective before a noun -

  e.g. pre-school education

- self-defence $\Rightarrow$ self + defence = a compound noun

- self-control $\Rightarrow$ self + control = a compound noun

- self- destruction $\Rightarrow$ self + destruction = a compound noun

- semicircle $\Rightarrow$ semi + circle = a compound noun

- semi-final $\Rightarrow$ semi + final = a compound noun

- ultrasound $\Rightarrow$ ulta + sound = a compound noun

- ultramarine $\Rightarrow$ ulta + marine = a compound noun

  ----

  brilliant pure blue colour

- A compound word may be written in one dictionary as a hyphenated word and in another as one word or as a pair of two or more words. It is best to be consistent with your own spellings and consult a reputable dictionary when in doubt.

. Singular and plural nouns

As a noun is a name, it can be used for a single thing **(singular)** or a number of the same things **(plural)**, but plural nouns differ from singular nouns in their endings. A large number of plural nouns end with **'s'** as exemplified in Table 6 below:

Examples of plural nouns with 's'

Singular	Plural	Singular	Plural
accident	accidents	animal	animals
bridge	bridges	candidate	candidates
camera	cameras	car	cars
chop	chops	competition	competitions
corner	corners	deed	deeds
desert	deserts	design	designs
director	directors	ear	ears
effect	effects	egg	eggs
exhibit	exhibits	eye	eyes
farm	farms	fool	fools
form	forms	gap	gaps
hand	hands	jacket	jackets
jug	jugs	length	lengths
lip	lips	pedestrian	pedestrians
marrow	marrows	opinion	opinions
pad	pads	spoonful	spoonfuls
tongue	tongues	waste	wastes
talk	talks	week	weeks
way	ways	writing	writings
word	words	work	works

Table 6

****

The above examples illustrate that many plural nouns are formed by adding 's' to the end of a noun. For instance:

• student $\Rightarrow$ singular and • students $\Rightarrow$ plural

• **A large number of singular nouns end with a letter -s, -ss, -sh, -tch, -x, -o other than 'e' but their plural nouns end with 'es' as exemplified in Table 7.**

Examples of plural nouns end with 'es'

Singular	Plural	Singular	Plural
actress	actresses	address	addresses
bonus	bonuses	box	boxes
crash	crashes	coach	coaches
harness	harnesses	hostess	hostesses
gas	gases	pass	passes
patch	patches	scratch	scratches
sandwich	sandwiches	splash	splashes
stitch	stitches	trench	trenches
tax	taxes	tomato	tomatoes
wash	washes	weakness	weaknesses

Table 7

• **Singular nouns which end with ' e' also form their plural with 'es'.**

Some examples of such nouns are given below:

• bone $\Rightarrow$ singular and • bones $\Rightarrow$ plural

• bristle $\Rightarrow$ singular and • bristles $\Rightarrow$ plural

• fare $\Rightarrow$ singular and • fares $\Rightarrow$ plural

.names $\Rightarrow$ singular and .names $\Rightarrow$ plural

. spectacle $\Rightarrow$ singular and . spectacles $\Rightarrow$ plural

. **Many plural nouns end with 'ies' as exemplified in Table 8.**

If you carefully study Table 8, you will learn that all singular nouns end with **a consonant** + **y**. Therefore, their corresponding plural nouns are formed by changing the last letter **y** to **ies**.

Examples of plural nouns end with 'ies'

Singular	Plural	Singular	Plural
army	armies	ancestry	ancestries
bakery	bakeries	blackberry	blackberries
community	communities	country	countries
comedy	comedies	family	families
folly	follies	irony	ironies
hobby	hobbies	glory	glories
lady	ladies	mercy	mercies
money	monies	nanny	nannies
nationality	nationalities	necessity	necessities
obscenity	obscenities	party	parties
oratory	oratories	perplexity	perplexities
possibility	possibilities	reality	realities
safety	safeties	worry	worries

Table 8

. **All singular nouns, which end with a vowel (a, e, i, o, u)and 'y', do not always form their plural with 'ies'.**

Here are some examples of such singular nouns and their corresponding plural nouns:

- way ⟹ singular and · ways ⟹ plural
- turkey ⟹ singular and · turkeys ⟹ plural
- ray ⟹ singular and · rays ⟹ plural
- journey ⟹ singular and · journeys ⟹ plural
- toy ⟹ singular and · toys ⟹ plural

· Irregular nouns

There are some smaller groups of nouns, which form their plurals in some different ways. These are illustrated below.

Examples of an irregular group of nouns which form their plural by replacing their 'f' with 'ves' (v+es)

Singular	Plural	Singular	Plural
belief	beliefs	leaf	leaves
half	halves	hoof	hooves
life	lives	loaf	loaves
shelf	shelves	thief	thieves
calf	calves	wolf	wolves
scarf	scarves (also scarfs)	wife	wives
dwarf	dwarves(also dwarfs	knife	knives

Table 9

Examples of another smaller irregular group of nouns
which form their plural in some peculiar ways

Singular	Plural	Singular	Plural
child	children	criterion	criteria
goose	geese	foot	feet
man	men	mouse	mice
penny	pence **or** pennies	stimulus	stimuli
tooth	teeth	woman	women

Table 10

- A very small group of nouns has two forms of plural. These plural are formed in their own specific way as shown in Table 11.

Examples of nouns which have two plural forms

Singular	Plural	Singular	Plural
appendix	appendixes appendices	formula	formulae formulas
focus	focuses foci	trauma	traumas traumata

Table 11

- A small group of nouns can be troublesome to some writers, as they

****

have their own peculiarities. In this group, some singular nouns have no plural. On the other hand, some nouns are used only as plural. Furthermore, some nouns can be used in singular or plural forms. The following examples illustrate the use of nouns surrounded by such inconsistencies:

• **Economics** $\Rightarrow$ **use as singular**

> • The economics of the Third World is in need of help from the First World.

• **Premises** $\Rightarrow$ **use as plural**

The premises were locked up when we arrived.

• **Mathematics** $\Rightarrow$ **uses as singular or plural**

> • Mathematics is the science of numbers, quantity and space.
> ------------------

use singular↵

> • Her mathematics are good.
> ----------------------

use as plural↵

• **litter** $\Rightarrow$ **uses as singular**

> • John's room was a litter of dirty crockery and old clothes.

• **Media** $\Rightarrow$ it is often used as **singular**, but some people think it should be used as plural only $\Rightarrow$ **plural** form of medium

> • The media has shown keen interest in this murder trial.
> -----------

singular↵

****

. The Internet is the modern medium of communication

----

here it is used as singular↵

. The media have shown keen interest in this murder trial.

----

plural use↵ - debateable

. **news** ⟹ plural but it is used as singular

. No news is good news.

. **jeans** ⟹ plural but it is used as singular with "a pair"

. He was wearing a pair of blue jeans.

. **scissors** ⟹ plural and its use is singular with 'a pair'

. Here is a pair of steel scissors for you.

. **wrinkle** ⟹ use as plural with 's' added as a suffix

. He is beginning to get wrinkles around his eyes.

. <u>Countable nouns</u>

A noun is considered as countable if it meets the following requirements:

(a) **.** <u>**It has both singular and plural forms**</u>
For instance:

cat ⟹ singular form	cats ⟹ plural form
shop ⟹ singular form	shops ⟹ plural form
judge ⟹ singular form	judges ⟹ plural form

(b) . **It is countable, i.e. can be counted (how many)**

    For example:

              four nurses, two answers, ten boys, etc.

(c) . **It can be preceded by such determiners as listed below**

        the, a, an, every, many, one, two, three, four, etc.

  Here are some examples:

. an organisation $\Rightarrow$ two organisations . a hospital $\Rightarrow$ many hospitals

. an apple $\Rightarrow$ two apples . a student $\Rightarrow$ many students

. a car $\Rightarrow$ a fleet of cars **or** 10 cars **or** many cars **or** every car, etc.

. a singular form agrees with a singular form of the verb:

           . Our car **is** parked in our garage.

    singular form of the verb ↵

. a plural form agrees with a plural form of the verb:

           . Three bicycles **are** for sale.

    plural form of the verb ↵

. Countable or count nouns form the largest group of nouns in English. In the plural form it can be used with or without a determiner. Some common countable nouns are listed below and on page 28.

---

*abacus, actor, adult, angel, angle, animal, article, artist, auditor, baby, bank, beach, bill, boat, boy, brother, bunch, buyer, campaigner, car, cat, child, cleaner, club, dancer, doctor, dream, drinker, elector, engine, expert, face, fan, farm, father, friend, garden, girl, grower, hat, headline, hospital, husband, icon, island, job, journey, jug, key, kitchen, ---

****

Some more common countable nouns are shown below:

---

knee, knife, lamp, leader, liar, library, lion, magazine, magic, map, motor, nail, nanny, native, nurse, offering, ox, page, parcel, park, plan, programme, queen, quiz (plural $\Rightarrow$ quizzes), report, river, roof, rota, scholar, shirt, sister, specialist, street, student, symbol, table, tent, tour, towel, tower, umbrella, uncle, valley, villa, volunteer, wall, week, weekend, wolf (plural $\Rightarrow$ wolves), year, zebra (plural $\Rightarrow$ zebras or zebra), zone (plural $\Rightarrow$ zones). Note: *abacus plural $\Rightarrow$ abacuses.

• <u>Uncountable (uncount or mass) nouns</u>

These nouns have the following attributes:

        (a) . they cannot be counted – refer to qualities and mass

        (b) . they do <u>not</u> have a plural form – they have only one form

        (c) . they can be used with or without a determiner

        (d) . some uncountable nouns are preceded by a **PARTITIVE** phrase or words. A partitive phrase or word refers to a part or quantity of something. For instance:

      • I have a piece of information.

     ------------------------ ----------------

partitive phrase ↵   ⇑

     piece   uncountable noun

    ----

partitive noun ↵ - as it forms partitive phrase

The reason is that information is not countable. However, you can refer to any amount of information as a part of the whole mass of information. It may be that you want to refer to the whole mass of information (no matter how little is the whole mass of information).

Here are some examples of uncountable nouns:

• There **is** still **some <u>wine</u>** in the bottle.

singular form of the verb⤶

       Since it is not counted as an individual thing, it
       is preceded by **some** (some is a determiner)

See ⟹ determiners

• There **are** three items of **<u>equipment</u>** for you.

  plural form of the verb   uncountable noun

Since equipment is not counted as an individual thing, it is preceded by
                            <u>three items of</u>

          partitive phrase ⤶

Indeed, for just one piece of equipment, one can say, for instance:

• There is a piece of computer equipment for you.

• **<u>History</u>** was my favourite subject at school.

uncountable noun

In this sentence, there is no need to precede the uncountable
noun with any determiner.

• It is common **<u>knowledge</u>** already.

uncountable noun ⟹ it is not preceded by '**a**'

• The tutor spoke in **<u>praise</u>** of her class.

uncountable noun ⟹ it is not preceded by '**a**'

• <u>**Sometimes, in accordance with the context, a noun may be either countable or uncountable.**</u>

The following examples illustrate this feature of nouns:

• In the hall, all <u>**lights**</u> are switched on.

in this context lights is a **countable noun** ⟹ preceded by **all**

• Have you got a <u>**light**</u>? (asking for a light for a cigarette)

here the noun light is **countable** ⟹ preceded by **a**

• This box contains a bedside <u>**light**</u>.

in this example the noun light is **countable** ⟹ here it means **one lamp**

• <u>**Light**</u> travels faster than sound.

In this sentence light is used as **uncountable**

• Would you like to have <u>**two pounds o f sugar**</u>?

Partitive phrase ↵   ⇑

                                                    uncountable noun

• Do you take <u>**one sugar**</u> or more?

determiner ↵   ⇑

          countable noun

• There is no personal <u>**sympathy**</u> between John and Jill.

in this context uncountable noun↵

Here sympathy means understanding between people with similar interests.

- Sandra has no **sympathy** for Barbara. It was her silly idea.
  ----

  in this context **countable** noun

Here sympathy implies feeling of being sorry for someone.

- You can have **two slices of** bread.
  -------------   -----

  partitive phrase ↵   ⇑

         uncountable noun preceded **by two slices of**

- **Some more common uncountable nouns are listed below:**

---

admittance, aggression, anger, backbiting, bidding, cancer, courage, coverage, disquiet, extinction, fitness, fun, gravity, happiness, health, independence, lawlessness, loneliness, luck, music, patience, racism, rot, spite, staff, tailoring, trading, traffic, training, travel-sickness, turbulence, unemployment, uproar, validity, vandalism, violence, visibility, warehousing, warmth, wastage, waste-paper, wealth, weaponry, weather, weightlifting, welfare, whipping cream, wisdom, worth, yarn.

- **Some nouns that have both count and uncountable meanings:**

---

benefit, billing, board, bubble bath, business, cake, capability, comfort, concern, confidence, danger, deceit, deduction, democracy, dinner, design, evil, explanation, experience, fashion, food, freedom, joy, marriage, power, prediction, pregnancy, practice, quality, reality, risk, sadness, sand, strength, stress, talent, technology, transport, trauma, voice, war, weight, whisky, white, wind, wit, work, yearning, youth.

****

.<u>Collective nouns</u>

A collective noun is a singular word, but it refers to a group of things. These things or objects in a group can be people, animals, animated things, ideas or concepts. Most collective nouns can take either a singular verb or a plural verb, but some take only plural verb form e.g., **cattle, police**, **people**, because they have plural meaning. <u>See page 375 for a list of some collective nouns.</u>

.Some examples of collective nouns agreeing with singular verbs:

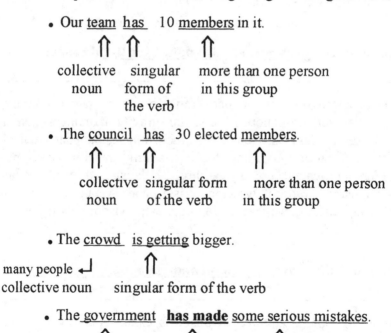

- Our <u>team</u> <u>has</u>   10 <u>members</u> in it.

      ⇑ ⇑   ⇑

   collective   singular   more than one person
    noun   form of   in this group
          the verb

- The <u>council</u> <u>has</u> 30 elected <u>members</u>.

       ⇑   ⇑   ⇑

    collective singular form   more than one person
     noun   of the verb   in this group

- The <u>crowd</u> <u>is getting</u> bigger.

many people ↵   ⇑
collective noun   singular form of the verb

- The <u>government</u> **<u>has made</u>** <u>some serious mistakes</u>.

       ⇑   ⇑   ⇑

   collective noun   singular form more than one mistake
            of the verb

- Our company's **<u>fleet</u>** of vans **<u>has</u>** a new depot.

               ⇑   ⇑

       collective noun   singular form of the verb

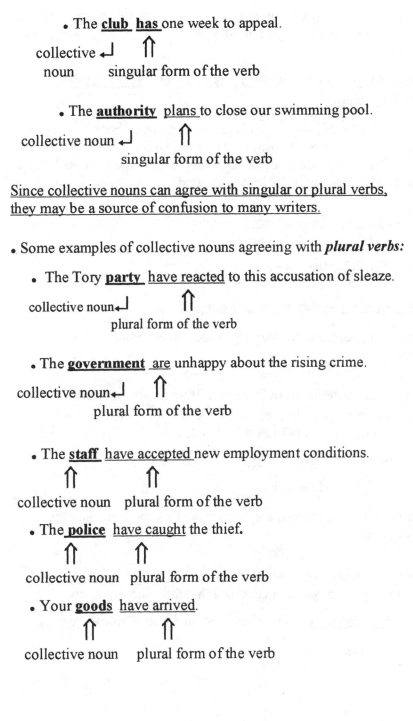

• The **club** **has** one week to appeal.

collective ↵ ⇑
noun   singular form of the verb

• The **authority** plans to close our swimming pool.

collective noun ↵ ⇑
              singular form of the verb

<u>Since collective nouns can agree with singular or plural verbs,
they may be a source of confusion to many writers.</u>

• Some examples of collective nouns agreeing with *plural verbs:*

• The Tory **party** have reacted to this accusation of sleaze.

collective noun↵ ⇑
              plural form of the verb

• The **government** are unhappy about the rising crime.

collective noun↵ ⇑
              plural form of the verb

• The **staff** have accepted new employment conditions.

⇑   ⇑
collective noun   plural form of the verb

• The **police** have caught the thief.

⇑   ⇑
collective noun   plural form of the verb

• Your **goods** have arrived.

⇑   ⇑
collective noun   plural form of the verb

'Goods' may be one thing, but it is used as a plural noun. For instance, a parcel may contain one item only. We still say, **goods have arrived**.

- ### When should you use either singular or plural verbs with a collective noun?

Usually, when one is thinking of the whole group or body of objects as a single unit, the singular form of the verb is used. On the other hand, if one refers to individuals or components, which make up the body or group, the plural form of the verb is applied.

- The <u>jury has/have returned</u> a verdict of guilty.

collective noun   either singular or plural form

- ### How can you test that a word is a noun?

The following tests can help you to determine whether a word is
a noun:

- A noun has a determiner in front of it. If you can justify placing one
  of the determiners such as **a**, **an**, **any**, or **the** in front of the word,
  then you know that it is a noun. For instance:
  - She was walking with _a_ dog.

         determiner↵

The determiner **a** precedes the word dog. This indicates that the word
dog is a noun.

- When you can justify placing one of the partitive words or phrases
  in front of a word, you can conclude that the word is a noun:
- I have **three pieces of** information that might be of some use to you.

partitive phrase ↵

In this case, the partitive phrase before the noun points to an uncountable noun ⟹ **information**.

- **Nouns can point to ownership**. For instance:

  - I do not know about his **sister's** marriage.

    this indicates ownership/possession

The word **sister's** is a **possessive form**. Now, isolate the word marriage and then place the determiner in front of it to read: **a marriage**. This is indeed another noun in this sentence.

Possessive noun form

When we add an -**'s** to a singular noun, we change its form to the possessive form. Here are some more examples:

- This is my **brother's** hat.

  possessive noun⤶

  - Our **team's** brilliant victory is good news.

  possessive noun⤶

  - Someone has smashed our **shop's** front door.

    possessive noun⤶

- When proper nouns end with –s, you have a choice of adding apostrophe s, or placing an apostrophe after the 's'.
  For instance:

- I have been invited to stay in the **Jones's** new home for the weekend.

- They went to **James'** office to see a demonstration of new office equipment.

- When a common plural noun ends with –s, just **add *an* apostrophe** to convert it into its possessive form.

For instance:

- Our history tutor often does not remember his **friends'** names.

- You can use our **customers'** car park until 17.00 hours every day.

- The idea of socialism was to make ordinary **workers'** lives easy.

- See ⇒ Noun Phrases

In summary, nouns are words that we use to give names to people, animals, natural and man-made objects. They are also used to name abstract things.

Common and proper nouns are the main groups of nouns. The other two groups of nouns are collective and abstract nouns. In order to use nouns correctly in both written and spoken English, it is important to understand noun gender (male, female and neuter) and number (singular or plural) of the same gender.

Over to You

1. Read the following passage in order to identify **proper**, **common** and **collective** nouns:

   Mr. John Smith, the secretary of the UK Branch of the International Association of Booksellers chaired a special conference. It was attended by 350 delegates from many countries.

It was held in the Forest Hotel situated in the heart of our beautiful Epping Forest, on the edge of London. The hotel was built some ten years ago. It has 400 bedrooms, each room with bathroom *en suite*. Its high standard facilities include:

a restaurant, a cafeteria, a large and well equipped conference hall, a number of seminar rooms and plenty of recreation amenities for adults and children.

At this conference, British delegates exchanged ideas and information about the book trade, and how to cope with the changing trading conditions and requirements both nationally and internationally.

The increasing pressure from multimedia electronic book publishers to sell their products have forced booksellers to form a forum called Multimedia Book Forum. The aims of this group are:

to agree an international trade discount structure with the representatives of multimedia publishers, distributors and wholesalers;
to discuss and agree goods ordering facilities; and
to settle their accounts with all the major multimedia publishers, distributors and wholesalers through the Booksellers Clearing House.

Mr. John Smith of Smith Booksellers, England, was appointed as its secretary and Miss Jane Clarke of Clarke Bookshop, Ireland, as its president. A team of ten persons drawn from ten countries was appointed as the forum's members.

2. Read the following text to identify compound nouns:

- I do not have alarm clock. I forgot to bring it with me.

- Almost every week I received some offers of credit card facilities from all kinds of finance houses.

- He is really humble human being. He lost his temper

because he was accused of something of which he had no knowledge.

- My brother-in-law came from Russia. He hardly speaks English, but he can still find his way around London.

- In the UK, letter-boxes are red. These boxes can be easily recognised. In some countries, we could not easily find a letter-box.

- He will be away from work for a long time because last night he suffered a heart attack.

- Police asked passers-by if they had seen the accident.

- I think more police constables should be out on the beat.

- Our breakfast time is 7-10 hours during weekdays.

- I would like to buy a new address book. Is there a good stationery shop in this town?

3. Sort the following nouns into concrete and abstract nouns:

answer, computer, hunger, relationship, desk, bird, king, allusion, village, allergy, beauty, college, admiration, love, remedy, factory, sympathy, bus, taste, yoghurt, navy, contrast, dislike, sunglasses, committee, human being, desire, need, guided missile, threat, human rights, manager, central heating, chocolate, dishonesty, aims.

4. Some collective/group nouns are also partitives. Give seven examples of partitives referring to such nouns.

5. The following table contains some singular nouns. Your task is to write plural nouns against the singular nouns listed:

Table - some singular nouns

singular Noun	Plural Noun	Singular Noun	Plural Noun
activity		army	
attempt		bonus	
authority		bridge	
beer		cloth	
coupon		demand	
effect		driver	
experience		foot	
goose		journey	
knee		kitchenware*	
lady-in- waiting		manner	
neighbour		ownership*	
a pair of pyjamas**		query	
reef		meeting	
a pair of ** trousers		sleeping bag	
tax		thoughts	
unemployment*		weatherman	

Chapter 3

Pronouns

• Introduction

A word used instead of a noun or a noun phrase is called a pronoun. Diagram 1 contains different types of pronouns. Personal pronouns occur more frequently than any other type of pronoun. In fact, pronouns do the work of a noun in naming a person or a thing. They take the place of a noun.

• Personal and possessive pronouns*

   * Some old grammar books describe possessive pronouns as
   possessive adjectives. Now consider the following example:

   • I would like to play tennis.
   ---

   personal pronoun

   refers to ⟹ **first person**

I stands for a single <u>first person</u> who would like to play (action) tennis. The first person is used by a writer or a speaker about himself/herself. It is the **subject** of this sentence, and for this reason, it is also known as a **subjective pronoun**. The subjective pronoun occupies the subject position in a sentence. <u>It comes before the verb.</u>

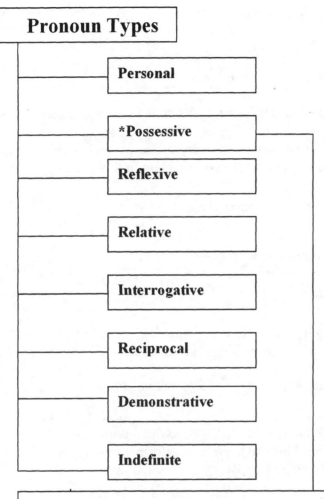

Pronoun Types

- Personal
- *Possessive
- Reflexive
- Relative
- Interrogative
- Reciprocal
- Demonstrative
- Indefinite

*. <u>Also known as Possessive Adjectives and do not</u> require apostrophe –s to indicate possession (see possessive nouns)

. They can function as determiners

<u>Diagram 1</u>

****

- **You** met her on a train.

  ---

personal pronoun – the second person

You is the <u>second person</u>. The second person in a sentence is the person to whom he/she writes or speaks. **You** can be singular or plural. Here, **you** is in the subject position. It also comes before the verb. Therefore, it is the **subjective pronoun** in this sentence.

- John has already informed **me**.

  ---

personal pronoun ↵

----

objective form ↵

me represents a single person. Here, **me** is the **object** of this sentence. Thus it is known as an **objective pronoun**.

<u>Note that the pronoun **me** occurs after the verb informed.</u>

- <u>It is worth mentioning that an objective pronoun may be in</u> the subject position. This can happen in informal writing, as shown by the following example:

  - **Me** and John are on speaking terms.
    ----

here objective pronoun used in the subject position

<u>This is not recommended because it is not standard English.</u>

In the following example, the possessive pronoun **my** comes before the noun **car**. Here, the possessive pronoun is used with a noun.

When a possessive <u>pronoun is used with a noun, then it is in</u>
<u>the dependent form.</u> In this example, **my** is a possessive
pronoun in the dependent form.

- **They** travelled to the airport in **my** car.

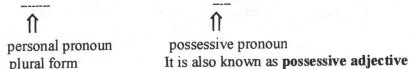

personal pronoun   possessive pronoun
plural form   It is also known as **possessive adjective**

See ⟹adjectives

My indicates that the car belongs to the person who writes or utters
this sentence.

They is in the <u>third person plural</u> form. The <u>third person</u> is the person
or thing/object/abstract idea about which the first person speaks or writes.
The third person can mean things, or objects or abstract ideas, as well as persons.

- Here are two copies of a recommended reading list.
  One is **mine** and the other is **hers**.

possessive pronoun   <u>possessive pronoun</u> - **independent form**

indicating noun's **gender** ↵

In this example, the possessive pronoun **hers** is used <u>without</u> any noun. In
fact, it is independent of any noun. <u>When a possessive pronoun is used in-</u>
<u>stead of a noun phrase then it is in the **independent form.**</u>

- **Theirs** is the red car parked in row A. **Ours** is a blue in row C.

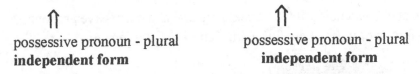

possessive pronoun - plural   possessive pronoun - plural
independent form   **independent form**

The classification of personal pronouns is given below in Tables 1.

* An apostrophe is not required in writing a possessive pronoun. For
  instance, it is wrong to write **their's**.

Classification of personal and possessive pronouns

Number	Subjective Pronouns	Objective Pronouns	Possessive Pronouns (*as above)	
Singular			Dependent form used with nouns	Independent form used instead of nouns
1st person	I	me	my	mine
2nd person	you	you	your	yours
3rd person	he, she, it, they	him, her, it, them	his, her, its	his, hers, its
Plural				
1st person	we	us	our	ours
2nd person	you	you	your	yours
3rd person	they	them	their	theirs

Table 1

- ## Is there any exception to the rule?

Yes, there is one exception worth mentioning:

- One must look after *one's* elderly parents. Here **one's** implies people in general.

- The above examples illustrate that personal and possessive pronouns perform a number of the following **functions** in a sentence.

    (a) <u>show the person</u>
    - **first person** - person (s) speaker (s) or writer (s).
    - **second person** - the person or thing being addressed.

It does not refer to the speaker or the writer.

. **third person** - It is the person or thing about which the first person is writing or speaking.

(b) indicate the gender of the noun which it renders – masculine, feminine or neuter
(c) denote the number – singular or plural
(d) substitute for the proper noun, e.g. Johnson
(e) point to the case of a sentence, e.g. possessive case
(f) identify a belonging , or belonging to, or a possession, e.g. **our**

. <u>Reflexive pronouns</u>

A reflexive pronoun refers to the subject. This is exemplified below:

. He dressed <u>**himself**</u> in his best clothes for this interview.

reflexive pronoun ↵

<u>Here, **himself** is a reflexive pronoun because the subject's action comes back on the person (pronoun) concerned.</u> This is to say that the action of the verb affects the person who has performed the action. In this example:

. he $\Rightarrow$ subjective personal pronoun $\Rightarrow$ singular 3rd person

. dressed $\Rightarrow$ reflexive verb

Here are some more examples:

. <u>**Sahara**</u> hurt <u>**herself**</u> as she fell off her bicycle.

⇑   ⇑

proper noun   reflexive pronoun

. <u>**You**</u> are so tired that you don't look <u>**yourself**</u> (your usual self).

⇑   ⇑

proper noun   reflexive pronoun

****

- I uttered these words to **<u>myself</u>**.

     reflexive pronoun ↵

- Each year Members of Parliament give **<u>themselves</u>** a big salary

  increment.   reflexive pronoun ↵

- We are enjoying **<u>ourselves</u>** very much. (= having a good time).

     reflexive pronoun

This example illustrates an idiomatic use of :

verb ⟹ **enjoy** and reflexive pronoun⟹ **ourselves**

- It is really important to look after **<u>oneself</u>**.

          Reflexive pronoun ↵

- It regulates **<u>itself</u>**.

 Reflexive pronoun ↵

<u>All above examples demonstrate that a reflexive pronoun refers
back to the subject of a sentence. Table 2 shows reflexive pronouns.</u>

<u>Reflexive pronouns</u>

Number	Singular	Plural
First Person	myself	ourselves
Second Person	yourself	yourselves
Third Person	himself, herself, one-self, itself	themselves

<u>Table 2</u>

- It is important to remember that there are two forms of the reflexive pronoun used for the second person as shown above. The plural form **yourselves** is used when you are referring to some persons or a group which includes the person to whom you are talking.

• <u>Relative pronouns</u>

A relative pronoun is a word, which links a subordinate clause to a main clause. These words are **that**, **who**, **whose**, **which**, and **whom**.

See⇒ clauses. Traditionally, **whom** was used as the object or a subordinate or relative clause. The modern practice is to use **who**. Both relative pronouns refer to people.

The following examples illustrate their application:

- He inherited a great deal of money, *which* he has used to set up a new business.

- This is the same person *who* sent us so many threatening letters.

- Joan is the lady *whose* son was tricked by the perpetrator.

- The car *that* I was to purchase was in poor condition.

- He is a man *whom* you can trust.

• <u>Interrogative pronouns</u>

Interrogative pronouns are used to ask questions. These words are also called **wh-words**. There are only five of them. These are exemplified below in *bold* characters:

- *Who* are you?

- *Which* of these bicycles do you wish to order?

- *What* is your prime aim now?

- *Whose* are those birds in a cage left in our front garden?

- By *whom* were you interviewed last week?

These interrogative pronouns also function as relative pronouns.

• <u>Reciprocal pronouns</u>

Reciprocal pronouns express a mutual relationship. They are like a two-way communication mode: one message going in one direction and one coming back from another direction. There are only two such pronouns: *each other* and *one another.* Here are some examples:

- The*y* **wrote to one another** for a number of years.
  ----

it means - each person wrote to the other person

- Jack and Jill always help **each other**.
  ----

it means - each member in this group of two helps the <u>other person</u>

- They can use **each other's/ one another's** computers without any password.------------------------------

use in possessive form ↵- apostrophe is before the -s in the possessive form

- Sometimes they stay at **one another's/each other's** country homes.
  ----

  use in possessive form ↵ - apostrophe is before the –s in the possessive form

<u>**The following rule is applied:**</u>

- more than two persons ⇒ **one another**

- two persons ⇒ **each other**

. <u>Demonstrative pronouns</u>

Demonstrative pronouns are those pronouns which indicate, show, or point to things. They are also used to refer to a particular person or people. These pronouns are:

- **this** $\Rightarrow$ singular demonstrative pronoun - indicates something within close reach

- **that** $\Rightarrow$ singular demonstrative pronoun - points to something further way

- **these** $\Rightarrow$ plural demonstrative pronoun - shows something nearby

- **those** $\Rightarrow$ plural demonstrative pronoun - refers to something further away

The following examples illustrate their usage:

- <u>**This**</u> is our car.

indicates <u>here</u> near the speaker <u>now</u>

- <u>**These**</u> chairs are no longer needed in this room.

shows a <u>present</u> situation in a <u>nearby place</u>

- <u>**These**</u> are our friends from Germany: Anne and Wolfgang.

refers to people <u>now</u> and <u>nearby</u>

- In my view **that** contract should be renewable.

refers to people's action <u>backward in time and space</u> (a contract is between people)

- **These** are slightly faulty goods for our summer sale next month.

  ⇑

refers to things <u>forward in time and space</u>

- **That** was Margo sitting at the end of the second row.

  ⇑

refers to a <u>person</u> <u>farther away in time and space</u>

- **That** was our sales forecast revealed by our sales manager

  ⇑

                                                        this morning.
refers to a <u>thing</u> <u>farther away in time and space</u>

- **Those** suitcases were found unattended by the airport police.

  ⇑

  refers to <u>things</u> <u>farther away in time and space</u>

- Sarah hasn't written to us from Sweden during the last six months.
  This is a worrying situation.

  ⇑

  <u>refers</u> to a person's action (Sarah's action) mentioned

earlier on ⇒person's action rather than just a person

- The motorways were very busy. **That's** why our coach arrived two

                              ⇑

                                                        hours late.
  refers to 'traffic' on the motorway to tell why their coach arrived late

- I'd like to say **_this_**. Our team displays enthusiasm but lacks a real

                      ⇑

                                                        talent to win tonight.
  use this when you are going to explain something

This way you **refer forward**. <u>Note **that** is not used this way.</u>

<u>In the above sentences, the meaning is relative to the context. The
reader can understand the meaning from the **context** of each sentence.</u>

- During a conversation, the speaker can also point to something without mentioning the noun or noun phrase. The following examples illustrate that the meaning is relative to the **speaker** who points to things <u>without mentioning the noun or the noun phrase:</u>

- I will take **this**. $\Rightarrow$ a speaker picks up a basket of straw berries without mentioning it – leave out the noun phrase

- She prefers **those**. $\Rightarrow$ a speaker points to a pair of shoes in a shoe shop

- Was **that** John on the telephone? $\Rightarrow$ it is used here to refer to a particular person $\Rightarrow$ John

- **These** will do. $\Rightarrow$ a speaker buys a bunch of flowers

Indefinite pronouns

Indefinite pronouns are those words which do not refer to any particular person or thing. There are a large number of words which can be used as indefinite pronouns. The following is a list of some commonly used indefinite pronouns.

Some commonly used indefinite pronouns

all	anyone	either	every-thing	little	nobody	several
any	any-thing	enough	few	many	none	some-body
another	both	every-body	least	much	no one	some-one
anybody	each	everyone	less	neither	nothing	some-thing

Table 3

- Some of these indefinite pronouns have exactly the same meaning.

This is illustrated by the following examples:

- In this room, **everyone** is aware of the class test this afternoon.

    it means all persons

- In this room, **everybody** is aware of the class test this afternoon.

it means all persons ↵
    Therefore:
        everyone = everybody = all persons or all the people

- **Someone** has removed my spectacles from the table.

    it means a person

- **Somebody** has removed my spectacles from the table.

it means a person
        Therefore: someone = somebody = a person

- **Nobody** has given me any message for you.

it means no person

- **No one** has given me any message for you.

it means a person

Note: In written English **no one** is more common than **nobody**
        no one is usually written as a two-word pronoun. Some
        people may write it with a hyphen.
All other indefinite pronouns listed above are compound words.

• <u>Numerals</u>

Numerals often function as pronouns. These are discussed under determiners.

In summary, pronouns are substitutes for nouns. It is worth mentioning here that at one time possessive pronouns were considered as possessive adjectives.

Over to You

1. Complete the following writings by inserting the correct pronouns. Also indicate the type of each inserted pronoun:

a) • We sell most national newspapers. ----- are also printed outside London.

b) • My friends wrote to me last month at the same time I wrote to -----.

c) • We have just received a copy of John's new publication. ----- has 500 pages.

d) • They telephoned us twice today. I cannot guess ------- reason for doing so after such a long time.

e) • He was here a few minutes ago. We were enjoying talking with -----.

f) • Certainly, this old car is not ---------. I have a new motorcycle.

g) • At last, we bought this house. It is ----.

h) • This job is not new for me. I have done ------- before.

i) • My wife and I have just entertained some guests. They were ----- old friends.

j) • There is a big difference between our opinions and ------.

2. Complete the following sentences. Also identify the type of the word inserted in the blank spaces:

a) • He could not force -------- to eat fish.

b) • On our arrival, we shook hands with our hosts and introduced---.

c) • Most people know that history repeats -------.

d) • You should think of ------ as one of us.

e) • She bore ------- with dignity throughout the funeral.

f) • John was thoroughly ashamed of -----, when he found out that I
knew his secret.

3.

Read the following statements and make corrections wherever
necessary:

a) • Jane, there are many quality shops in our town. You can
buy for yourselves the latest fashionable clothes.

b) • As a group you must decide yourself and let me know your
decision by 13.00 hours today.

c) • I have not shaved myself since last Monday.

d) • She is dressing herself to go out with her friend.

e) • My grandfather is recovering well and he can wash himself.

f) • I cooked the meal myself.

g) • She saw the burglar with her own eyes.

4.

Fill in the pronouns in these sentences:

a) • Neurologists ------ research and treat diseases of the nerves earn
a great deal of money.

b)• A French sportsman ------ I met at a restaurant in London.

c) . He is the same person ----- I saw stealing from the shop yesterday.

d) . Can you recognise the person ----- you asked for the direction?

e) . -------- is your house?

f) . This is the house in----- our present Prime Minister was born.

g) . These are the only four new cars----- we would like to export.

h) . ------- telephoned us?

i) . A car is parked in our driveway. ----- is it?

j) . ------horse came first, Indian Summer or Red Rose?

k) . ------ does she want from her estranged husband Martin?

l) . Here are four cameras. ------ one do you like?

m) . The manager asked Doreen to----- she had supplied a copy of the confidential report.

n) . To----- should I approach for your character reference?

o) . -------- gentleman is my old colleague.

p) . This parcel contains some books. ------- are in French.

q) . Anne and I have written to --------- for several years.

r) . Some students want to communicate with ----------

s) . I am surprised ------- has paid us today.

t) . -------- in the office is thinking of you. Get well soon!

Chapter 4

Verbs(1)

• <u>Introduction</u>

The word verb is derived from the Latin word **verbum.** In Latin, it means 'the word'. A verb is a central part of speech and writing. A verb can be a word or a group of words. The reason for its pivotal importance is that as a word or a group of words, it is required to construct a sentence. Generally speaking, people think of a verb as a **doing** or **action** word. Indeed, most readers would have learnt this idea of a verb at school. In fact, verbs are also used to describe the *state* or **condition** of something. Now, consider the following two sentences:

> • Andrea <u>**received**</u> a large bouquet of fresh roses.

> verb

Here the verb clearly shows the physical action of Andrea, **'doing'**. Many verbs are used for this type of **action** of doing something.

> • John **<u>believes</u>** in her good character.

> verb

In this example, the verb indicates '**John's state of mind**', which is not his physical action of doing something. There are many such verbs in English that indicate a state or a condition.

<u>If a word can be marked by **inflection for tenses**, then the word is a verb.</u> This is the major difference between verbs and any other classes

****

of words. Tenses are discussed under tenses in Chapter 5. Like nouns, many verbs have more than one form. The verb is at the heart of sentences and clauses, and thus it is the most important part of speech.

See $\Rightarrow$ inflection.

. <u>Verb forms</u>

Verbs have the following forms:

. **Base form**   . **s/es-form**   . **Participle**   . **Past Participle**

. <u>Base form</u>

Verbs in a dictionary are listed in their base forms. The base form is also known as **bare infinitive**, **root form** or **stem**. It is without the particle **to**. For instance, the following verbs are in their base forms:

be, sing, dance, laugh, work, run, wonder.

Sometimes, the bare infinitive is preceded by **to**, e.g. to wash, to wish, to go, etc. For instance:

. I <u>wanted</u> **to wash** my hands.

verb⤶   ⇑ = to +verb

verb $\Rightarrow$ to-infinitive form of the verb $\Rightarrow$ **wash**

. I **promised** **to send** some flowers to Anne.

verb⤶   ⇑ = to + verb

verb $\Rightarrow$ to- infinitive form of the verb $\Rightarrow$**send**

When a verb is preceded by the word *to*, it is known as **<u>to-infinitive</u>**. The word **to** is used as **<u>to-infinitive marker</u>**. It also functions as an adverb and a preposition. See $\Rightarrow$adverbs and prepositions

. <u>'s/es'-form</u>

The bare infinitive form is inflected in relation to the third person singular(subject form) by adding –**s/es** to the verb. This is discussed under concord or agreement. Here are some examples of verbs inflected this way:

- look ⇒ looks
- play ⇒ plays

- run ⇒runs
- smile ⇒ smiles

- go ⇒ goes
- laugh ⇒ laughs

The following examples demonstrate the use of the s/es -form of the verb:

- She **seems** happy.

s- form of the bare infinitive ⇒ **seem**

- Frank **loves** Elene.

s- form of the bare infinitive ⇒ **love**

- She **wishes** you good luck.

es- form of the bare infinitive ⇒ **wish**

• **Participle –ing form**

It is that part of the verb which ends in **-ing**, e.g. **going, coming, seeing, missing, jumping**, etc. Its use is illustrated below:

- I am **writing** a letter.

-ing participle form of the verb↲ - **write**

- Alexander is **playing** with his toys.

-ing participle form of the verb↲ - **play**

• <u>Past participle form</u>

It is that part of the verb which ends in **-ed** in <u>regular verbs,</u> e.g. **happened, disappeared**, etc. For instance:

> • I **joined** him at London Victoria Underground Station.
> ---------

simple past tense form of the verb ⇒ **join**

> • They have **worked** for us.
> ----------

present perfect tense: past participle form of the verb ⇒ **work**

• <u>In irregular verbs the past participle ends with **-en'** or **some other**</u>
endings, e.g. **fallen, struck, undergone, laid,** etc.

For instance:
> • She **became** his wife.
> ------------

simple past tense: past participle form of the

verb ⇒ **become** (irregular verb

• <u>Inflection</u>

Inflection means changing the ending of a word or spelling of it in accordance with its grammatical function. In English, as exemplified above, many words have inflected forms. Here is another example of an inflected verb:

• Prince Charles has **made** an enthusiastic speech tonight.

verb inflected from $\Rightarrow$ **make** (present perfect tense)

• <u>Regular and irregular verb forms</u>

Verbs are divided into regular and irregular verb forms. The forms of
<u>regular verbs</u> are determined in accordance with the changes they un-
dergo in order to explicit tense(time) or mood(a category of verb).
These verbs are also known as weak verbs. The reason for calling them
weak is that they follow rules to express tense or mood. The four different forms of regular verbs and how they are formed are shown in
Table 1. A vast majority of verbs are regular. In fact, there are thou-

sands of regular verbs. See $\Rightarrow$ tenses and moods

• <u>Irregular verbs</u>

 Irregular verbs are so stubborn that they do not follow any set of rules.
Like regular verbs, irregular verbs also change their shapes, but unexpectedly as shown in Table 2. There are three forms of irregular verbs,
as you can see in Table 2.

As these verbs do not obey any set rules, they are also known as <u>strong
verbs.</u> A good thing is that most verbs are regular. The total of irregular verbs comes nowhere near to the total of regular verbs. In fact,
there are about 300 irregular verbs. You may find all these listed towards the end of your quality English Dictionary.

Tables 1 and 2 on pages 61 and 62

Some regular verbs

Base Form or Infinitive (bare) Form or Root or Stem	Present Form -s /es added to infinitive form	Participle Form 'ing' added to infinitive form	Past Participle Form 'ed' added to infinitive form
abuse	abuses	abusing	abused
accuse	accuses	accusing	accused
advise	advises	advising	advised
blame	blames	blaming	blamed
cease	ceases	ceasing	ceased
disturb	disturbs	disturbing	disturbed
enter	enters	entering	entered
guide	guides	guiding	guided
help	helps	helping	helped
interview	interviews	interviewing	interviewed
join	joins	joining	joined
knock	knocks	knocking	knocked
look	looks	looking	looked
manage	manages	managing	managed
note	notes	noting	noted
owe	owes	owing	owed
push	pushes	pushing	pushed
rate	rates	rating	rated
scatter	scatters	scattering	scattered
turn	turns	turning	turned
unfold	unfolds	unfolding	unfolded
vanish	vanishes	vanishing	vanished
work	works	working	worked
yearn	yearns	yearning	yearned
zoom	zooms	zooming	zoomed

Table 1

Some irregular verbs

Base (Basic) Form (infinitive)	Past Tense Form	Past Participle Form
arise	arose	arisen
be	was, were	been
become	became	become
begin	began	begun
bet	bet or betted	bet or betted
bid	bade or bid	bidden or bid
catch	caught	caught
come	came	come
dream	dreamt or dreamed	dreamt or dreamed
fall	fell	fallen
feel	felt	felt
forecast	forecast or forecasted	forecast or forecasted
get	got	got
hang	hung or hanged	hang or hanged
hold	held	held
keep	kept	kept
know	knew	known
lay	laid	laid
mislead	misled	misled
overlay	overlaid	overlaid
overthrow	overthrew	overthrown
quit	quit or quitted	quit or quitted
read	read	read
ride	rode	ridden
saw	sawed	sawn
tear	tore	torn
tell	told	told
undertake	undertook	undertaken
wake	woke or waked	woken
wear	wore	worn

Table 2

. <u>Moods of the verb</u>

The word 'mood' is a derivative of **'modus'**, a Latin word. In both speech and writing, verbs enable us to express the '**mood**'. There are three types of moods in English, namely:

- **<u>Indicative mood</u>** – it is used to make a statement, state a fact or ask a question. In the following examples verbs are in the indicative mood:

    - Spring is already here.

    - Am I allowed to ask a question?

    - He is writing a letter to his bank.

- **<u>Imperative mood</u>** – it is used to give a command or an order. The command or order can also be of a polite nature, e.g. **forgive me**. The following examples illustrate this type of mood:

    - Go away.

    - Sit down.

    - Excuse me.

- **<u>Subjunctive mood</u>** – it is used to express a possibility, uncertainty, condition, wish, hope, etc.

    The following examples illustrate their use.

    - They wished they were at the meeting

    - I would have liked to come with you.

    - It is conceivable that he could have met us here.

. <u>Tenses and verb agreement</u>

The following examples illustrate that verbs help us to express the time when the action or the state or condition of a verb takes place. The present tense means **now**. It enables us to communicate the action or the state of something at the present time. Similarly, the past tense means **then**. It assists us to put into words the action or the state of something which took place in the past. The verb is vital in any sentence.

In English, the verb tense is marked by inflection for only the **present** and **past tenses**. However, the form of the verb is controlled by the person or thing and number of the subject. The future can be expressed by the present time. The way it is formed is discussed under Future Tense, Future Progressive Tense, Future Perfect Tense and Future Perfect Progressive tense. All these ideas about tenses are discussed in the next chapter.

• See ⟹ Verbs(2)

Now examine the following sentences:

• Janet **hates** no one.

subject - singular third person ⤶   ⇑

present tense –s form of the regular verb ⟹ **hate**

state of mind/behaviour/attitude ⤶

• She **held** my hand in her soft hand.

subject ⤶   ⇑

⇑   past tense ⟹ - irregular verb ⟹ **hold**

singular third person   action⤶

As **hold** is an irregular verb, it is inflected without the **'ed'**.

•Active and passive verbs and voices

Verbs may be classified as active and passive verbs. When the subject performs the action or experiences state or condition, it is called an **active verb or active voice.**

****

When the subject is affected by the action or state or condition of the verb, it is called a **passive verb or passive voice**. For instance:

- The writer <u>sent</u> the proposal. ⇐ **active sentence/active voice**

  active verb ↵

Who **sent** the proposal? The writer. Therefore, the **subject - the writer** is doing the action.

- The proposal <u>was sent</u> by the writer. ⇐ **passive**

  passive verb ↵   **sentence/passive voice**

Who **sent** the proposal ? The writer - doing the action is directed at the proposal ⇒ **subject**

Active sentences are the **active voice**. The active voice means being active or doing something. The active voice in both written and spoken language is considered as a good style. The **passive voice** is just the opposite of the active voice. The passive voice involves the use of the **auxiliary verb to be**. This may be stated as:

Passive voice = auxiliary verb to be + past participle

- The diploma <u>was gained</u> by me from our local university.

  ⇑ - passive voice

  auxiliary verb + past participle = passive verb

- I <u>gained</u> my diploma from our local university. ⇐ **active form**

  ⇑

transitive verb functioning as active verb

- She broke the cup. ⇐ **active form**
- The cup was broken by her. ⇐ **passive form**
- Someone has to answer the phone. ⇐ **active form**
- The phone has to be answered by someone. ⇐ **passive form**
- He handed me a letter of employment. ⇐ **active form**
- A letter of employment was handed to me. ⇐ **passive form**

. Germany invaded Poland in 1939. ⇐ **active form**

. Poland was invaded by Germany in 1939. ⇐ **passive form**

. <u>Verb classes</u>

Diagram 1 shows a basic classification of verbs. In English there are thousands of verbs. Here we are concerned with the verb form and its use from different grammatical views. Most verbs may be labelled as main verbs/lexical, but a small number of verbs are known as <u>auxiliary verbs.</u> The basic auxiliary verbs are **be**, **do,** and **have**.

. <u>Auxiliary verbs</u>

The word 'auxiliary' is derived from the Latin word **auxilium**, which means help. Indeed, this is exactly what the auxiliaries do in a variety

of ways. For instance: . She is dancing to night.

--- --------------

auxiliary verb derived from be↵   ⇑

it is helping the main verb   main/ lexical verb

Continued below Diagram 1

. <u>The primary auxiliary 'do'</u>

. <u>To ask a question:</u>

. Where **do** you <u>**live**</u>?

⇑

main verb supported by the auxiliary verb ⇒**do**

. <u>To emphasise a point:</u>

. Ursula <u>**does**</u> <u>**show**</u> a sign of worry.

auxiliary do in the form of **does** ↵   ⇑ show ⇒**main verb**

main verb supported by the auxiliary verb ⇒**does**

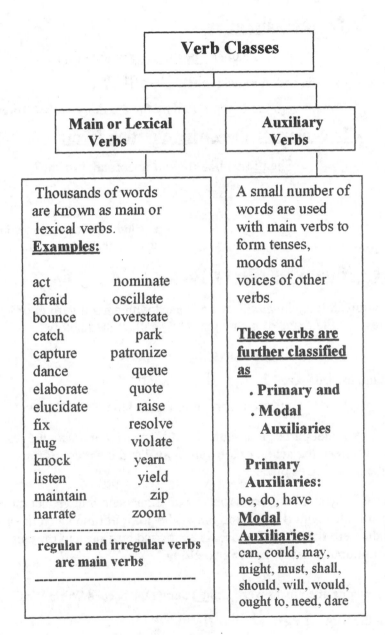

Verb Classes

Main or Lexical Verbs

Auxiliary Verbs

Thousands of words are known as main or lexical verbs.
Examples:

act	nominate
afraid	oscillate
bounce	overstate
catch	park
capture	patronize
dance	queue
elaborate	quote
elucidate	raise
fix	resolve
hug	violate
knock	yearn
listen	yield
maintain	zip
narrate	zoom

regular and irregular verbs are main verbs

A small number of words are used with main verbs to form tenses, moods and voices of other verbs.

These verbs are further classified as

. **Primary and**
. **Modal Auxiliaries**

Primary Auxiliaries:
be, do, have
Modal Auxiliaries:
can, could, may, might, must, shall, should, will, would, ought to, need, dare

Diagram 1

- **To state a negation:**

  - James **does not** **care** about Jane.

  auxiliary do is in does form with **not**↲   ⇑

  main verb **care** supported by the auxiliary verb ⇒**does**

- **To construct a negative question form:**

  - She **didn't** like travelling abroad, **did** she?

  negative ↲- past   ⇑

  past form
  question tag – a short question
  added to the end of a statement

• The primary auxiliary 'be'

In its various forms, the auxiliary *be* is used with a main verb in order to express a wide range of meanings. This is illustrated below:

  - We **are** **travelling** to France.

'be' in the form of **are** ↲   ⇑

  present participle form of the verb ⇒**travel**

Here **are** is a vital part of this sentence. It helps us to indicate the relationship between the action of the verb **travel** and the point of time when the action takes place.

In this case, the auxiliary **are** assists us to understand that the action is not yet complete, but it is still ongoing. The point of time when the action of the verb **travel** takes place, is expressed by a present progressive /continuous tense form **are travelling**.

  - Millions of civilians **were** **killed** during the Second World War.

'be' in the form of **were** ↲   ⇑

  past participle form of verb ⇒**kill**

This example illustrates the application of the auxiliary **be** in its form

were. Here it is helpful in showing us the relationship between the action of the verb <u>kill</u> and the point of time when the action was complete. In this case, the point of time when the action of the verb <u>kill</u> takes place, is expressed by the past participle tense form <u>were killed</u>. Furthermore, this example includes a passive verb phrase '<u>were killed</u>' whose subject **millions of civilians** is the recipient of the action 'killed'. See active and passive verbs.

- <u>The following examples illustrate the use of 'be' in order to express</u> a negation (negative meaning):

    - We **are** not *aware* of his whereabouts.

  'be' in the form of **are** ⤶   ⇑

            main verb supported by the auxiliary with 'not' for negation

    - The burglar **was not caught**.

    - She *isn't coming* tonight.

    - She **isn't present** here, <u>is she</u>?

                                    ⇑

                        a question tag

                                    ⇑

        a short question added to the end of a statement

• The primary auxiliary 'have'

In its three forms (**have, has, had**) is used with a main verb in order to construct the past tense. This is illustrated below:

- I **have walked** all the way from Hyde Park to Piccadilly Circus.

auxiliary verb   past participle form of verb ⇒ **walk**

The main verb is supported by the auxiliary **have** to construct the present perfect tense. The use of **have** is crucial as it shows that the **action** walk is complete. In this case, the point of time when the action of the

****

verb **walk** took place is expressed by the_**present perfect tense**.

> • She **has** **resigned** from her post as head teacher.

auxiliary form of have↲   ⇑

> past participle form of verb ⇒**resign**

The use of **has** is decisive as it helps us to understand that the action (termination of employment) is complete. In this case, the point of time when the action of the verb **resign** took place is expressed by the **present perfect tense form.**

> • I **had** **passed** secondary school examinations some years a
>
>   ⇑   ⇑

> auxiliary form   past participle form of the verb ⇒ **pass**
>   of have

This example illustrates the application of 'have' in the form of 'had'. In this case, the auxiliary indicates that the action of achievement at secondary school is complete. In this example, the point of time when the action of the verb *pass* took place is expressed by the_**past perfect tense form.**

• Verb aspects

The primary auxiliary 'be' and 'have' are used to form the verb aspects. The aspects are subtle meanings expressed by the verb forms as demonstrated below. There are two verb aspects:

> • **progressive aspect** and
>
> • **perfect aspect**

• The progressive aspect shows that the action is in progress or continuous or ongoing. The progressive aspect can be visualised as:

The progressive aspect = be + present participle

This is exemplified below:

- John **is returning** home today from France.

- Anne **was studying** at Moscow University for one semester.

- <u>The perfect aspect implies that the action has been completed.</u>
  <u>The perfect aspect can be stated as:</u>

The perfect aspect = have/had + present participle

This is exemplified below:

- Julia has written a letter to us from Norway.

- Sarah has/had no money to buy a cottage in the country.

- <u>**Can you use both the progressive and perfect verb aspects**</u>
  <u>**in a sentence?**</u> Yes, you can. This is demonstrated below:

- **He has been writing** for a living for the last ten years.

- She **had been visiting** her mother.

- Stewart **had been playing** cricket for England until he was 44 years old.

. <u>Modal auxiliaries</u>

Modal verbs help main verbs to indicate a range of meanings as exemplified in Tables 3 and 3A. From the above examples, you can see that auxiliary verbs enable us to use main verbs in some specific ways in order to express a variety of meanings. In general, modal auxiliaries are helpful for expressing your attitude towards someone or some situation and the effect of your speaking or writing on someone or the situation concerned. For example:

He <u>**might**</u> be the right person we are looking for to fill this vacancy.
  ⇑

The modal indicates that in your opinion it is possible **'he'** is the right person for the job. This example clearly illustrates your attitude to the person 'he' and the situation – **vacancy** and the likely effect – **suitable for the job**.

If you say: He **is the right person** we are looking for to fill this vacancy. It clearly states that you are sure that ' **he**' is suitable for the job. It shows certainty as opposed to possibility.

Examples of range of meanings rendered
by some modal auxiliaries (cont. on next page)

Modal Auxiliary	Use of Modal Auxiliary	Meaning Rendered
can	He **can** play cricket.	ability
cannot	John **cannot** dance.	ability/ negative form
could	Joan **could** swim when she was only six years old.	ability
could not	James **could not** run fast enough.	ability/ negative form
can	**Can** I go now? She **can** stay with us for two weeks.	permission permission
could	The nurse on duty said, 'You **could** go out for some fresh air.'	permission
may	**May** I ask you a question?	asking for permission
should	I **should** study hard as I want to gain high grades	obligation
ought to	I **ought to** take a holiday now if I am to get over this sudden loss of business.	necessity/ obligation
must	I **must** return home by 16.00 hours as we are expecting some guests from Paris for the weekend.	necessity

Table 3

Examples of range of meanings rendered
by some modal auxiliaries(cont. from last page)

Modal Auxiliary	Use of Modal Auxiliary	Meaning Rendered
will	I **will** attend the annual office party this year.	intention
shall	I **shall** spend my long summer holiday in Spain.	intention
would	She **would** have gone to see her mother if she had had a day off from work.	conditional intention/wish
may	I **may** see you tonight at the club if I can finish my work early.	possibility
might	I **might** consider leaving this job if they do not promote me soon.	possibility
could	Your parents **could** at least have written to us about your trip to England	ability
will	I **will** fly to Frankfurt in July providing I can re-arrange my work schedule.	prediction
should	I **should** write to you soon from Japan.	prediction
would	She **would** buy a mansion in Kensington if she had two million pounds in her bank.	condition/ prediction
could	I am so tired of mountaineering that I **could** fall sleep.	prediction/result
could	**Could** you repeat what you have just told us?	strong request/ demand/ instruction
could	You **could** telephone us from the airport.	suggestion
could	**Could** you lend me five pounds until this after-noon?	request
need	**Will** I need to carry with me a full British pass-port when I am in Russia?	necessity/ obligation

Table 3A

****

.Transitive and intransitive verbs

An intransitive verb does not take an object or a complement. It can stand alone. If necessary, it can be followed by a prepositional phrase.

In contrast, **a transitive verb** is followed by an object because it cannot stand alone. The difference between these types of verbs is exemplified below:

> • She **smiles**.

intransitive verb↵

Without any other words after the verb, this simple sentence makes sense. The action of this intransitive verb is complete. **It is intransitive because it can stand alone.**

> • I **speak**.

intransitive verb ↵

The action of the transitive verb is complete as the sentence makes sense. It can stand alone.

> • It **happens**.

intransitive verb ↵

It is meaningful and there is no need for an object after 'happens'. **It can stand alone.**

• **An intransitive verb is not followed by an object, but if it is required, it can be followed by a prepositional phrase.**

Here are some examples:

> • She **smiles** at you.

intransitive verb↵   ⇑
                    prepositional phrase

****

- Our trainee staff **complained** to the manager.

           intransitive verb   prepositional phrase

- **The action of the transitive verb affects the person or thing. For this reason, it is followed by an object (person or thing).**

This is exemplified below:

- He <u>appointed</u>.

⇑

   transitive verb

It does not answer the question: who? or what? Therefore, it does not stand alone to be meaningful. To be meaningful, this sentence must have an object:

- He <u>appointed</u> **me** to this post.

transitive verb ↵   ⇑

         object

There is no need to add anything after the object as 'He appointed me' is also perfectly meaningful.

- I <u>enjoyed</u> **my meal**.

transitive verb ↵   ⇑

         object

Without the object, **I enjoyed** does not make much sense. The verb **enjoy** refers to feelings. There are many transitive verbs, which can express feelings and other aspects besides actions.

- **There are many verbs that can be either transitive or intransitive.** For instance:

- He <u>played</u> cricket.

⇑

   functioning as **transitive** verb

****

In this context, it requires an object **cricket**. Here the action of the subject **he** is transferred by the transitive verb to the object *cricket*. This sentence conveys intended meaning.

• She **plays** in the school playground.
⇑ ⇑
functions as intransitive verb   prepositional phrase

Here there is no object, and thus the action of the verb is not transferred to the object. The prepositional phrase qualifies the verb.

See ⇒Prepositions

• Our doorbell **rang**.

functioning as intransitive verb ↵

• A caller **rang** our door bell.

functioning as transitive verb ↵

• **The following verbs are among those many verbs that can be transitive or intransitive:**

begin, break, breathe, bum, close, cook, continue, divide, drive, end, explode, finish, fly, go, hang, hurt, increase, join, mend, open, pour, qualify, ride, roll, run, rush, saw, say, separate, shine, smash, sound, stand, start, stop, talk, taste, tear, unite, weaken, work.

• **The following verbs are among those many verbs that are intransitive:**

advance, arrive, blush, collapse, cry, depart, die, dine, doze, elapse, exist, fall, flinch, flourish, gleam, happen, itch, labour, laugh, occur, pause, prosper, rise, roar, shine, slip, snore, stink, sulk, swim, throb, vanish, weep, yawn.

• The following verbs are among those many verbs that are transitive:

address, affect, afford, bear, believe, build, calm, carry, concern, damage, demand, design, desire, do, enjoy, exchange, expect, express, fear, fill, free, get, give, grant, have, hit, include, isolate, introduce, knee, lease, love, make, manifest, reign, reject, respect, revalue, waste, wrap, wring.

• Linking or copular or copula verbs

A linking or copular or copula verb links the subject with the complement. The Latin word **copula** means a 'bond', hence its derivative is linking. The basic linking verb is **'be'** with its most used forms: **am, is, are, was** and **were**.

• Here are some more linking verbs which can link the subject with the complement:

appear, become, come, fall, feel, get, go, grow, look, keep, prove, remain, seem, smell, sound, stay, taste, turn.

The vast majority of verbs are ordinary verbs which take an object when constructing clauses and sentences. On the other hand, a very small number of words which are copular verbs are followed by the complement. However, It should be noted that **appear**, **prove** and **seem** may be followed by '**to be**' and a **complement** as demonstrated in Tables 4 and Table 5.

A complement may be just one word as shown above. It is equivalent to an object. See ⟹ Complement under Phrases

Linking verbs exemplified

Subject	Linking Verb	Complement
It	is	Monika. ⇐ noun
They	remained	silent. ⇐adjective
She	became	a teacher. ⇐noun phrase
He	proved to be	a helpful person. ⇐ noun phrase
Our aim	proved	right at last ⇐adjective phrase
She	appears or appears to be	intelligent . ⇐adjective
Our journey	looked	very long. ⇐adjective phrase
The old lady	feels	a lot of pain. ⇐noun phrase
She	looked	all right to me .⇐adjective phrase

Table 4

- * Linking verbs **prove, seem, smell, sound** and **taste** are often used to give a viewpoint. You can do so by adding a prepositional phrase beginning with 'to' and placing it after the complement as shown below in Table 5.

- **An adverbial phrase after a linking verb also relates to the subject:** linking verb + adverbial. For instance:

   - My chair was **here 10 minutes ago**.

   adverbial phrase of place ↵ + time

• She felt ill before her meal time.
   ----

prepositional phrase of time ↵ see ⇒ adverbial phrase

Some linking verbs describing actions other than of doing something

His son	grew	tall and handsome. ---------------------- ⇑ adjective phrase
His wife	seems **to be**	a very kind person. --------------------- ⇑ noun phrase
It	gets	cold and windy ------------------ ⇑ adjective phrase
It	sounds	perfect to me* ------- ⇑ prepositional phrase

Table 5

• **It should be noted that the following linking verbs are used with only certain adjectives which describe something as illustrated below:**

. **taste** is only used with some adjectives which describe taste.
   For example:

. This bread tastes <u>**salty**</u>.

describing the taste of the bread↵ - **adjective**

. **fall** is used with ill, asleep and silent. For example:

. During the lecture, he often falls asleep.

. **go** as a linking verb is used with some adjectives to describe that something has become different in a particular way, especially a bad way, e.g., mad, blind, bald, bankrupt. For example:

. He has gone <u>**bald**</u>.

⇑ - **adjective**

indicating change in a particular way to someone's appearance

. Our milk has gone <u>**sour**</u>.

describing the change of state of milk ↵ -**adjective**

. <u>Participles</u>

The idea of present and past participles has been introduced in relation to regular and irregular verbs. You know by now that the **present participle** and **past participle** are two important parts of the base form of the verb. For instance:

. listen   ⟹ **base from of the verb**

. listening ⟹ **present participle**

. listened ⟹ **past participle**

Let's examine the following examples:

1 . I <u>**listen**</u> to you.   2 . I <u>am</u> <u>**listening**</u> to you.

⇑   ⇑

base form   <u>auxiliary form + participle-**ing**</u>

of the verb   present participle form ↵

3 . I **have listened** to you.

auxiliary form + past participle –**ed**

past participle form ↵

Examples (2) and (3) show **present** and **past participle forms**. Both present and past participles forms with the auxiliary verbs are used frequently as verbs.

(4)**.** I **listened**.

past tense ↵

Here the verb *listened* is not functioning as the past participle, despite the fact that 'listened' is also the past participle form. To function as a past participle verb, the verb requires an auxiliary verb as illustrated above. Participles cannot work in their own rights as verbs. They can function as **verbals**. This is discussed towards the end of this chapter.

Example 4 demonstrates the difficulty associated with participles that can function in a variety of ways.

• **Participles are frequently used in clauses.**

For example:

• **Flying in the air,** he conceived the idea of his latest innovation.

participle clause↵ - phrase does not have a finite verb

• She was at that bus stop for 30 minutes **waiting for him patiently**.

participle clause ↵

• **Smoking is prohibited** in public places.

participle clause ↵ - clause has a finite verb

In this last example, smoking is functioning as a noun but it is a participle. When a participle functions as a noun, it is a gerund. It is getting somewhat complicated. Let's discuss gerunds because gerunds and participles are very close to each other.

. <u>Gerunds</u>

When a participle verb formed with -**ing** is used in a clause or a sentence as a noun, it is known as a **gerund**. In other words, a gerund is a verb form that functions as a noun. The following examples show that gerunds can function as the subject, object or form a phrase.

> • <u>**Running**</u> keeps you healthy.

unaccountable noun ↵- **ing** form of the verb ⟹ **run**

<u>In this example, Running is functioning as a noun, subject and **gerund**.</u> In contrast, in the following example, **running** is only a participle.

> • He <u>**is running**</u> for his local charity.

present participle ↵- **ing** form of the verb ⟹ **run**

> • <u>**Dancing**</u> is her favourite hobby

gerund ↵ - it is a noun functioning as ⟹ **subject**

> • <u>**Washing**</u> is a burden.

gerund ↵ - here it is a noun functioning as ⟹ **subject**

> • Alison loves <u>**laughing**</u>.

> gerund ↵ - functioning as a noun ⟹ *object*

> • I enjoyed <u>**having**</u> you.

> gerund ↵ - forming a noun phrase ⟹ having you

> • I wouldn't mind <u>**waiting**</u> for you.

> gerund ↵ - forming a noun phrase ⟹ waiting for you

> • Hazel is very good at <u>**cooking.**</u>

gerund *forming a noun phrase*↵ - at cooking

- It is important to remember that <u>only possessive nouns and pronouns can modify a gerund.</u> This is exemplified below:

  - I don't like Barbara's **laughing** at the old lady.

    gerund ↵– Barbara's ⟹ possessive noun modifying gerund Barbara possesses *laughing*

<u>**Barbara laughing is incorrect**</u>

  - Hazel's **choosing** the colour won't be a good idea.

    gerund ↵ - Hazel's ⟹ possessive noun modifying gerund

<u>**Hazel choosing is incorrect**</u>

. <u>Verbals</u>

A verbal is derived from a verb. Verbals are related to verbs. A verbal may look like a verb, but it is never used in a sentence as a verb. In a sentence, it can function as a noun, adjective or adverb. There are three classes of verbals. These are **participles, gerunds** and **infinitives**. A gerund has the same form as the present participle. This can be a source of some confusion. Here are some examples of each class of verbals:

  - I find the show **amusing**.

    participle ↵ - verbal

it is functioning as an adjective and modifying the noun ⟹ **show**

  - We were given a talk by a very **interesting** speaker.

    participle ↵ -verbal

it is functioning as an adjective and modifying the noun ⟹ **speaker**

  - It was a **frightening** scene.

    participle ↵ - verbal

it is functioning as an adjective and modifying the noun ⟹ **scene**

• We sold our shop as a **going** concern.

participle↵- verbal

it is functioning as an adjective and modifying the noun ⟹ **concern**

The above examples demonstrate that when a participle is functioning as an adjective, it is placed next to its noun.

• **The to-infinitive can be used to form noun and adverbial phrases**. For instance:

  • **To take a train** is the easiest means of transport tonight.

  verbal ↵

Here the verbal is functioning as a noun phrase. It is also the subject of the sentence.

  • She wished **to be the beauty queen**.

  verbal ↵

In this case, the verbal fulfils the function of both the object of the sentence as well as acts as a noun phrase.

  • **To take a train**, they didn't know the location of the rail station.

  verbal ↵

Here the verbal is functioning as an adverbial phrase. It can also be called an infinitive phrase.

  • He telephoned me **to break the news**.

  verbal ↵ - functioning as an adverbial phrase

These examples may not be easy to grasp. It will help you to understand these if you read about finite and non-finite clauses.

See ⟹Clauses.

• **The gerund can be used as a verbal noun.** For instance:

  • **Walking** in the evenings is our daily routine.

verbal noun ↵- functioning as a noun as well as the subject

Verbs(1)   **85**

****

- **Arriving late at work** is not recommended.

verbal use of gerund↵

- **To run a small business** is difficult.

prepositional phrase ↵ - verbal use of infinitive

In this example, the infinitive phrase is functioning as a noun phrase. It is also the subject of the sentence.

- She wished **to get another job**.

prepositional phrase ↵ - verbal use of infinitive

The infinitive phrase is functioning as a noun phrase. It is also the object of this sentence.

- **Should you always use to-infinitive?**

The use of *to* with the base infinitive depends on the grammatical structure. For instance:

- I am pleased **to meet** you.
- I did not see Jane **enter** through this gate.
- She is always lucky **to be winning**.
- She likes **to touch** flowers. It means that she likes to touch flowers, as a 'one-off'.
- She likes touching flowers. – it means that she always likes touching flowers, as a 'habit'.

- **Sometimes the omission of 'to' is not considered as an error, but an ellipsis. It means shortening.** For instance:

- My husband helped Mrs. Williams**(to) carry** her shopping.

to is not essential ↵

- They wanted us **to run** faster than we could.

to is required ↵

- It is better if you do it now than **(to) leave** it till tomorrow.

    to is not essential ⏎

. <u>Split infinitives</u>

Placing of a word or words between the **to** and the **verb** creates a split infinitive. Some people do not like the idea of a split infinitive. In fact, sometimes it is desirable to use a split infinitive as it helps to show the verb is modified. For instance:

- In order **to precisely reply** to your letter, I must consult my staff.

    split infinitive⏎- precisely is causing a ⟹ **split**

Adverb **precisely** is modifying the verb **reply**.

- **To fully appreciate** your ideas, I must read your book.

    split infinitive⏎ - appreciate is causing a ⟹ **split**

Adverb **fully** is modifying the verb **appreciate**. The writer of this sentence may consider it necessary to use a split infinitive.

- **Sometimes the use of split infinitives can result in the clumsy construction of a sentence.** For instance:

    - Caroline began **to slowly cry** until she became hysterical.

    - The interview panel wanted **to again interview** me.

The above two examples are re-written without split infinitives. The following re-constructions are simple and sound better:

- Caroline began *to cry slowly* until she became hysterical.

- The interview panel wanted *to interview* me again.

- There are no rules regarding the use of split infinitives. If you are sure that a split infinitive is needed, split the infinitive. If you think that it may create some ambiguity, re-write the sentence without it.

Verbs(1)   **87**

****

• <u>Misuse or omission of infinitive, participle and gerund</u>

When we write or talk about verbs, we refer to them as **to drink**, **to eat**, **to love**, **to go**, etc. Misuse of infinitives, participles and gerunds often happens. Here are some examples:

> • <u>**Watching** from the window, the procession got bigger and bigger.</u>

    participle clause ↵   main clause ↵

This construction suggests that **the procession** was watching from the window. This is meaningless. It can cause misunderstanding. The reason for this misunderstanding is that the subject of the main clause is **the procession** which is the implied subject of the participle.

<u>In order to avoid the danger of misunderstanding, we can rewrite it correctly as:</u>

> • Watching from the window, **we saw** the procession getting
>   bigger and bigger.

Here it means: We were watching...., we saw the .... bigger.

> • <u>Standing by the bus stop, the car hit a lamp post.</u>

    participle clause ↵   main clause↵

This sentence implies: the car was standing ......stop,
the car hit......post.

<u>The following re-construction is correct</u>:

> • Standing by the bus stop, **we saw** the car hit a lamp post.

• <u>When using gerunds, writers often ignore the fact that a gerund can</u> only be modified by **a possessive noun or pronoun**. For instance:

• Annemarie does approve of her husband buying another new car.

<u>The correct statement of this example:</u>

• Annemarie does approve of her **<u>husband's buying</u>** another new car.

                possessive noun ↵   gerund↵

- The misuse of an infinitive happens, when it is separated from the word it is expected to modify. Sometimes an infinitive is placed in an inappropriate place in a sentence. For instance:

- All of us had electrical blankets **to sleep** when camping in the forest.

                              misuse ↵

In this sentence, the infinitive is connected with blankets instead of the subject. This is not the purpose of using it here. The following re-construction is grammatically correct:

- All of us had electrical blankets enabling us to *sleep* when camping in the forest.

In the following example, the infinitive is incorrectly used:

- The idea is that you use German **to manage** local branches.

                         inappropriate use ↵

This construction suggests that you use German person or German language which will manage **(action)** local branches. This is ambiguous. This is not the intention. The intended meaning is that you use German language to manage local branches **(action)**. The *action* of the verb is to be performed by the subject.

The following sentence is correct:

- The idea is that you use German language in order **to manage** local

  branches.   the language which enables you to manage ↵

  This communicates the intended meaning.

- Some people feel strongly about the use of split infinitives as a contentious issue. This does not mean that you should avoid using them.

.**Phrasal verbs**

****

A phrasal verb is a multi-word verb. Phrasal verbs form a special group of verbs, which consist of verbs made of two or three words. For instance:

- Please **fill in** an application form.

phrasal verb ↵ - **fill** + **in**

verb ↵ + ⇑

adverb

- Usually my grandfather **dozed off** in front of the fire.

phrasal verb ↵ - **dozed** + **off**

verb↵ +⇑

adverb

- We do not **deal with** this company.

phrasal verb ↵ - **deal** + **with**

verb↵ + ⇑

preposition

---

deal with means to do business with a company, an organisation or an individual. It has some other meanings. See ⇒ a dictionary.

- I **feel for** her as she has lost her job.

phrasal verb ↵ - **feel** + **for**

verb↵ + ⇑

preposition

---

feel for means to have sympathy for somebody

- It was when he joined our club that he really **came out of himself**.

phrasal verb ↵ -**came** + **out** + **of**

verb↵ + ⇑ + ⇑

adverb preposition

> **came out of himself** means to relax and become friendly with other
> people and have more confidence in himself

• He is upset as his girlfriend **walked out on him**.

  phrasal verb ↵ - **walked** + **out** + **on**

  verb↵   + ⇑ + ⇑

  adverb preposition

The above example illustrate that phrasal verbs are formed by either
two or three words.

• The construction of phrasal verbs can be described as follows:

a) When it is a formed by two words, the first word is a verb which
   is followed by either an **adverb** or a **preposition**. This is
   illustrated by the first four examples above.

b) When a phrasal verb is made of three words, the first word is
   a **verb**, the second word is an **adverb** and the last one is a
   preposition.

   The last two examples clearly demonstrate this construction.

c) Simple words such as **out**, **in**, **off** which help to form phrasal verbs
   are described in Chapter 1 under Particles Class. It is necessary
   to repeat that these words are classed as adverbial particles or
   just particles. Indeed, these words can be put into more than
   one word class.

.**Warning**

The above six examples show that a combination of two or three words
creates a phrase. Since a particular phrase has a verb in it, it is called a
phrasal verb. A phrasal verb gives a specific meaning, which may or
may not be obvious. It may not be possible to work out the meaning
from the words within the phrasal verb, because the meaning of the
phrasal verb is almost idiomatic. For this reason, the meaning of
phrasal verbs used in some examples are shown in boxes above.

• Where can you to find Phrasal Verbs?

There are very many phrasal verbs in English. You can even buy a dictionary of phrasal verbs in a reputable bookshop. Furthermore, a good dictionary lists phrasal verbs at the end of those entries that have such phrases. Here are some phrasal verbs for you to make use of them:

Some phrasal verbs

back down, balance out, bear up, boil down to, bounce back, call out for, come down, come forward, come up, creep in, cut in, die away, die down, do away with, drop by, drop out, ease up, end up, face up to, fade away, fall apart, fall behind, fight back, fool around, get about, get along, go along with, hang together, hold on, inflict yourself/somebody on somebody, inform on somebody, insist on doing something, keep under, live up to, match up to, mess about, push around, play around with, run away with, run off, show off, shy away from, wriggle out of.

In summary, the verb is the most important element in a sentence. Without a verb, we cannot express action (working), and condition, or state (alive).

Over to You

1. In English many verbs have inflected forms.
   What is verb inflection?
   Write six sentences using inflected verbs.

2. Make a distinction between regular and irregular verbs.
   Illustrate your answer with the help of two examples of
   each type of verb.

3. Identify verbs in the following sentences and list each under
   transitive, intransitive and verbs that can function as transitive
   or intransitive. Also state the main feature of transitive and
   intransitive verbs.

a) Unfortunately this accident happened.
b) We were waiting for you for nearly two hours.
c) During the meeting she coughed several times.
d) Her mother cried.
e) The police arrested him.
f) Silvia loves Ralf.
g) They granted me leave.
h) It was designed by a famous architect.
i) We rejected their offer.
j) She talked for a long time.
k) We are united.
l) He rushes.
m) It is closed.
n) I cook.

4. The following sentences contain both active and passive voices. Identify each voice. Also make a brief distinction between these voices:

a) The interim report was sent to me by the Board Secretary.
b) He rode his new bicycle first time today.
c) We do not wish to be left behind.
d) The letter was sent by First Class post from England.
e) The meeting has been closed.
f) We debated this topic last night.
g) He won the First Prize tonight.
h) I wanted to take my driving test this week.

5. The following sentences contain some verbs. Find in these sentences bare infinitive, to-infinitive, participle and gerund. Give the main feature of each type of these verb forms:

a) A short break from work is better for you than working
b) We have got these Christmas cards to post.
c) You were asked to finish this job first.
d) Today I have so many things to do.
e) Gardening is hard work for me.
f) Our director ordered staff to finish early today.
g) Walking is good for you.

****

h) Going to town by car is not easy today.

i) It was not easy buying tickets for tonight's performance.

j) Do you mind waiting a moment?

6. The following incomplete sentences contain phrasal verbs.
Fill in the blank spaces in order to complete the sentences:

a) Can you ----------- up a meeting?

b) We were looking ------ the photo.

c) Their car's noise woke us ------.

d) Please do not ----------- away these papers.

e) Mary -------- after her sick mother.

f) Fame has crept ------ on him after just one television appearance.

g) Don't just fool ------.

h) I do not wish to hang ------- here.

i) I cannot put ---------with this sort of behaviour.

h) You ought to get ------- of the house more.

i) She gave ---------- one million pounds to charity.

j) We must set ----- a new system for dealing ----------so many claims.

k) He is so humble that he always talks --------- his own achievements.

7. Why do you think auxiliary verbs are a vital part of the language?
Explain the use of some auxiliaries in the following sentences:

a) They have visited China several times in the last five years.

b) Could I borrow your spare chair for my guest, please?

c) If you should miss the train, we will take you to the airport by car.

d)   You must show your boarding card before you get on a plane.

e)   Our manager told John, 'You ought to work hard.'

f)   Our French guests might have found it difficult to follow.

g)   You should have heard that I helped your guests.

h)   You may go now.

i)   Could you show me how to solve this puzzle?

j)   Don't travel by car tonight. It could snow heavily.

k)   Next year, prices will increase again.

l)   I shall be leaving my office as soon as I complete this order.

m)   After his heart operation, he could hardly walk.

n)   I will be able to send you a message from New York.

o)   If we go on quarrelling like this, we cannot hope to unite together
     in achieving our aim.

p)   May I help you madam?

q)   Can I help you sir?

r)   Shall we travel to London to meet them face-to face to resolve
     this matter?

s)   We won't/will not leave this place without the refund of
     our deposit.

t)   Somehow, we have t to resolve our differences.

****

Chapter 5

Verbs (2) – Formation of Tenses

. <u>Verb tense</u>

A verb phrase always has a verb as its head. A verb always has a tense. Therefore, it is important to understand the relationship between tenses and phrases. Let's consider the following examples:

       . Janet <u>**laughs**</u> a lot.

present tense - verb <u>**laughs**</u> $\Rightarrow$ present tense

       –s form of the regular verb **laugh**

       . I <u>**work**</u> here.

       present tense - the verb <u>**work**</u> $\Rightarrow$ present tense

base form of the regular verb **work** ↵

       . I <u>**proved**</u> that he was wrong.

past tense - the verb proved $\Rightarrow$ past tense **-ed form** for the irregular verb - **prove**

       . Jane <u>**left**</u> the office a few minutes ago.

past tense - the verb **left** $\Rightarrow$ past tense **-ed form** for the irregular verb **leave**

These examples illustrate that verbs are used to express the time when the action of a verb takes place. The word **'tempus'** is a Latin word, which means time. The word **tense** is a derivative of this Latin word. Therefore, the **present tense** means the present time (now). Similarly, the **past tense** means the past time (then).

• **The tense** is a form of a verb as shown above. It indicates a
              particular point in time in the present, past, or future.

• In English, the verb tense is marked by **inflection** (change in the form of a word, especially the ending) for the **present tense** and **past tense** only.

• There are other tenses, which are marked by other means. All sixteen tenses are summarised in Table 1 in this chapter. Before we discuss tenses, it is desirable to understand what we mean by verb concord or verb agreement.

.Verb concord or agreement

Verb concord or agreement is a rule, which states that the form of the verb is dictated by the person and number of the subject. Let's apply this rule to the following examples:

• I **travel** today.
   ⇑   ⇑
   1   2

1 is a subject **I** ⟹ first person and single (number)
2 is a verb **travel** ⟹ It is the **base/infinitive** form of the verb
In this example, in accordance with the verb concord, the verb form is agreed with the person and number of the subject.

• She **speaks** German well.
   ⇑   ⇑
   1   2

1 is the subject **she** ⟹ third person and single (number)

****

2 is a verb ⟹ It is *–s* **inflection** which marks the third person singular of the **present tense** as demonstrated above. This way, the verb form agrees with the third person singular.

> • They **work** in a restaurant.

1   2

1 is the subject **they** ⟹ third person and plural

2 is a verb ⟹ it is the **basic/infinitive** present form of the verb. Here, the verb agrees with the third person and is plural (number).

> • I **lived** in London some years ago.

1   2

1 is a subject **I** ⟹ first person and singular

2 is a verb ⟹ it is the **-ed past or participle form** ⟹**regular form**

> • You **left** England yesterday.

1   2

1 is the subject **you** ⟹ second person and singular

2 is a verb ⟹it is the **-ed past or participle form** ⟹ **irregular form**. In this case, the verb agrees with the person and number of the subject. **Past tense**.

• The essence of concord is that the subject controls the form of the verb. This rule is applied in all sixteen tenses discussed in this book.

• Finite and non-finite verbs

In the following examples, the verb is marked for tense. When a verb is marked for tense, it is called a **finite verb or a finite verb phrase**. A finite verb may be the only verb in a sentence. You can have a finite

verb in both main and sub-ordinate clauses. See ⟹ Clauses
Here are some examples:

- He **breeds** ducks.

finite verb ⟹ present tense form
The relationship between the verb '**breeds**' and the subject 'he' is
in concord/agreement.

- Anne **travels** to Russia twice a year.

finite verb ⟹ present tense form
The relationship between the verb '**travels**' and the subject '**Anne**' is
in concord/ agreement.

- I always **buy** some flowers for my wife.

finite verb ⟹ present tense

The relationship between the verb '**buy**' and the subject '**I**' is
in concord/ agreement.

- We **love** their new cottage in the country.

finite verb ⟹ present tense
The relationship between the verb '**love**' and the subject '**we**' is
in concord/ agreement.

- I **joined** your book club.

finite verb ⟹ past tense
The relationship between the verb '**joined**' and the subject '**I**' is
in concord/ agreement.

****

• You **interviewed** her the other day for a job.

finite verb ⟹ past tense

The relationship between the verb **'interviewed'** and the subject **'you'** is in concord /agreement.

• We **went to** Switzerland last year.

This verb phrase contains a finite irregular verb

The finite irregular verb **go** changes its form for the past tense by becoming **went**. This is equivalent to the past participle **-ed form**. There are many such irregular verbs.

The relationship between the verb phrase **'went to'** and the subject **'we'** is in concord/ agreement.

A sentence must have one finite verb. See ⟹ Clauses and Sentences.

• **A non–finite verb is not marked for tense. The non-finite verb phrase can contain one of the following verb forms:**

   • **infinitive** – both bare and to-infinitive forms

   • **gerund** - the –**ing** form of a verb

   • **participle** – it has two forms:

         (1) • the -**ing** from = the present participle or

         (2) • the – **ed** from = the past participle

The non-finite phrase does not give information in the same way as the finite phrase gives on tense (time). It does not take a subject. All verbs except modal auxiliaries have non-finite forms. See Modal Auxiliaries. The following examples illustrate non-finite phrases:

- serious <u>to study</u>

to- infinitive form $\Rightarrow$ non-finite phrase

- slow <u>going</u>

gerund form $\Rightarrow$ non-finite verb

- <u>appearing</u> on screen

participle form $\Rightarrow$ non-finite verb

- The bare infinitive and the past participle form of the verb are not often used.

- The past participle **'–d' form**, depending on the context, can function as finite and non-finite:

  - Some young hooligans **<u>attacked</u>** Maria in the street.

    finite verb ↵ - past tense

  - We saw Maria **<u>attacked</u>** by some young hooligans in the street.

    non-finite participle verb – it has no subject and tense

- **<u>A sentence can have both finite and non-finite phrases</u>.** This is exemplified below:

  - We **<u>wished</u>** **<u>to travel</u>** together.

  finite verb phrase↵
                      non-finite verb phrase

  - The doorman **<u>asked</u>** us **<u>to show</u>** our tickets.

  finite verb phrase↵
                        non-finite verb phrase

Now we can examine tenses in some detail.

****

1. Present tense or simple present tense

The present tense is used to express a present action or state that exists now. Let's first examine the following examples:

. I **walk** all the way.

present tense⏎ - formed from the base form of the verb ⟹**walk**

. You **talk** to him.

present tense ⏎ - formed from the base form of the verb ⟹**talk**

. He/she **runs** fast.

present tense⏎ - formed by an **-s inflection** in the third person

singular verb ⟹**run** subject ⟹ **he/she**⟹ third person singular

. They **sing** nicely.

present tense⏎ - formed from the base verb ⟹ **sing**

subject ⟹ **they** ⟹ third person plural

These examples illustrate that the **base form** of the verb is used for all persons, except the third person singular. For the third person singular the verb form changes by – s inflection. Here are some more examples:

. He **lectures** on Russian literature. ⟹ indicating a recurrence

. We **arrive** the next day.   ⟹ implying some future time

. He **loves** his family very much.   ⟹ specifying an emotion

. This car **belongs** to my brother.   ⟹ showing ownership

. Water **is** essential for our survival. ⟹ indicating a truth at all times

. I **think** it's a great idea.   ⟹ pointing to an opinion/state

2 . Present progressive/continuous tense

The present progressive tense shows that the action is continuous. It is still happening. The present continuous can also be used for present states which last for some time. For permanent states, use the simple present tense. The following examples demonstrate the use of this tense in verb phrases:

- I **am working** hard to pass my examinations.

indicating action ↵ - ongoing action over a period of time

- She **is cooking** our lunch.

suggesting someone in the middle of doing something

- They **are coming** to stay with us tomorrow.

telling us about some future arrangements – stay

- We **are** <u>always</u> **dining** in that restaurant every Friday.

pointing out that something has been happening for some time

- After answering a telephone call, she **is feeling** depressed.

expressing a temporary state of one's mind ↵

- This afternoon our car sales **are looking** poor.

implies a temporary state of a business ↵

- In order to construct the present progressive tense, place the present form of the auxiliary **be** before the participle form **'ing'**. It is easy to remember it as:

The present progressive tense = present form of **be** + participle form **'-ing'**

---

3. Past tense

The Past tense describes an event which has already happened or a

****

state of something which existed at a particular time **(then)** before the present time**(now)**. The following examples illustrate the construction of verb phrases indicating the past tense, which is also known as the <u>**simple past tense**</u>.

- I <u>walked</u> to <u>Chelsea</u>.

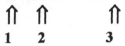

   1   **2**   **3**

In this example:

   1 = subject first person singular. Also I is a **pronoun**

   2 = signifying the past tense formed from the past participle **–ed**

      (-ed inflection) the regular verb ⇒**walk**

  3 = **noun phrase** ⇒ the preposition **to** can occur before a noun.

     - Robin <u>**managed**</u> his family business well.

     past tense⤶ - formed from the past participle **-ed** form

     (-ed inflection) the regular verb ⇒**manage**

  Robin ⇒ subject **and** third person singular

    - You <u>**led**</u> your team successfully.

past tense formed from the past tense form of the <u>irregular verb</u>

lead ⤶

you ⇒ subject **and** second person singular

   - We <u>**bought** a cottage in Wales</u>.

verb phrase indicating past tense formed from the past tense form of the irregular verb ⇒**buy** and the subject ⇒ first person plural

These examples demonstrate the use of both regular and irregular verbs to form the simple past tense. Here are some more examples of using the past tense in verb phrases:

- She **said** that she **was** an actress. ⇒reported speech

* They announced that our train **arrived** on time. ⇒reported speech

* We **went** to school everyday by car. ⇒describes a past event

* Once upon a time we **lived** in that house.

     tells us about a past circumstance

* Was he unconscious when the police **appeared** at the scene?

     enquires about the past condition/state of a person

* There **was** no rain. ⇒describes the environmental condition

4. Past progressive tense

The past progressive/continuous tense is used to express what was happening at some point in time in the past. In order to express the past continuous state such as feelings, normally the simple past tense is used. Sometimes for a temporary state, one can use the past progressive tense. The following examples illustrate the use of this tense:

* I **was swimming** in the sea.

indicating an action over a period of past time

* He **was working** every day seven days a week.

indicating an action over a whole specific period

* We **were training** our staff when the fire broke out.

shows a sudden occurrence when in the middle of doing something

* Due to an industrial strike, we **were working** from home that day.

     pointing to a temporary action for a short period

****

• She **was crying**.

expressing a temporary feeling. (she cried = past tense)

> The construction of the past progressive tense is stated as:
> Past progressive tense = past form of be + participle form 'ing'

5. Future tense

The future tense expresses actions or states which will happen in the future. It also describes the future in the past. The future tense is formed using an auxiliary verb with the bare infinitive form of the verb.

> We can visualise the construction of the **simple future tenses** as:
> **Future tense = auxiliary will or shall + bare infinitive verb form**

Here are some examples of verb phrases with the future tense:

• I **shall visit** you soon in Germany.

will may be used with first person ⟹ singular subject

• He **will help** you.

• They **will come** to see us next year.

• *We* **'ll telephone** you on our arrival.

• It **will go** by airmail tonight.

• **The future in the past is expressed by the future tense by using would form of the auxiliary will:**

• Angelica <u>told</u> Thomas that he <u>would arrive</u> on time.

past tense ↵   future in the past↵

• You <u>promised</u> that we <u>would write</u> this article together.

past tense ↵   future in the past ↵

It is important to know:

Traditionally

shall $\Rightarrow$ it was used for the first person subject

will $\Rightarrow$ it was used for the second and third person subject

---

|

Present-day

For the first person subject $\Rightarrow$ use either **shall** or **will**

For other subjects $\Rightarrow$ use **will**

See $\Rightarrow$ Shall and Will

- **Are there some other ways of expressing the future besides the future tense?**

The future can also be expressed without using the future tense in the following ways:

1).
    If something is about to happen soon, or you think it will happen or you intend to do something very soon, you can state it as:
        a) be going to + bare infinitive form of the verb. Or
        b) **be** going to be.
    This is exemplified below:

            - Our French guests <u>are going to visit</u> us this afternoon.

indicating the event will happen fairly soon ↵

bare infinitive form of the verb $\Rightarrow$ visit

- Sonia Gandhi <u>is going to be</u> the next Prime Minister of India.
              ⇑

indicating the future occurrence which will happen in the near future

2).

If you expect planned events will happen soon, you can specify these by using any of the following future markers:

a) be about to + bare infinitive of the verb form
b) be about to be + past participle form of the verb
c) be due to + bare infinitive of the verb form

For instance:

- We **are about to leave** London.

- Our company is **about to be** taken over by a German company.

- I **am due to start** my night shift at 20.00 hours.

6. Future progressive tense

The future progressive expresses an action that is continuous over a period in the future. It is constructed as:

Future progressive tense = shall/will + be + participle form – ing form

The following examples of the future progressive tense express the relationship between the information conveyed by the verb phrase and time/tense, when these were uttered:

- I shall/will be going to see my mother soon.

- We shall/will be drinking in that pub over there.

- Everyone will be cheering when you appear on the stage.

- They will be serving us as soon as we take our seats.

7. Perfect or present perfect tense

The perfect or present perfect indicates that the action or state is complete in the near past up to the present time. This is just the opposite to the simple past, which denotes that the action or state ended in the past. For instance:

- Our guest **arrived**.

It means that the action was completed in the past.

- **When did they arrive?**

The only conclusion we can draw from this statement is that they arrived in past time. It does not tell us that the past was a day ago, a month ago or whenever. Thus, the action of arrival finished in the past.

- Our guests **have arrived**.

It means that the action was completed in the near past that is up to the present time.

- **When have they arrived?**

It means that our guests have arrived presently and that they are here now (present time).

- She **felt rotten** for leaving her children behind.

The action was completed in the past. We do not know when in the past.

- She **has felt rotten** for leaving her children behind.

It implies that the action was completed in the near past up to the present time.

The construction of the present perfect tense can be visualised as:

Present perfect = present of auxiliary verb have + past participle

This is further illustrated below:

* He **has sheltered** his manager from criticism.

present perfect ↵

In accordance with the concord, the verb is in agreement with the subject **he**. The word **has** is the singular form of the primary auxiliary verb **have**.

* We **have written** to them for a copy of the contract.

present perfect ↵ - irregular verb ⟹ **write** its past participle

form ⟹**written**

* Our hosts **have shown** us the area by car.

present perfect ↵ - irregular verb ⟹ **show** its past

participle form ⟹shown

8 . Present perfect progressive tense

The present perfect continuous/progressive is used to express an action over a period of time in the past and is continuing up-to the present time. Its method of construction can be outlined as:

Present perfect progressive tense = present of have + been + participle form ing

The following examples illustrate the application of this mode of expression:

* She **has been working** with us for four years.

present perfect continuous ↵ - shows repeated action - working up to now/present time.

* We **have been living** in this building since it was built.

present perfect continuous ↵ - shows repeated action

* They **have been singing** on stage for a living for the last five years.

present perfect continuous ↵ ⟹ shows repeated action

****

The present perfect continuous is not used to express state
('I believe you.' believe = state).

9. Past perfect tense

The past perfect tense is used to express an action or a state that happened or existed some time ago in the past. It is constructed as:

Past perfect tense = past of auxiliary verb have + past participle

The following examples exemplify the use of the past perfect tense:

- I **had received** many such requests before.

past perfect ⏎ - shows an action in the distant past

- This was a request for money. I **had received** such requests before.

      past perfect relates to an action which occurred
      in the distant past

- They **had planned** their trip some time ago.

past perfect ⏎ - action before a past time

- They **had thought** about their own families.

past perfect tense ⏎- points to a state that existed in their minds
in the distant past

- We **had admired** their courage.

past perfect tense ⏎- shows a state ⟹ approval in the distant past

- We **had had** a new car then.

past perfect tense⏎-shows a state ⟹ownership/own in the
distant past

Note that sometimes the past perfect is called **the pluperfect** **(Latin:Plūs quam Perfectum)**

****

10 . <u>Past perfect progressive tense</u>

The past perfect progressive is used to indicate a continuous action over a period of time in the past. It is described as:

> Past perfect progressive tense = past of have + been + participle form – ing

This is illustrated below:

> • I **had been travelling** all day.

      past perfect progressive ↵

It expresses a continuous action(travelling) in the past - it happened in the distant past.

> •We **had been running** early in the morning to get fit for this race.

      ⇑

past perfect progressive

> • In those days, our business **had been doing** very well.

      past perfect progressive ↵

> • When I met her, she **had been shopping** at Harrods.

      past perfect progressive ↵

- This does not mean that I met her during her shopping at Harrods of Knightsbridge, London, but after her shopping. If you wish to say that you met her during her shopping period/time, use the **past progressive tense** as shown below:

> • When I met her, she **was shopping** at Harrods of Knightsbridge
>
> past progressive tense ↵   London.

> • When our guests arrived, I **had been cooking** for them.

      past progressive tense ↵ - <u>points to an ongoing action</u>

           in the distant past ↵

- In all these cases, it implies a continuous action in the distant past. The continuity in the distant past is at the heart of the past perfect continuous tense. Here are a few more examples for you:

- We were in France. We had been enjoying our long weekend in Paris.

- She had been studying at Warsaw University when I moved to Poland.

- When we saw Robin last time, he had been distributing leaflets for another musical show on the doorstep of the Carlton Club.

These examples illustrate that the past perfect continuous tense is used only in the past context.

11 . Future perfect tense

The future perfect tense is used when the speaker or the writer is thinking about the future, and then looks back when something will be completed at a specific point in the future time. It is constructed as:

Future perfect tense = will/shall + have + past participle
(- ed/en/ other ending)

For example:

- By next month, they **will have submitted** our report to the director.

⇑   ⇑
thinking about the future   saying by next month specific point
in future time
report will be submitted ⇒ looking back into the future

- Three days' stay is enough in Berlin, as you will have seen
1   2
its main attractions within this time.
. In this example: 1 ⇒   projecting into the future
2 ⇒ predicting the future outcome in a specific duration in the future
looking back into the future ↵

- In <u>two months' time</u>, we **will/shall have** gone to Austria.

⇑   ⇑

projecting into the future   <u>predicting the future outcome</u>
<u>in a specific period in the future</u>

looking back into the future ↵
- saying in two months' time(specific point in future time)

we will be in Austria ⇒ looking back into the future

<u>You can use shall with the first person.</u>

- They <u>will have replied</u> to our letter <u>by now</u>.

⇑   ⇑

predicting the future   <u>a particular time in the future</u>

looking back into the future ↵

12 . <u>Future perfect progressive tense</u>

The future perfect progressive tense is used when the speaker or the writer is thinking about something and then looks back when something will be completed at a specific point in the future time. It is constructed as:

Future perfect progressive tense = will/shall + have +been + participle –**ing** ending

- At the end of January, I <u>shall/will have been living</u> in London.

- Tomorrow night, we <u>will have been crossing</u> the English Channel by a night ferry.

- She wants us to marry next summer, as we <u>will have been living</u> in our new home.

- You <u>will have been staying</u> with us in three weeks' time.

Future perfect progressive tense shows continuity in the future.

13 . <u>Future in the past</u>

The future in the past is looking forward to the future from the past.
You can imagine it as your intention of doing something in the future but in
the past time. For instance:

- I <u>should/ would travel</u> to France to see Paris.

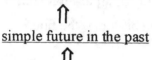

<u>simple future in the past</u>

travel in the future ahead of the present time but in the past time

- I <u>should/ would be travelling</u> to France to see Paris.

<u>future progressive in the past</u>

travel in the future ahead of the present time but in the past time

- I <u>should/ would have travelled</u> to France to see Paris.

future perfect in the past

- I <u>should/ would have been travelling</u> to France to see Paris.

future perfect progressive in the past

Tenses show that there are many facets of verb phrases. When an **auxiliary verb** is added to the **lexical verb** (main verb) to construct a verb
phrase, the auxiliary verb helps us to make a statement. Indeed, tenses
contain verb phrases. Tenses enable us to express an extensive range of
astonishing meanings.

In Table 1, you can see at a glance the full working of all tenses. It is a
summary of the information embedded in each statement, and the relationship between the **information** and the **time** (tense) when it was
enacted or spoken.

A Summary of Tenses (Active Voice)

Present Simple	Past Simple	Future Simple	Simple future in the Past
I go	I went	I shall/will go	I should/would go
Present Progressive	**Past Progressive**	**Future Progressive**	**Future Progressive in the Past**
I am going	I was going	I shall/will be going	I should/would be going
Present Perfect	**Past Perfect**	**Future Perfect**	**Future Perfect in the Past**
I have gone	I had gone	I shall/will have gone	I should/would have gone
Present Perfect Progressive	**Past Perfect Progressive**	**Future Perfect Progressive**	**Future Perfect Progressive in the Past**
I have been going	I had been going	I shall/will have been going	I should/would have been going

Table 1

In summary, when we make a statement about a situation that exists now, in the past or will happen in the future, we are referring to **a point in time.** This specific idea of point in time is at the heart of tenses. Thus, all learners of good grammar should be able to construct tenses summarised in Table 1. See also page 389 for another table.

****

> . For More Example See ⟹ Phrases
>
> . Passive Voice Tenses See ⟹ Exercise 3 below

Over to You

1. The following sentences contain finite and non-finite verb phrases. Identify these verb phrases. Give two reasons for the identification of these types of verb phrases.

a) Please leave this room.
b) Our manager took action to remedy the situation.
c) The suspect murderer has been interrogated for the last three days.
d) He tried to help us.
e) Definitely, we want to know the truth in this matter.
f) She categorically denied her involvement in that car accident.
g) He wished to come home tonight.
h) They wanted to be assured of their place in the semi-final.
i) Our shopping centre was crowded with day trippers.
j) They had been trying to telephone us from Moscow.
k) A passer-by found an elderly man bleeding on the roadside.
l) Jane reported to work twenty minutes late twice last week.
m) He prepared his speech very carefully to deliver it tonight.
n) He wondered what to do next for a living.
o) Neither Anne nor I recalled ever having seen them.

2. Each of the following sentences has one or two blank spaces. Your task is to fill in these spaces. These completions will result in different tenses. Identify each completed tense.

a) I ----- happy.

b) They ------ going to the beach now.

c) Two years ago, she ------- in England for three years.

d) Recently, Harry ------ written to us from Cambridge.

e) On my arrival, I ------ write to you from Spain.

f) Now we ------ watching a film.

g) Last week they --------skiing in Switzerland.

h) Not long ago, they --------- travelled to France.

i) Last year, we -------- the Indian summer in the UK.

j) She -------- never ridden a horse before she joined our club.

k) You must believe me I did not think that I ----- come First
     in London Marathon Race this year.

l) The Indian summer --------- returned today.

m) We will ------ arriving at 14.000 hours at Victoria Coach Station.

n) Most certainly, I --------- be staying at The Regents Hotel in Paris.

o) By that time, we will have retired.

p) The weatherman told us that it --------- going to rain all that day.

q) He had ----- talking to me.

r) At that time our train will ------- been travelling through
     the tunnel.

s) By that time, We ----- have returned to France.

t) At the end of this year, we -------- -------- been living in this house
     for ten years.

u) Indeed, she promised that she --------- be writing to me soon about
     our plans for the future.

v) During our visit to Paris last year, you indicated that you ------ ----
     been moving to another flat.

w) We all knew Jane would ------- working at the post office.

x) Your father told me you -------- served your country in Bosnia.

118   **Verbs(2) – Formation of Tenses**

****

y) I have ----- showing our learning resources to new colleagues.

z) We ---------having torrential rain now.

3. Table 1, in this chapter 1, is a summary of tenses in the active voice. Your task is to design a table similar to this table but in the passive voice by inflecting the verb eat.

4.

The following four sentences are incorrect. Correct these and state their tenses:

a) There is three reasons for not accepting their invitation.

b) If we had been requested for help in this matter, we have taken all the necessary steps to protect her.

c) She was disappointed that her daughter will not be travelling to England to see her mother.

d) They asked her if she will be accepting this post.

****

Chapter 6

Adjectives

• Introduction

Adjectives are words used with a noun or a pronoun to modify the noun or the pronoun. In doing so, they tell us what something is like. There are many thousands of words that are classed as adjectives and function as adjectives only. In addition, many more thousands of words which function as nouns, adverbs and so on also function as adjectives. Adjectives change their forms when a comparison is made. They <u>do not</u> do so for a gender or number (singular or plural). Some adjectives are shown in List 1 below.

Some adjectives

awful, beautiful, big, busy, cheap, clear, clever, dangerous, dark, difficult, easy, expensive, extraordinary, famous, foreign, gloomy, glorious good, happy, harmful, harmless, huge, inaccessible, inaccurate, incapable, jealous, jobless, jolly, kind, lovely, loving, low, mean, medium, mental, native, nice, noble, nosy (or nosey), obnoxious, obscene, opportune, painful, passionate, popular, quick, quiet, quizzical, recent, relentless, religious, short, smooth, straight, tall, three-quarters, tiny, ugly, unfit, unfriendly, vain, vast, vivid, weary, wedded, wide, yellow, young, youthful, zonal.

List 1

Let's consider first the following two examples:

- I can see a **tall man** standing in front of our house.

    --- ------

adjective ⌐   ⇑

         noun

In this sentence, the word **tall** gives some information about the man by describing him as tall. Since it is used with the noun **man,** its function is considered as modifying or qualifying the noun **man.** Here the adjective is a modifier. If you wish, you can think of modifying as defining the noun **man.** The adjective in this position in this sentence is giving us information about an attribute (tall) of the noun man.

- I can see a **very tall man** jumping up and down.

    ----- ---- ------

intensifier ⌐   ⇑   ⇑

      adjective noun

Here **very** is preceding the adjective **tall** and is thus functioning as an intensifier. The reason for placing it in front of the adjective is to grade the height of that particular man who is jumping up and down. By placing **very** in front of tall, we have graded the adjective on an imagined scale. **Very** is an adverb of degree that tells us about the measurement on an imagined scale as it does not specify the height in any recognised unit of measurement. This example shows that adjectives are **gradable**. Here are some more examples:

- She is a **most generous person**.

    ------ ------------ ---------

intensifier ⌐   ⇑   ⇑

      adjective noun

- You are **kind** to me.

    ------ -------- ------

   ⇑   ⇑   ⇑

   1   2   3

      1 is personal pronoun – subject form
      2 is adjective
      3 is personal pronoun – object form

In this example, the adjective **kind** refers to the personal pronoun **you**. This way, it is modifying the personal pronoun by giving information (that is kind) about the pronoun.

- It is a **nice new** car for us.

adjective ↵ ⇑
      adjective

In this example, **nice** is modifying the adjective **new**. The adjective **new** is modifying the noun car. When two or more adjectives occur before a noun, their position is fairly fixed as above.

The following examples further illustrate that adjectives modify pronouns:

- **She** was **happy** to hear the news about her son.

- **They** arrived home **hungry** and **angry** due to traffic congestion on the M1 motorway.

- **It** is a **cold**, **wet** and **stormy** night.

• The position of adjectives

Most adjectives can occur in two particular positions in a sentence or a clause. Certainly, some adjectives can be placed in one particular position, but not in the other position in a sentence or clause. These rules are explained below:

• **An adjective can occur before a noun**. Here are some examples:

- John lives in an **old** house.

adjective before the noun ↵

122   **Adjectives**

****

The adjective **old** relates to the house. In fact, it defines or modifies the noun 'house' in terms of its age. The word age as an attribute is giving information about the house. <u>When an adjective modifies or defines a noun, and it comes before the noun, such a word is called an **attributive adjective**.</u> This is further illustrated by the following examples:

      . We are having a **lovely** time.
                      ------

   attributive adjective ⤶

     . It is certainly a **big** day for all of us.
                      ----

   attributive adjective ⤶

     . This is an **expensive** property.
               ----

   attributive adjective ⤶

     . I do not like **loud** music.
                -----

   attributive adjective ⤶

     . It was a **memorable** holiday for all of us in France.

     . It is a **beautiful** garden for a wedding party.

     . They have two **lovable** daughters.

. <u>**An adjective can occur in the predicate.**</u>

This is demonstrated below:

     . This crime is the **worst** in our city's history.
            -------   -------

noun to which the⤶   ⇑
adjective relates   adjective

In this sentence, the adjective occurs between a noun and a verb. Here the adjective is in the **predicate**.

> • See ⟹ sections on Subject Element and Complement Element
>
> for Predicate ⟹ under Clauses

In this sentence, **crime** is the subject. The remainder of this statement is the **predicate.** Since after the subject, the remainder of the sentence describes the **crime** (subject) as the **worst** (adjective), and thus the adjective occurs in the predicate.

> • The **house** in which John lives **is old**.
>   -------   --- ----

noun to which the ↵   verb↵

adjective relates   adjective ⟹ occurs in the predicate

When an adjective occurs in a sentence in the predicate as illustrated above, it is called a **predicative adjective**. In each example, the adjective is placed after the noun.

Here are some examples of adjectives that occur only in the attributive position:

• A number of countries of the **former** Soviet Union are now
  independent countries.   ---------
                  ⇑

        attributive position - **former** ⟹ attributive only

• The proposed new road will link the **principal** cities in our
  part of the country.   -----------
               ⇑

        attributive position - **principal** ⟹ attributive only

• Her bank overdraft **upper** limit is £2500.
            ----

attributive position - **upper** ⟹ attributive only

• On the other hand, **unwell, alone, contented** and some other adjectives occur only in the predicative position:

- I am very sorry that he is **<u>unwell</u>** and will not be able to come

  to work today.

         predicative position - **unwell** ⟹ predicative only

- He lives **<u>alone</u>** in a big house.

     predicative position - **alone** ⟹ predicative only

- He was a **<u>contented</u>** person.

  ⇑

predicative position - **contented** ⟹ predicative only
(contented used with nouns)

• <u>Comparisons of adjectives</u>

The only time adjectives change their forms is when a comparison is made. There are three comparative forms of adjectives. These are shown above in Table 1. These forms are graded by degree, which shows the extent of comparative qualities.

- **<u>Descriptive form</u>** is the form of the adjective as listed in dictionaries. It is also known as the **positive form**.

- **<u>Comparative form</u>** is used for comparing two objects.

- **<u>Superlative form</u>** is for comparing three or more objects.

Objects are people, animals, animated and natural things .

<u>Table 2 on page 127 shows some examples of these adjective forms.</u>

The following examples illustrate the use of these forms of adjectives:

          - He is a **<u>tall</u>** person.

     descriptive ↵ - no comparison is intended

- He is **taller** than you.

comparative form of adjective $\Rightarrow$ a comparison is made between two persons

- He is the **tallest** in our group of 10 persons.

superlative form of adjective $\Rightarrow$ compares a person with more than two other persons

• Irregular forms

Some adjectives have irregular forms. Table 1 contains the most commonly used irregular adjectives.

<u>Some irregular adjectives</u>

Descriptive	Comparative	Superlative
good	better	best
little	less	least
bad	worse	worst
many or much	more	most

<u>Table 1</u>

• Intensifiers

These are words like **extremely**, **fairly**, **incredibly**, **quite** and **very**. Sometimes an adjective can be preceded by an intensifier in order to emphasise the quality of the adjective.

By means of intensifiers we can strengthen the meaning or the quality of the adjective to a desirable degree of comparison. The following examples illustrate the use of intensifiers:

- You can say about someone:

    - He is **very** clever.

    - He is **fairly** clever.

    - He is **quite** clever

    - He is **extremely** clever.

    - He is **incredibly** clever.

- You can describe a place as:

    - It is a **large** cricket ground.

    - It is **quite** a large cricket ground.

    - It is a **fairly** large cricket ground.

    - It is a **very large** cricket ground.

    - It is an **incredibly** large cricket ground.

- You can compare one person or thing with another:

    - James was **more** intelligent than John.

    - Today the crowd was **much** bigger than any other crowd I have ever seen.

    - His speech proved **less** formidable than yours.
    -----

lower degree comparison.↵

    - Europe's Express Coach Network is the **least** expensive travel system in Europe.   -------

lowest degree of comparison - cheapest mode of travel ↵

    - He is the *least* successful in our group in this tournament.

Some examples of adjective forms

Descriptive (Positive)	Comparative	Superlative
beautiful	more beautiful	most beautiful
black	blacker	blackest
big	bigger	biggest
cold	colder	coldest
difficult	more difficult	most difficult
endearing	more endearing	most endearing
few	fewer	fewest
great	greater	greatest
intelligent	more intelligent	most intelligent
large	larger	largest
long	longer	longest
loud	louder	loudest
lovely	lovelier	loveliest
many	more	most
nice	nicer	nicest
noisy	noisier	noisiest
old	older	oldest
poor	poorer	poorest
quiet	quieter	quietest
short	shorter	shortest
sunny	sunnier	sunniest
tall	taller	tallest
ugly	uglier	ugliest

Table 2

. Absolute adjectives

There are some adjectives that cannot be graded by degree in the same

****

way as shown above. Such adjectives exist only in their basic form.
They do not have comparative, or superlative inflections. The following examples demonstrate this characteristic of some words used as
adjectives:

> • You are **right** this time.

descriptive or basic form↵- no other forms exist

It means that you cannot be more or less right if you are right. It is the
highest degree of quality implied by this adjective. Just the opposite is
wrong. For instance:

> • Robert is **wrong** to suggest that John is guilty.

descriptive or basic form ⟹ no other forms exist

It means what it implies no more no less. It cannot be graded. It is
incorrect to say **very wrong**.

> • This is a **unique** occasion in our lives.

descriptive or basic form – no other forms

It means one specific occasion. It is incorrect to grade it as **a very
unique** occasion or **more unique** than the other occasions.

> • It is **impossible** for you to reach Manchester from here by

⇑   car in 60 minutes.

descriptive or basic form

You cannot say less impossible, fairly impossible or add anything else
to it in order to grade it. Therefore, you cannot compare absolute adjectives. The following words are also examples of absolute adjectives:

absolute, dead, elder, infinite, only, perfect, real

• When can a word function as an adjective?

There are a great many words which can function as adjectives. A noun can be used as an adjective. Similarly, an adverb can function as an adjective. Pronouns can do the work of adjectives. Furthermore, some words can be used as participles and adjectives. Indeed, you can also create many adjectives by adding suffixes to many words. For the sake of understanding words that can function as adjectives, we can discuss them as follows:

. **<u>Descriptive</u>** - These are descriptive words and easily recognised. Some of these are listed below:

> handsome, good, beautiful, green, black, ugly, bad, rough, smooth

. **<u>Demonstrative</u>** – **this, these, that** and **those** are demonstrative adjectives. They point out to the noun which they modify.
For instance:

- . this ship $\Rightarrow$ ship is modified by $\Rightarrow$ this
- . those books $\Rightarrow$ books is modified by $\Rightarrow$ those
- . that car $\Rightarrow$ car is modified by $\Rightarrow$ that
- . That car is mine. $\Leftarrow$ **That** is modifying the noun $\Rightarrow$ car
- . This house belongs to John's sister. $\Leftarrow$ **This** is modifying the <u>noun</u>

                                         house↵

. <u>When **this, that, these** and **those** are used with nouns as shown above, they are known as **demonstrative adjectives**; otherwise they function as pronouns. This is illustrated below:</u>

> . You can have **<u>this</u>**.
>
>   pronoun ↵   See $\Rightarrow$ Pronouns

. **<u>Interrogative</u>** -What? Which? These words are used with nouns to ask questions. For instance:

> . **<u>What</u> time** was it when you saw her?

interrogative adjective↵ ⇑
                 noun

•**What** arrangements have you made for your Easter break?

•**Which** newspaper do you read?

•**Which** car did you buy the other day?

In these examples, both **what** and **which** as adjectives are connected with one attribute of a noun that is next to them in each sentence. By asking a question, the speaker is inquiring about the quality/ attribute of a noun. This is how they function as adjectives - when they are asking for information about the noun next to them.

• **These interrogative words can perform different functions under other word classes as illustrated below:**

(1) • **What** went wrong ?

pronoun↵ - no noun here

(2) • **What** job will you do first?

determiner↵

(3) • I have several products. **Which** do you want?

pronoun↵ - non noun here

(4) • **Which** teacher is your tutor?

determiner↵

In examples 2 and 4 **what** and **which** are before nouns and thus they are functioning as **determiners**(2 and 4 may be described as interrogative adjectives). On the other hand, in examples 1 and 3, **what** and **which** are not used with nouns next to them and thus these are functioning here as **pronouns**.

• **Adverbs** – some words can function as adjectives as well as adverbs. For instance:

• She talks **fast**.

adverb ↵ - modifying verb ⇒ talks

****

- It is a **fast** train.

  adjective ↵ - modifying noun ⟹ train

Fast can also function as a verb and as a noun.

- We will most **likely** miss her now.

  adverb ↵ - modifying verb ⟹ miss

The word **miss** is also a noun. The word **likely** means expect or probable. Note that **likely** as an **adverb** must be preceded by any of these intensifiers: **most, more, or very.**

- The most **likely** outcome is a draw.

  adjective ↵ - modifying noun ⟹ outcome

Note that **likely** as **an *adjective*** is usually preceded by more or most.

- **Nouns** – some nouns can function as adjectives. Conversely, adjectives can also function as nouns. The following examples show how this happens in practice:

  - From my **past** experience I'd say it is more likely to happen.

  adjective ↵ - modifying noun ⟹ experience

  - During the **past** month I was in Italy.

  adjective ↵ - modifying noun ⟹ month

In both examples, past means gone by in time.

- He often looks back on the **past** with a mixture of regrets and joys.

  functioning as a noun ↵

- I have travelled on this route in the **past**.

  functioning as a noun ↵

In the last two examples, past means the time that has passed away ; and things that you have done in an earlier time. The context of these examples illustrates in what capacity a word is functioning in a sentence.

- **Sometimes adjectives can function as nouns if they are preceded by a definite article 'the'.**

  For instance:

  - Our government must do more to help the **homeless**.

    functioning as a noun ↵

  - There have been many failed government attempts to help **homeless** people.

    ⇑

    functioning as an adjective

- **Participles** – some participles(**verb + - ing ending**) can function as adjectives. Here are some examples:

  - The current international political crisis is **worrying**.

    functioning as an adjective ↵

  - Marion's forthcoming travel to Siberia alone is **worrying** her parents.   functioning as a participle↵

    See Participles

- ### How can you recognise an adjective?

Words such as **cold, good, bad** and **wonderful** are descriptive adjectives. Such adjectives are easily recognisable. The English language has thousands of adjectives. There are some common word endings that help you to recognise adjectives. Some of these word endings, together with some adjectives, are listed in List 1.

- # A word of warning

Words ending with –**ly** and –**y** often cause confusion as many adverbs and adjectives have these endings. For instance: **holy** is an adjective but **yearly** is both an adjective and an adverb.

Some adjectives and their recognisable word endings

Word Ending	Adjective
– *able*	breakable , fashionable, desirable, comparable
– *al*	commercial, brutal, dismal, natural
– *ar*	circular, perpendicular, popular, solar
– *ed*	worried, excited, subdued, inexperienced
– *ent*	intelligent, excellent, urgent, negligent
– *ful*	joyful, wonderful, harmful, careful
– *ible*	incredible, sensible, compatible, horrible
– *ic*	alcoholic, athletic, classic, idiotic
– *ing*	dying, laughing, charming, encouraging
– *ish*	Irish, foolish, childish, selfish
– *ive*	decorative, demonstrative, adhesive
– *less*	meaningless, harmless, childless, defenceless
– *like*	childlike, warlike, businesslike, ladylike
– *ous*	dangerous, courageous, nervous, marvellous
– *some*	awesome, troublesome, handsome
– *worthy*	newsworthy, praiseworthy, roadworthy

List 1

• Compound adjectives

There are thousands of single word adjectives in English. There are also many adjectives which are made of two or more words. These adjectives are usually written with hyphens between them. For instance:

> • She is really a **good-looking** lady.
>   --------------------
>   compound adjective ↵

- I cannot trust him as he is **two-faced***.

  compound adjective ↵
* It is used for a person who says different things to different
  people about something and is thus not a trustworthy person.

  - You must remember that fame can be a **two-edged** sword**.

                               compound adjective ↵
* It means two possibilities – one good and one bad.

    - He borrowed some money from me because he is **hard-up***.

                               compound adjective ↵
** It means having very little money for a short time.

- The following is a short list of some compound adjectives:

absent-minded	clear-cut	hard-wearing	penny-pinching
accident-prone	close-fitting	ill-advised	quick-tempered
action-packed	close-cropped	kind-hearted	quick-witted
air-worthy	deep-frozen	light-hearted	run-down
back-door	easy-going	low-cut	run-of-the-mill
back-to-back	far-reaching	mouth-watering	stuck-up
big-headed	fancy-free	narrow-minded	two-dimensional
cack-handed	good-tempered	open-minded	well-tried

In summary, some adjectives only identify the noun as in the phrase
first chapter. Many adjectives describe nouns as in the phrase **a green
coat**. It is telling us about the noun which is of a green colour. There is
a widespread tendency to use adjectives, when they do not add any information to the meaning of the nouns they modify (in **serious crisis**,
both words mean the same).

See⟹ Adjective Phrases. Answers ⇓ contain some further information

Over to You

****

1. Read the following sentences. If you find any of these sentences using an incorrect adjective, correct it; otherwise write against it 'correct'.

a) She says that she feels stronger than she did yesterday.

b) What a loveliest surprise!

c) Chelsea football ground was fuller of spectators.

d) We specialize in clothes for a fuller figure.

e) The amount of money involved is quite smaller.

f) John's weekly salary is less than the salary of any of us.

g) He was very ill on his wedding day.

h) Which of the two boxers will be most successful?

i) We think it would be wiser to meet them.

j) It would be rather advisable to calm down tonight.

k) The plane was almost empty from Stockholm to London.

l) She was quite tall and thinnest.

m) He feels somewhat depressed about his future.

n) After the accident, she was confused.

o) In our class she was most clever.

p) In our old town the streets are extremely narrow for cars.

q) He loved her brighter blue eyes.

r) Is £1000 sufficient for your trip to Italy?

s) It is the most perfect timing.

t) We could have travelled by bus, or an underground train or just walked down to the British Embassy, but we preferred the latter.

2. In the following sentences pick out modifiers(words which are before nouns) and adjectives.

a) I am so tired today.

b) In my opinion, she was absolutely right in accepting his sincere apology.

c) I must say that the lecture was not at all informative and interesting.

d) It was really the nicest place I ever visited in that part of the world.

e) He is by far the best candidate for this job.

f) She is feeling no better today.

g) We were warm enough that night.

h) In Paris underground trains were somewhat crowded.

i) I am pretty sure that they will accept our offer this time.

j) We quite enjoyed travelling by train to Paris.

3. Explain to a friend the use of adjectives and adverbs in the following statements.

a) Warsaw has a very interesting old town.

b) At the present, our weather is depressing.

C)) His employers have sent him a cautiously worded letter.

d) Those nice people came from Egypt for the conference.

e) Which local hotel are you booking for the party?

****

Chapter 7

Adverbs

•**Introduction**

An adverb is a word that modifies or qualifies another word, which may be a verb, an adjective or another adverb. It can also modify or extend an adverbial phrase, prepositional phrase and conjunctions. Indeed, the adverb has the largest range of functions of any part of speech. Note that word class and parts of speech mean the same.

Adverbs can be difficult to identify. However, the most common function of adverbs is to modify the main verb in a sentence. Therefore, it is reasonable to assume that this is a reason for giving it this name. There is a large number of adverbs for expressing reason, time, manner, place, order, etc. Some of the adverbs are listed below:

Some adverbs

abruptly, absolutely, accordingly, afterwards, again, aggressively, carefully, early, easily, frightfully, fully, gently, ghastly, heavily, here, however, just, nevertheless, nervously, now, quickly, quietly, perfectly, roughly, slowly, so, softly, sometimes, successfully, suddenly, then, there, therefore, too, truthfully, unintelligently, unintentionally, vaguely, vastly, very, violently, why, wholly, widely, willingly, worriedly, yearly, yearningly, yesterday, yet.

List 1

The following examples illustrate the use of adverbs:

> • We walked **<u>slowly</u>**.

adverb of manner ↵ – modifying the verb ⇒ **walked**
It tells us how we walked. The adverb **slowly** has affected the meaning of this short sentence.

> • **<u>Soon</u>** we will leave home.
>

adverb of time ⇒ expressing time ⇒ it tells us about **when** we will leave in the future

> • He said **<u>almost</u>** nothing new to protect his reputation.
>

adverb of degree – it means here scarcely

almost nothing = scarcely anything
Here **almost** is modifying the quantifier **nothing** (= no single thing = not anything)

> • Some people go to bed **<u>early</u>**.

> adverb of time ↵

> • Have you anything **<u>else</u>** to do this afternoon?
>

adverb modifying the question (else = any other things)
Here **else** means in addition to something already known.

> • If you **<u>ever</u>** wish to visit Berlin, you can stay with us.
>

adverb of frequency - modifying the verb ⇒**wish**
<u>Note that ever = at any time</u>

> • You knew where I was. **<u>Moreover</u>**, you knew who had done it.
>

> adverb – here its function is to support the previous statement
> Here moreover = in addition

- <u>**Somehow**</u>, I do not feel she can convince them of her honesty.

adverb of reason – related to an unspecified reason
Note that somehow = reason unknown

- During the boring seminar, he answered the question **<u>drowsily</u>**.

  adverb of condition – indicating sleepy state ↵

- That red car could **<u>easily</u>** be our motor.

  adverb of possibility – indicating possibility

- There was a road accident but **<u>luckily</u>** no one was injured.

  adverb expressing ⟹ wish

- Silvia spoke **<u>very</u>** quickly.   ⟸ **Silvia or Sylvia**

  adverb modifying another adverb⟹**quickly**

- That little girl looks **<u>very</u>** pretty.

  adverb modifying adjective ⟹**pretty**

The above examples demonstrate that adverbs are useful words to enhance the meaning of both written and spoken statements. Many adverbs give information about **when**, **where**, **how** and the extent of
something. In addition, there are many other adverbs of other meanings. Some of these are exemplified above and more examples are
given later in this chapter.

. <u>Position of adverbs</u>

You can see in the above examples that adverbs can be positioned at the beginning, in the middle or at the end of a sentence. However, if you place an adverb without thinking about which word the adverb should modify, you can change the meaning of the sentence unintentionally. For instance:

- John spoke to us **<u>clearly</u>** in English.

adverb modifying verb $\Rightarrow$ **spoke**
in this position, the adverb **clearly** = **distinctly**

Here the adverb **clearly** is functioning as an adverb of quality. It is specifying how distinctly/clearly John spoke to us in English.

- **<u>Clearly</u>,** John spoke to us in English.

adverb of certainty

- In this position, the adverb **clearly** = **certainly**

In this sentence, the adverb is modifying the whole sentence. It refers to the entire context of this sentence. It is implying that <u>without doubt John spoke to us in English</u>.

It shows that an adverb can modify different parts of the sentence. It is, therefore, important to position it correctly in order to avoid ambiguity. You may come across some rules of placing the adverb in a sentence. There are no universally laid down rules. In general terms, you can place an adverb before the word it is modifying. This rule is not workable in many cases. However, before using an adverb, make sure that it does not lead to an unnecessary vague meaning.

. <u>Adverb forms</u>

1. <u>Many words exist as adverbs</u>

These adverbs are not related to adjectives or any other classes of words. Many adverbs of this group are commonly used. Some adverbs of this category are listed below:

> again, almost, always, else, elsewhere, ever, evermore, hence, henceforth, how, however, moreover, often, perhaps, quite, really, seldom, soon, somehow, somewhat, therefore, thereby, thus.

2. Many adverbs have the same form as adjectives

The following words can function as adjectives and adverbs:

Adjective	Adverb
alike	alike
backward	backward(s)
clean	clean
early	early
far	far
fast	fast
forward	forward(s)
full	full
further	further
hard	hard
late	late
long	long
next	next
only	only
straight	straight
weekly	weekly
well	well

List 2

- The following examples illustrate the use of some words as adjectives and adverbs:

  - It is a **straight** street.

    adjective ↵

  - I went **straight** home as we were expecting a guest.

    adverb ↵

- You must cook it for a **further** 3 minutes.

  adjective ↵

- I had walked **further** than I had planned.

  adverb ↵

- It is **hard** work for me.

adjective ↵

- You must try **hard** to pay back my money.

  adverb ↵

- From London to Edinburgh by coach is a **long** journey.

  adjective ↵

- You can stay here as **long** as you like.

  adverb ↵

- How far is it to the **next** underground station?

  adjective ↵

- Who will jump **next**?

  adverb ↵

- He was the **only** person at the scene of the accident.

  adjective ↵

- I **only** arrived a few minutes before the meeting started.

adverb ↵

- Since the car accident, she is not a **well** woman.

  adjective ↵

- Nothing was going **well** without him.

  adverb ↵

3. Many adverbs are formed from adjectives as:

adverb = adjective + ly

The following examples illustrate how adverbs are created by applying this rule:

Adjective ⇒ **Adverb derived from adjective + ly**

Adjective	Adverb
articulate	articulately
bold	boldly
certain	certainly
descriptive	descriptively
excessive	excessively
glorious	gloriously
jealous	jealously
memorable	memorably
quick	quickly
serious	seriously

• In addition to the above, the following spelling rules for converting adjectives into adverbs are applied:

4. To form an adverb from an adjective ending in a consonant + y:

insert i after the consonant and replace y by ly

The following examples illustrate how adverbs are generated by applying this rule:

Adjective ⇒ Adverb derived from adjective - ily form

Adjective	Adverb
bloody	bloodily
bloodthirsty	bloodthirstily
cheery	cheerily
drowsy	drowsily
dry	drily (also dryly)
easy	easily

Adjective ⇒ Adverb derived from adjective - ily form

---

gloomy	gloomily
haughty	haughtily
hearty	heartily
lazy	lazily
lucky	luckily
patchy	patchily
risky	riskily
shy	**shyly** (exception as it does not obey the rule)
sly	**slyly** (another adverb formed against the rule)

• It is worth mentioning that the adjective **gay** has a vowel 'a' before 'y'. It becomes an adverb **gaily** in the same way as adverbs derived above. This is another exception to the above rule.

5. <u>To form an adverb from an adjective ending in a consonant + le , replace e with ly.</u>

The following examples illustrate how adverbs are created by applying this rule:

Adjective ⇒ Adverb derived from adjective – ly form

---

agreeable	agreeably
able	ably
ample	amply
credible	credibly
debatable	debatably
equable	equably
humble	humbly
laughable	laughably

Adjective ⟹ Adverb derived from adjective – ly form

probable	probably
possible	possibly
reasonable	reasonably
simple	simply
subtle	subtly
terrible	terribly
understandable	understandably
vulnerable	vulnerably

6. <u>To form an adverb from an adjective ending in -ic, add -ally to the word.</u>

The following examples illustrate how adverbs are created by applying this rule:

Adjective ⟹ Adverb derived from adjective + ally form

apologetic	apologetically
artistic	artistically
basic	basically
bureaucratic	bureaucratically
characteristic	characteristically
dramatic	dramatically
frantic	frantically
heroic	heroically
historic	historically
idiotic	idiotically
intrinsic	intrinsically
optimistic	optimistically
organic	organically
periodic	periodically

Adjective $\Rightarrow$ Adverb derived from adjective + ally form

prosaic	prosaically
symbolic	symbolically
sympathetic	sympathetically
systematic	systematically
telepathic	telepathically

• Here is an example of an exception to the above rule:

public $\Rightarrow$ publicly

7. To form an adverb from an adjective ending in l, just add -ly to the word.

The following examples illustrate how adverbs are created by applying this rule:

Adjective $\Rightarrow$ Adverb derived from adjective + ly form

awful	awfully
beautiful	beautifully
boastful	boastfully
careful	carefully
eventual	eventually
material	materially
meaningful	meaningfully
medical	medically
punctual	punctually
respectful	respectfully
successful	successfully
wonderful	wonderfully

7. To form adverbs from adjectives ending in -ll, just add -y to the word.

For instance:

- full $\Rightarrow$ fully (also full)

- shrill $\Rightarrow$ shrilly

- There are not so many adjectives which end in double –*ll*

• Adjunct word or phrase

An adverb or phrase that adds meaning to the verb in a sentence or part of a sentence is called an adjunct. When additional information is given by the adjunct in a sentence, it is modifying or qualifying. Therefore the adjunct acts as a modifier. It may be removed from the sentence without making the sentence ungrammatical. It is usually an adverbial or a prepositional word or a group of words. For instance:

- He came **fast**.

fast is an adverb and adjunct

- He telephoned us **in a great hurry**.

a group of words - adjunct phrase

Both the adverb and the phrase add further information to the verbs **came** and **telephoned** respectively.

• Functions of adverbs

- The most common function performed by many adverbs is to **modify the verb.** Here are some examples:

- She drives **safely**.

adverb modifying the verb drives by adding further

information $\Rightarrow$ **safely**

safely enhances the central meaning conveyed by this statement.

• He walks **gently**.

adverb modifying the verb walks

Here the adverb adds further information by way of highlighting **how** this particular person walks.

• We are **very** pleased to meet you.

adverb modifying the verb pleased

Here the adverb **very** places emphasis on the meaning of the whole sentence.

• Due to noisy people in the room, I could **hardly** hear you.

phrase ↵

adverb modifying the verb hear

In this sentence, the adverb **hardly** adds meaning to the verb in the clause(part of a sentence).

• She was seen **recently**.

adverb modifying the verb was seen

Here the adverb adds further information to the meaning of this statement by pointing out the time when she was seen.

• **An adverb modifies another adverb:**

This is exemplified below:

• Police arrived at the accident scene **very quickly**.

first adverb↵

second adverb

<u>In this sentence:</u> • quickly $\Rightarrow$ adverb modifies verb $\Rightarrow$ **arrived**

• very $\Rightarrow$ adverb modifies second adverb $\Rightarrow$**quickly**

In this case, the adverb **very** acted as an intensifier. It is one of the adverbs of degree. Its use in this sentence has graded the adverb **quickly**, and thus placed greater emphasis on the meaning of the other adverb.

- He has performed <u>**unexpectedly**</u> <u>**well**</u>.

       first adverb ⤶   ⇧

                 second adverb

In this sentence:

- well ⇒ adverb modifies verb ⇒ **performed**

- unexpectedly ⇒ adverb modifies adverb ⇒ **well**

Here the adverb **unexpectedly** is a descriptive adverb. Its function is similar to that of adjectives modifying nouns. It adds an extra layer of meaning to the central meaning of this statement.

- He left home <u>**most resentfully**</u>.

     first adverb⤶   ⇧

             second adverb

- resentfully ⇒ adverb modifies verb ⇒left

- most ⇒ adverb modifies adverb ⇒**resentfully**

- We visited John <u>**quite often**</u>.

      first adverb ⤶   ⇧

           second adverb

- often ⇒ adverb modifies verb ⇒ **visited**

- quite ⇒ adverb modifies adverb ⇒ **often**

Here the adverb **quite** adds extra meaning conveyed by **often** which is an adverb of time.

- Sarah answered questions <u>**more fully**</u> than Jane did.

      first adverb⤶ ⇧

           second adverb

- more **fully** $\Rightarrow$comparative use

- fully $\Rightarrow$ adverb modifies verb $\Rightarrow$ *answered*

- more $\Rightarrow$ adverb modifies adverb $\Rightarrow$ *fully*

In this example, **more** is acting as an intensifier by placing emphasis on the meaning of the adverb **fully**.

• An adverb can modify an adjective:

The following examples show this action:

- He is <u>**fairly**</u> <u>**happy**</u>.

  adverb⤶   ⇑

        adjective

- fairly $\Rightarrow$ adverb modifies happy $\Rightarrow$ **adjective**

The adverb **fairly** is placed before the adjective **happy** in order to intensify the meaning of this adjective.

- This suitcase is <u>**really nice**</u>.

  adverb⤶   ⇑

       adjective

  - really $\Rightarrow$ adverb modifies adjective $\Rightarrow$ **nice**

The use of the adverb **really** adds further information to the meaning of the adjective **nice**.

- This car is <u>**too long**</u>.

  adverb⤶   ⇑

       adjective

- too $\Rightarrow$ adverb modifies adjective $\Rightarrow$ **long**

- You're <u>**absolutely right**</u>.

  adverb⤶   ⇑

       adjective

- absolutely $\Rightarrow$ adverb modifies adjective $\Rightarrow$ **right**

- This is a **quite** **small** office.

     adverb↲   ⇑   ⇑

              adjective   noun

- **quite** $\Rightarrow$ adverb modifies adjective $\Rightarrow$**small** modifies $\Rightarrow$<u>office</u>

                                         noun↲

When **quite** is used with an adjective, before a noun , it must be preceded by **a**, or **an** as illustrated above.

- **An adverb can modify a preposition:**

This is exemplified below:

- He is sitting <u>**right beside**</u> his father.

     adverb ↲   ⇑

                preposition

- **right** (right = exactly) $\Rightarrow$ adverb modifies preposition

- **beside** (beside = next to)

- The car <u>**just** **in front of**</u> me stopped suddenly causing this accident.

 adverb↲   ⇑

           preposition

       - **just** (= exactly) $\Rightarrow$adverb modifies preposition

       - **in front of** (= ahead but near)

- When you called, I was <u>**really in**</u> the garden shed without my mobile phone.   adverb↲   ⇑

                        preposition

    - **really** (= truly or in reality) $\Rightarrow$ adverb intensifying the meaning of the preposition $\Rightarrow$ **in**

- They are <u>**always**</u> <u>**at**</u> home in the evenings.

        adverb↲   ⇑

                 preposition

- always (= at all times) ⟹ adverb modifies preposition ⟹**at**

- He entered the hall **quietly from** the back door, which was unlocked.

                       --------- -------

          adverb↲   ⇑

                   preposition

- **quietly** (= without any sound or noise) ⟹ adverb modifies

  preposition ⟹ **from**

- <u>**Adverbs can also modify prepositional phrases.**</u> See ⟹ phrases.

• <u>Types of adverbs</u>

The prime function of an adverb is to support the central meaning of a statement by supplying further information. Indeed, the inclusion of an adverb in a sentence can enhance the meaning of a statement. The examples given above illustrate this role played by adverbs in sentences. The following types of adverbs cover a wide range of functions performed by adverbs:

. <u>Adverbs of manner</u>

The adverbs of manner describe <u>**how**</u> something happened or was done. This is exemplified below:

            • Andrew approached Jane **calmly**.

                       ----

             adverb of manner ↲

It gives us information about **how** Andrew approached Jane. It answers the question:

- <u>**How** did Andrew approach Jane?</u> It modifies the verb **approached**.

* He drives **smoothly**.
  ----

adverb of manner ↵

It answers the question:

* How does he drive? **smoothly**. It modifies the verb ⟹ **drives**

    * Tell us **frankly**, what's the matter with you.
      ----

  adverb of manner↵

* How did she tell him? **frankly**. It modifies the verb ⟹ **tell**

* Most adverbs of manner end in *ly* as illustrated by the above examples. Some adverbs of manner do not end in *ly* as demonstrated by the following examples:

  * Cars were running fast **on** the motorway.

    adverb of manner ↵

  * How were cars running? **fast**.- modifying the verb ⟹ **were running**

  * Robert walks **straight**.
    ----

  adverb of manner ↵

  * How does Robert walk? **straight**. - modifying the verb ⟹ **walks**

* Sometimes the adverb of manner can be without **ly**. For instance:

  * She told him the **loudest** in front of their guests that she didn't

    adverb of manner ↵   love him.

    - **loudest** modifying the verb ⟹ **told**

* **Louder, loudest are used in informal style.**

  * You should walk **slowly**.

    adverb of manner ↵ - modifying the verb ⟹ **slow**

• <u>Some adverb of manners are listed below:</u>

---

absolutely, awkwardly, beautifully, brilliantly, carefully, clearly, comfortably, correctly, dramatically, efficiently, frankly, honestly, incidentally, nicely, patiently, politely, properly, quietly, roughly, sensibly, softly, thoroughly, truthfully, urgently, voluntarily, warmly, willingly

---

. <u>Adverbs of time</u>

Adverbs of time state **when** something or some action has taken place or will take place. The following examples illustrate how adverbs of time can be used:

• We enjoyed a group discussion **afterwards**.
                              ----

                         adverb of time⤶ - modifying the verb ⟹ **enjoyed**

It answers the question:

                  •When did you enjoy group discussion? **afterwards**

• We discussed this matter **yesterday.**
                      ----

             adverb of time ⤶ - modifying the verb ⟹ **discussed**

               • She is ill **now**.
                      -----

           adverb of time ⤶ - modifying the verb ⟹ **ill**

• This news programme is broadcast **nightly**.
                            ----

               adverb of time⤶- modifying the verb ⟹broadcast

         • **Soon** I will finish this job.
          ------

adverb of time ⤶ - it modifies the verb ⟹ **finish**

In this example, the adverb is the first word. Often, the adverbial of time goes in the end position as illustrated above. It usually happens that place and time are mentioned together. Let's examine adverbs of place now.

• <u>Adverbs of place</u>

Adverbs of place tell us **where** something occurs or happens or shows a direction(place). The following examples show the use of adverbs of place:

    • We will meet **here**.
      ------

    adverb of place ↵ - it is modifying ⟹ **will meet**

  • They live **upstairs**.
     ----

adverb of place ↵ - it modifies the verb ⟹ **live**

    • We parked our car **somewhere**.

    adverb of place ↵ - it modifies the verb ⟹ **parked**

  • Sylvia is **abroad** for her friend's wedding.
    ----

adverb of place ↵ - it modifies the verb ⟹ **is**

  • The bad weather kept us **indoors** over the weekend.
      ----

    adverb of place↵- it modifies the verb ⟹ **kept**

  • Please go **upstairs** where she is waiting for you.
    ----

adverb of direction↵- indicating direction to the person who is being talked about

  • You must not **look down**, if you feel dizzy on this cliff.
    ----

adverb of direction↵- direction to a place

• **Adverbial phrases are made of more than one word.**

For instance:

---
round and round, to and from, back and forth, anti-clockwise,

in and out.   See ⇒ Phrases.

• Some adverbs of place are listed below:

---

ahead, ashore, backward, close, downtown, in, inland, locally, nationally, near, next door, northward, outdoors, overseas, southward, there

---

• Adverbs of reason and purpose

Adverbs of reason and purpose inform us why an action or something has happened. The following examples show their application:

> • He said it **deliberately** to annoy me.
>   ----------------

adverb of purpose ↵ - it modifies the verb ⇒**said**

It tells us the reason why he said it and thus answers the question:

• Why did he say it? **deliberately** ⇒ it means intentionally.

• **Inevitably**, our journey was cancelled because of late payment.

⇑

adverb of reason

• **Why?** **inevitably** means something certain to happen or occur. The cause is given in this statement.

> • I broke it **accidentally**.
>   ---------------

adverb of reason ↵

****

- You made it difficult for us **purposely**.
  ----

adverb of reason ↵

- I did not hurt your feelings **intentionally**.
  ----

adverb of reason ↵

. <u>Adverbs of frequency</u>

Adverbs of frequency tell us about the repetition or occurrence of something. Some adverbs of frequency are used in the following examples:

- The class **always** begins at 9.15.
  ----

adverb of frequency ↵ - How often ? **always**

- I come to this park **often**.
  ------

adverb of frequency ↵ - How often? **often**

- It's **usually** the manager's responsibility.
  ----

adverb of frequency ↵- How often? **usually**

- I eat rice **rarely**.
  ----

adverb of frequency ↵ - How often? *rarely* (seldom = rarely)

- Nothing **ever** happens in this place for young people.
  ------

adverb of frequency ↵
<u>**Ever** is used with negative statements and questions. It expresses doubt or condition. It usually comes before a verb as shown above.</u>

. <u>Adverbs of degree</u>

Adverbs of degree show the **extent** to which something has happened.

These adverbs are often used. Here are some adverb of degree:

> altogether, awfully, considerably, dreadfully, easily, enough, forever, fully, greatly, hard, incredibly, just, less, least, more, most, noticeably, perfectly, quite, rather, remarkably, so, strongly, sufficiently, totally, too, truly, unbelievably, very, well, wonderfully.

These adverbs include words like: **easily**, **enough**, **forever**, **somewhat**, and **twice**. The following examples show how to use such adverbs:

- He visited us **fairly** recently.

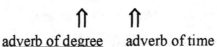

adverb of degree   adverb of time

modifying **recently** ↲ - intensifying the meaning of the adverb of time

- I **<u>hardly</u>** knew his intention.

adverb of degree modifying the verb ⟹ **knew**

- This pair of shoes is **rather** expensive.

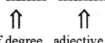

adverb of degree   adjective

modifying **expensive** ↲

- She fell **<u>right</u>** <u>to</u> the bottom of the stairs.

adverb of degree   preposition

modifying **to** ↲

- The lecture hall was **half** full.

  ----

  adverb of degree ↵ - modifying adjective ⟹ **full**

Adverbs of degree can also be a fraction (half) or percentage, e.g. thirty percent wrong.

• <u>Adverbs for other functions</u>

In addition to the above types of adverbs, there are adverbs for indicating the following wide range of functions:

- <u>**Adverb of viewpoint**</u> expresses a particular view concerning a specific state or situation. Some adverbs of viewpoint are: **financially**, **economically**, **personally** and **strictly**. Here are some examples:

  - This trip is **financially** bearable.

    ----

  adverb of viewpoint ↵ - expressing financial state

  - **Economically**, the USA is the strongest country.

    ----

  adverb of viewpoint ↵ - expressing economical status/state

- <u>**Adverb of focus**</u> is used to highlight the word or a phrase which the writer or the speaker wants to focus on. Some adverbs of focus are: **also**, **even**, **especially**, and **only**. For example:

  - I **only** visited him once in London.

    ----

  adverb of focus ↵ - focusing on the verb⟹ **visited**

<u>**Only** is the word the writer wanted to focus on.</u>

****

- She **especially** loves his wealth.

----

adverb of focus ↵ - focusing on the phrase ⟹ **his wealth**

- **Adverbs of different attitudes** relate to a comment on someone's behaviour, feeling, truth, falsity and similar attitudes. Some relevant adverbs are:

curiously, fortunately, honestly, possibly, naively, surprisingly, wisely

Some of these are exemplified below:

- He was in the lecture hall, but **curiously**, I did not see him.

adverb of attitude ↵

In this sentence, the adverb **curiously** (= strangely) indicates the truth the writer/speaker knows.

- She **naively** trusted the caller.

adverb of attitude – indicating behaviour

- **Honestly**, I have no idea where he has gone for his lunch.

adverb of attitude – emphasizing the truth spoken

- **Possibly**, they will reject our invitation.

adverb of attitude – predicting feelings of some people

- **The linking adverb** relates to the previous sentence or clause. Some linking adverbs are listed below:

anyway, besides, further, furthermore, however, moreover, nevertheless.

These are exemplified below:

- You say the balance is zero. **However,** I think one invoice is still unpaid.
                        ----

             adverb of linking↵ linking the previous sentence

- We are late for the meeting. **Anyway,** we must attend it.
                        ----

             adverb of linking↵ linking the previous thought/statement

- **The comparison of adverbs** is similar to the comparison of adjectives. Some adverbs have the same form as adjectives. Adverbs take the comparative and superlative forms with such endings:

---

er/est, more/most, farther / farthest, further, furthest, better/best

---

In practice, there is hardly any difference between these and adverbs of degree. These are illustrated below:

- Tomorrow you should start your work ten minutes **earlier** than usual.
             comparative form of adverb↵

- She likes him **more** than his wife.

comparative form of adverb ↵

- His complaint is **worse** than I thought.

comparative form of adverb↵ - comparative of ⟹ **badly**
                                            (badly, worse, worst)

- Friday is the **soonest** I can contact you by telephone.

superlative form of adverb↵ - it means here as soon as possible

- Which car do you like **best**?

superlative form of adverb ↵ - superlative of ⟹ **well**

• The railway station is **farthest** from where our car is parked.

superlative form of adverb ↵ - superlative of ⟹ **far**
                                          (**farthest = very long distance**)

As you have already noticed that many adverbs are single words. In addition, there are many groups of words that can function with and without adverbs as **adverbial elements**. These adverbials form phrases and clauses. For instance:

Yesterday morning, I saw him. In this sentence, the adverbial element is highlighted. In fact, it is an adverbial phrase as it has no finite verb.

See ⟹ Phrases

• When is a word an adjective or an adverb in a sentence?

Both adjectives and adverbs have some common features and differ in some respects. In order to understand adverbs as a word class, it is vitally important that you appreciate their specific functions as discussed in this chapter.

Certainly, there are many adjectives and adverbs, which perform the same function of describing something in a sentence. However, from the context of a sentence you can find out whether it is an adjective or an adverb. For instance:

• She had a **long** wait at Heathrow due to an industrial strike.

adjective↵ -**long** is placed before a noun to modify the **noun**

                                                                    wait ↵

• She had to wait **long** at Heathrow due to an industrial strike.

adverb↵ **long** is placed after the verb wait modifying the **verb**

                                                                    wait ↵

Sometimes, it can create some confusion in recognising when a word is an adjective or an adverb. Furthermore, this may lead to the incorrect use of a word.

In summary, adverbs can enhance the overall meaning of a statement. Even so, most of the time, they are not essential components for structuring sentences. You can construct a meaningful and grammatically complete sentence or statement without any adverb. However, there are occasions when the inclusion of an adverb in a sentence is desirable.

Over to You

1. The following sentences contain adverbs and their functions. List these under adverbs and the type of function that they are performing:

a) She softly held my hand in her gentle hand and smiled.

b) He regularly telephones her daughter in France.

c) This equipment is too expensive for our small business.

d) There was so much disagreement that our meeting ended abruptly.

e) I must add that you have certainly made good progress this year.

f) The profit margin will hardly cover our costs.

g) Afterwards we took the last train to get home.

h) In the UK shops are open, even on Sundays.

i) The summary is given below.

j) An EU financial grant will be economically beneficial to our region.

k) She sings much better than I do.

l) Where will we meet?

m) She drove anti-clockwise on a one-way street.

n) It is most likely that they will not accept our invitation.

o) Please do not think that the mess was created intentionally.

2. The following words are adjectives. Some words function as both
   adjectives and adverbs. Some adverbs are closely related to some
   adjectives. In the following list, write against each adjective its
   corresponding adverb.

   alarming, brilliant, continual, depressing, extreme, elegant,
   frightening, gross, horrible, immense, independent, light-
   hearted, misleading, nationwide, off-hand, ragged, underground,
   worried, wrongful.

3. Exemplify the use of adjectives listed above in example 2. Also
   construct sentences using their corresponding adverbs so that
   the nature and function of these adjectives and adverbs are easy
   to understand.

4. The following statements contain adverbs and adverbials. If
   you find any of these either in the wrong place or incorrect,
   you should correct them and give a reason for doing so.

a) Often one can buy fruit cheaper in the market.

b) She told the grocer that she could buy this cheaply at
   a supermarket.

c) On the left, the gentleman is my uncle.

d) Usually this car park is full

e) He probably does not care very much about her health.

f) He purposely did not exchange greetings with his opponents.

g) How is she? She is kind and we like her very much.

h) The business conditions improved themselves even more
   rapidly than was expected.

Chapter 8

Prepositions

• Introduction

A preposition is a word or a group of words used before a noun, pronoun or noun phrase. It also shows the relation of a noun, pronoun, noun phrase or clause to the rest of a sentence. There are many simple words and groups of words which act as prepositions. Some of these are listed below under simple and group prepositions:

Some prepositions

Some simple prepositions

about, above, across, along, among, at, bar, before, behind, beside, by, circa, down, during, except, for, from, in, inside, into, minus, near, notwithstanding, of, on, out, over, per, plus, pro, to, since, towards, under, with, without(it is listed as one word in some dictionaries).

Some group prepositions

according to, ahead of, apart from, because of, due to, instead of, near to, as far as, in accordance with, in addition to, for the sake of, in favour of, in front of, in a hurry, in terms of, in view of, on behalf of, with reference to, with regard to.

List 1

As shown above, the basic form of a preposition is just one word. This form is known as a **simple preposition**, e.g. **at**. A **group** or **compound** or **complex preposition** consists of two or more prepositions, e.g. **in accordance with**. It is worth mentioning here that sometimes two or more simple prepositions merge together to form a complex word preposition, e.g. **onto**. See above. The following examples illustrate their specific feature of coming before a noun, pronoun or noun phrase:

- **Anne left the office** before lunch.

preposition before a noun ↵   ⇑

                      noun

In this sentence, the preposition before joins the first part of the sentence (highlighted) with its second part. This is how it shows the relationship between these two parts of the sentence. It also meets the specific requirement of a preposition, e.g. a preposition comes before a

noun ⇒ lunch. Similarly:

- **They shouted my name** across the road.

                preposition ↵   ⇑

                          noun phrase

preposition occurred before a noun phrase↵

- We live **next to** him.

          preposition ↵   ⇑

             personal pronoun

Prepositions express a variety of relationships between a noun, pronoun, noun clause or noun phrase and the rest of a sentence. They cover a wide range of meanings. The most typical are the relationships of **place** and **time**. Some of these relationships are illustrated below:

. <u>Prepositions of place</u>

This is illustrated by the following examples:

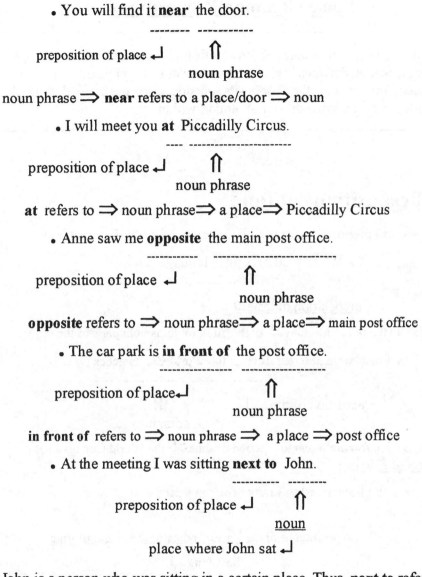

• You will find it **near** the door.

preposition of place ↵   ⇑
                    noun phrase

noun phrase ⇒ **near** refers to a place/door ⇒ noun

• I will meet you **at** Piccadilly Circus.

preposition of place ↵   ⇑
                    noun phrase

at refers to ⇒ noun phrase⇒ a place⇒ Piccadilly Circus

• Anne saw me **opposite** the main post office.

preposition of place ↵   ⇑
                        noun phrase

opposite refers to ⇒ noun phrase⇒ a place⇒ main post office

• The car park is **in front of** the post office.

preposition of place↵   ⇑
                        noun phrase

in front of refers to ⇒ noun phrase ⇒ a place ⇒ post office

• At the meeting I was sitting **next to** John.

preposition of place ↵   ⇑
                        <u>noun</u>
        place where John sat ↵

John is a person who was sitting in a certain place. Thus, **next to** refers to the place where John was sitting.

• Some common prepositions which relate to place and direction are listed in List 2. Some of these are consist of more than one word.

Some Common Prepositions

about, above, across, ahead of, away from, before, behind, below, beneath, beside, between, by, close by, down, from, in, inside, in between, into, near, off, on, opposite, outside, over, past, round, through, throughout, to, towards, out of, under, within.

List 2

. Prepositions of time

We use prepositions of time in a variety of ways. For example:

- We arrived here **on** Monday.

preposition of time↵   ⇑

refers to the time - Monday↵- preposition **on** joins both parts of the sentence

- Roads were deserted **during** the World Cup matches.

preposition of time ↵   ⇑
                                 noun phrase

Preposition **during** refers to a period of time⟹ the World Cup matches –
a definite time

- We have lived in France **for** ten years.

preposition of time↵ - **for** indicates the length of time
how long ↵

- You should arrive **before** the weekend.

preposition of time↵ - **before** refers to the time
no later than the weekend ↵

• My contract will not expire **until** the end of next month.

      preposition of time↵ - **until** refers to the time

      when an event/ **contract** will expire↵

• A sentence can have both place and time prepositions. For instance:

    • We will meet you **at** breakfast **in** our hotel.

    preposition of time ↵ ⇑   ⇑   ⇑

refers to breakfast ↵   noun preposition noun phrase

    ⇑   ⇑

it is at a particular time   refers to a place ⇒ **our hotel**

    • We have been living **for** three years **in** this house.

      preposition of time ↵   ⇑

     refers to a period of time   preposition of place

        refers to a place - this house↵

    • We lived close **to** their shop **in** 1995.

  preposition of place ↵   ⇑

refers to a place = shop   preposition of time - *in* refers to time ⇒ **1995**

• Prepositions of other meanings

Here are some other prepositions related to other meanings. These are discussed under some appropriate headings below.

• Prepositions of cause, reason and purpose

These are described below with the aid of the following examples:

    • The brutal crime was committed **without** a motive.

      preposition of reason ↵   ⇑

                        noun phrase

The preposition **without** is followed by the noun phrase, which points to a **motive** $\Rightarrow$ **reason**

- Our Prime Minister is anxious **about** the predicted unfavourable

    election result.   ⇑
                                    preposition of **reason**

Note that **a cause** produces **an effect**, e.g. an event or something that happens. On the other hand, a reason has a much wider scope. For instance, you can give a reason for something which is done. A reason can be a justification for something happening. The following examples illustrate the use of some prepositions of cause:

- I am happy <u>because of</u> <u>a return to normal working hours</u>.
            ⇑   ⇑
    <u>preposition of **cause**</u>   noun phrase – describes an event
            ⇓
    indicates the effect of an event described by the noun phrase on

    I **(subject)** as $\Rightarrow$ **happy**

- His lateness was **due to** <u>a traffic jam in the town</u>.
            ⇑   ⇑
    <u>preposition of **cause**</u>   noun phrase – describes an event
            ⇓
    indicates the effect of an event stated by the noun phrase on

    his lateness $\Rightarrow$ **subject**

- <u>It is worth mentioning that the word **purpose** means an intention or</u> determination to do something. The following examples illustrate the use of such prepositions:

    - **Despite** the rain, we will travel to London for Jane's wedding.
    ⇑
    preposition of **purpose**

Here the preposition **despite** points to travel without being deterred by rain.

****

- She went to work **contrary to** her doctor's advice.

preposition of **determination**↵ preposition **contrary to**

shows her determination for work↵

- **Prepositions of exception, addition, support, opposition, etc.**

The following examples show how to use such prepositions:

- We have paid the loan **except** for the commission

⇑   and interest charges.

preposition of exception - refers to ⟹ an exception

It can also be a verb meaning **exclude** or **exempt**.

- All guests have left **except** John Smith from England.

preposition of **exception**↵- implying that only John Smith is still here

- We have no close friends in this area **other than** Jack and Jill.

preposition of **exception**↵- implying **only** or **except**

Here is another example to demonstrate its further use:

- Jane seldom seems **other than** cheerful.

preposition of **exception**↵ implying only or except (seldom = not often)

- She is beautiful, **apart from** her height

preposition of **exception**↵ - implies that the height is excluded

- I have completed all orders **apart from** the one received just now.

preposition of **exception**↵

⇑

apart from implies the order just received is not yet completed

- In the last two examples, **apart from = except for**. On the other hand, in the following examples **apart from** has a different meaning.

In these examples: **apart from = in addition to = as well as**

* **Apart from** his inherited wealth, he owns this global enterprise.

  ⇑ - apart from implies ⇒ in addition to something
  preposition of addition

* **Apart from** his well-paid full-time job, he has a part-time job.

  ⇑ - apart from implies ⇒ in addition to something
  preposition of addition

* Our trainer was **with** us throughout the race.

preposition of support⤶ - or preposition of ⇒**possession**

* I saw Eric walking **with** a girl **with** red hair.

       ⇑   ⇑

preposition of accompaniment   preposition of possession

The last example indicates that sometimes prepositions can express different meanings. In this sentence '**with red hair**' means '**who has red hair**'.

* His age is **against** him for this travelling salesman's job.

       ⇑

  preposition of opposition

* Among the most common prepositions are **of** and **with**. These are used to denote possession or belonging as demonstrated below:

      * Sarah is a young pianist **of** rare talent.

  preposition of possession ⤶

* **There are prepositions for almost all kinds of meanings.**

  Here are some examples:

  * You can pay for your travel **by** cheque or **by** credit card.

                    1 ⤶   2 ⤶   ⇑

                                        implies 'any card'

  1 = 2 = preposition of **manner**

- Some parents stay together <u>despite</u> their differences <u>for the sake of</u> their children.   ⇑   ⇑
                    preposition of concession   preposition of reason/purpose

- <u>**Some prepositions are not easy to recognise, e.g. via and vis-à-vis**</u>.

These are exemplified below:

- We came to know about your success **<u>via</u>** your sister.

                    preposition of manner↵

- It is claimed that Microsoft has an unfair commercial advantage **<u>vis-à-vis</u>** other software companies in the world.

preposition of comparison ↵ - this is of French origin

<u>The preposition **vis-à-vis** means in comparison with or in relation to</u> <u>something. Here is another example of its use:</u>

- Nurses' earnings *<u>vis-à-vis</u>* the national average are very low.

preposition of comparison↵ -relation

. <u>Prepositional idioms</u>

Many prepositions are used with idioms. You have to learn the use of idioms. Here are a few examples of prepositional idioms.

- John and Jill began to argue loudly, and I thought it was time I **<u>stepped in</u>**.
        ⇑

preposition of idioms - idiom⟹ **step in = to intervene**

- She is **<u>at heart</u>** a very kind person.

prepositional idiom ↵ idiom ⟹ **at heart = really**

- He thanked us **<u>from the bottom of his heart</u>** for all our help.

                    prepositional idiom↵

idiom ⟹ from the bottom of one's heart = very sincerely

- The manager wants to talk to all of us **one by one**.

                                    prepositional idiom↵

    idiom ⟹ one by one = individually

- The resolution was passed by the board of directors.
  on the nod.

prepositional idiom
on the nod = all agreed without taking a vote

- <u>**When is a word a preposition, an adverb or a conjunction?**</u>

A word can function as a preposition, an adverb or a conjunction. The main feature of a preposition is that it is followed by a pronoun, noun or noun phrase. If you apply this rule to a sentence, you should be able to find any preposition in a sentence. The following three examples illustrate the use of the word **before**.

- John had left home <u>**before**</u> his wife's arrival.

  Preposition of time ↵   ⇑

                              noun phrase

- <u>The adverb modifies a verb, an adjective, another adverb or an adverbial phrase.</u>

For instance:

- That happened <u>**before**</u>.

  adverb of time ↵ - modifying the verb happened

- <u>The function of a conjunction is to join clauses to form compound and complex sentences.</u>

For instance:

- <u>It may be a long time</u> **before** <u>we meet again.</u>

  clause 1↵   conjunction ↵   clause 2 ↵

clause 1 + conjunction + clause 2 = complex sentence

You have to examine the context in which the word is used in a sentence to determine if the word is a conjunction, adverb or preposition.

A standard dictionary should be consulted if you are not sure of the meaning and usage of a preposition.

In summary, prepositions have a wide range of meanings and many different uses. They can be a source of confusion. For example, **by** can express time, place, manner and action. For instance:

. The computer was repaired **by** me. ⇐ Preposition of **action**
. It must arrive **by** next day. ⇐ Preposition of **time**
. It is laying *by* the table. ⇐ Preposition of **place**
. They went away **by** taxi. ⇐ Preposition of **manner**
  by is also an adverb. For example:
. Time goes **by** so quickly. ⇐   **by** is an **adverb**.

English has a large number of prepositions. Some are long-winded such as **for the reason that**. Its equivalent is **because**. When possible, use a short one. See ⇒ Phrases   and   See ⇒ Clauses

Over to You

1. Fill in the prepositions in the following sentences:

a) The lady who is sitting almost ---- the end of the second row.

b) When he was waiting ---- his wife outside the supermarket.

c) You must be ready ------ I arrive ---06 hours.

d) We drove ---- the Channel Tunnel --- France.

e) My desk is ---- Karen's desk ---- the third floor.

f) When I was going ----- the stairs and she was coming-----
the steps, we spoke to each other.

g) She wrote to my boss angrily ----- his cleaning rota schedule.

h) ---- that time, we went ----- the cinema ----- our French guests.

i) We were walking ------ the path, when we suddenly appeared.

j) During the tea break, he came ------ me and introduced himself.

k) ---- winning the lottery jackpot, she became famous overnight.

l) The intruder disguised himself ---- a policeman.

m) Silvia is more intelligent ----- Clair.

n) She is a colleague ----- my wife.

o) Our government ought to do everything ------- their power
   to stop increasing gun related crimes.

p) You will find a package ----- the main gate.

q) I wandered ----- their beautiful garden.

r) Please take your hand --- -- my shoulder.

s) I cannot copy it now as our machine is ------order.

t) ----- ---- way to Scotland, we had lunch in the Lake District in
   England.

2. The following sentences have some **highlighted** words. List these
   under adjective, adverb and preposition.
a)
Although there is no right or wrong way to apply this technique, it does help
to have a **basic** understanding **of some applied** principles.
b)
Kissing and worshipping the feet **of** divine or eminent souls is **still** a sign **of**
respect that was, **for** centuries, evident in cultures **worldwide**.
c)
The social smile is **quite distinct from** the genuine smile of pleasure.
For a start, the one you conjured **up just now** has **almost certainly**
by now disappeared **without** trace. A **spontaneous** smile lingers, and fades
more evenly and **slowly**.
d)
With life **constantly** changing, and people striving to progress, this

understanding makes it easier to be **hard working** and **healthy**.
e)
Just as you shouldn't take a polite letter **for** an **encouraging** one,
don't let a harsh letter do more damage **than** necessary.

3. The following statements have some errors. Re-write these
   with corrections.

a) At the garden everything was very colourful.

b) Our plane landed on Frankfurt Airport on time.

c) This is my Hungarian friend whose home I stay in.

d) We are looking what ought to be ordered.

e) Has the medical nurse been sent?

f) There is something strange in him.

g) My wife was very much worried what to wear tonight.

h) I told the policeman that I did not have my driving licence on me.

i) To be successful in life, you must believe yourself.

j) They cut their tree a month ago.

k) I have received some DVD's from a friend to listen.

l) I haven't met him from last Christmas.

m) We arrived in time on 23.00 hours.

n) Our guests arrived on time for the evening meal.

o) Could I please use this desk instead the other desk?
p) During the course of our discussion, she became rather angry.

q) How long did you stay in Berlin? I stayed in Berlin during
   the week.

r) I was lucky **that** I had a friend in Warsaw to call for help.

Chapter 9

<u>Determiners & Interjections</u>

• <u>Introduction</u>

A determiner is a word that comes before a noun or a noun phrase. It is used to determine which person (s) or thing(s) are being referred to in a statement. Let's consider the following examples:

> • **The** chancellor.
> ----- ---------------
>
> determiner ↵   noun↵

There are chancellors' posts in many countries. In this sentence, it refers to a unique chancellor in one country. Here the determiner indicates a unique position.

> • **The** House of Commons.
> ----- --------------------------------
>
> determiner ↵   noun phrase↵

The United Kingdom has only one place called the **House of Commons**. This is the only recognised place of this name in the country. In this case, the determiner refers to a unique status for a unique building.

The above examples show that some words are called determiners because they determine how nouns and pronouns are being used. In the above examples, it determines how the noun the **chancellor** and the phrase **House of Commons** are used. A determiner by itself does not make much sense, but when it is used with nouns and noun phrases it amplifies their meaning.

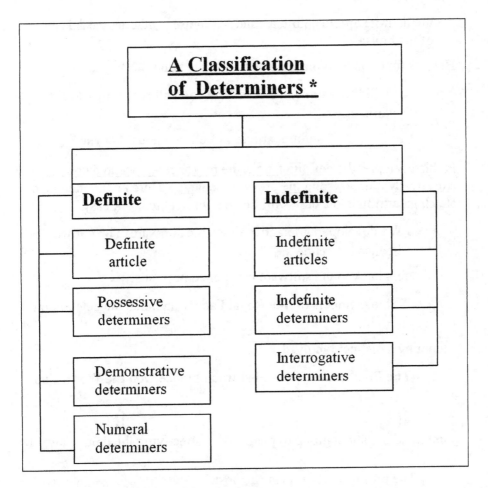

Diagram 1

* sometimes called demonstrative adjectives.

• The definite article

Its use is exemplified and explained below:

- It is **the** house where I was born.
  ----

the definite article before a noun ⟹ **house** - indicates the uniqueness
of the house

Here its function is to place emphasis on the noun ⟹ **house**

- I will buy a **car** tomorrow. **The car** will make my travel to
  work easy.   ----

  definite article ↵ before a noun ⟹ **car**

In this example, <u>the definite article **the** makes reference to a noun a
car already mentioned in the previous sentence.</u> Here its function is to
attach an attribute to a car: "will make my travel to work easy"

- We developed interactive timetable software. **The** software is
  licensed to schools.   -----

refers back to the software mentioned previously↵

- Some members of **the** Royal Family attended the celebration
  tonight.   ---

denoting a distinct family↵

- **The** French nation was glad when France won **the** World Cup.
  ----   ----

pointing to a distinct group of people   specifying the unique award

- The promised letter is in **the** post.
                        ----

indicating that the noun **post** is a communication organisation

Here the **post** is not thought of as a particular post office, but as an organisation in the communication business.

****

- **The** highest mark in the psychology test was gained by Anne.

⇑ - noun phrase

the precedes the superlative adjective ⟹ **highest**

Here **the** is modifying the superlative adjective **highest**.

- June 21ˢᵗ is **the** longest day each year.

⇑

the preceded the superlative adjective *longest* in this noun phrase

In this example, **the** is modifying the superlative adjective **longest**.

- Margaret Thatcher has been **the only** female British prime minister.

⇑

the preceded the adjective **only** in this noun phrase

⇑

modifying the adjective ⟹ **only**

- Now is the turn of **the next** person.

⇑

the preceded **next** in the noun phrase ⟹ **the next person**

In this case, **the** is modifying the adjective **next**.

- It was **the** summer of 2000, when I went to Poland.

----

phrase of time ↵

It is not preceded by an adjective but by **the**.

- A phrase of time containing a noun begins with **the** as illustrated

182   **Determiners & Interjections**

****

above. <u>The condition is</u> that the noun must not be preceded by an adjective. Some more examples to illustrate this rule are:

- We visit our parents at **the** weekend.

  ⇑

  phrase of time without an adjective before the noun

- They married **the** following Saturday.

  ----

  the preceded the phrase of time ↵

- <u>Use **the** before the name of a country, if its name ends with kingdom or republic</u>: For instance:

  - This book was published in **the** United Kingdom.

  - **The** Republic of Ireland is in Europe.

- Use **the** before a plural name of countries: For example:

- In 1958, **the Netherlands** became a founding member of the EEC.

- **The United States of America** consists of 50 administrative states.

- <u>If the name of a region is not modified by another word (an adjective)</u>, **the** comes before it: For instance:

  - Birmingham is situated in the Midlands.

- <u>The definite article can be used to express how something is</u> measured. This is illustrated below:

  - In these days, potatoes are sold by **the** kilogram.

- <u>The definite article precedes the names of entertainment places, trade and similar centres, galleries and museums.</u>

Here are a few examples:

* We met in **the Tate Gallery** some years ago.

* **The World Trade Centre** is situated near London Bridge.

----

the is not needed before this name ↵

Many bridge names are without **the**, but there are exceptions to this rule. For example, the Humber estuary in North East England has a bridge over it. This bridge is called 'The Humber Bridge'. It is the longest single-span suspension bridge in the world. The Humber Bridge (1981)

* I have been to **the Albert Hall** several times.

----

an entertainment hall in London↵

* **The Dorchester** is a well-known hotel in London, England.

* A definite article comes before a noun, if it indicates a unique position/status: For example:

  * As **the secretary** of this club, I am responsible for administration.

* **The** is used with an unaccountable noun, providing an unaccountable noun refers to some particular person(s) or object(s). For instance:

* **The petrol** in the United Kingdom is more expensive than in Spain.

----

unaccountable noun - preceded by **the** ⇒definite article

  * Their cat loves **the music** played on radio.

----

unaccountable noun↵- preceded by **the** ⇒definite article

* **The** is used with a plural noun when a noun refers to some specific meaning: For instance:

- Michael Jackson and **the children** were shown together.

> plural noun↵ – here it means some particular children

- **The books** we received from Poland are not in English.

plural noun↵ – refers to some specific books

• <u>Indefinite articles</u>

The indefinite article has two forms: **a** and **an**. Their functions are exemplified below:

- Yesterday was **a bit** warmer day.

indefinite article↵   ⇑

                       noun phrase

- When a noun phrase describes something or a person, the indefinite article precedes the noun phrase as shown above. On the other hand, in the following example *an* is essential. The reason is that the article **an** precedes the noun if a singular noun begins with a vowel (a, e, i, o, u). For instance:

- **An** elephant from India has ears like **the** map of India.

⇑   ⇑

indefinite article   definite article

In the last example, four nouns (elephant, India, ears, map) are mentioned five times. Only on two occasions indefinite and definite articles are used respectively. On the other three occasions, there is no need to insert any of these determiners.

<u>Both examples show that the indefinite article stands for *one* or in other words, **a** and *an* function as one.</u>

****

. She is **a** nice girl, isn't she?

 --- ---------

indefinite article↲   ⇑

noun phrase with a singular noun ⇒**girl**

. My son is **a** student.

 ----

indefinite article↲ - preceded a singular noun ⇒**student**

● A phrase of time begins with *a* if a noun is preceded by an adjective.

This is illustrated below:

. *A* very cold winter day is here. Or : *A* very cold winter day!

 ----------------------   ------------------------

⇑   ⇑

phrase indicating time   phrase of time forming no sentence

winter ⇒ noun is preceded by the adjective ⇒**very**

. **very** is both an adjective and an adverb. Here it is functioning as an adjective of degree

. **cold** is both an adjective and a noun. Here it is used as an adjective

See ⇒ adjectives

. **A** wonderful day when England won the World Cup.

 ----

phrase of time↲-day ⇒ noun preceded by the adjective **wonderful**

. **A** remarkable **day!**

In this phrase, the noun is preceded by the adjective. For this reason, the indefinite article *a* started this phrase.

* The indefinite article comes before a noun if it does not indicate a unique position/status: For instance:

    * As *a* member of this union, I am entitled to free admission.
    ----

essential in this phrase ↵

Since a union has many members, the status of a member is not unique.

* The indefinite article a/an precedes a noun expressing prices and similar rates: For instance:

    * Bananas are eighty pence **a kilogram**.
                            ----

                  essential in this phrase ↵

* The indefinite article can come before a noun in place of **one**. For example:

    * I would like to buy **a** car.
                        ---

              here a = one↵

* The indefinite article is used to indicate someone's job or profession or any attribute that describes the person: For instance:

    * Jane is *a* **belly dancer** in Cairo.
    ----

a is essential here↵

    * Before he joined the Labour Party, he was **a communist**.
                                            ----

                        a is essential ↵

* The indefinite article can be used instead of **any**.

    For instance:

• Just buy **a book** on psychology.

----

a book = any book ↵

• <u>Many idiomatic phrases embody both definite and indefinite articles.</u>
Here are some examples of idiomatic phrases:

    • **an** angel of mercy   • **a** bag of nerves   • **a** fair crack of the whip

    • **the** top brass   • **the** iron curtain   • **the** golden rule

• <u>Possessive determiners</u>
(Sometimes called possessive adjectives)

Possessive pronouns function as determiners if they **<u>qualify a noun</u>**.
The following examples illustrate their function as determiners.

         • This is **my** book.

Possessive determiner ↵ - qualifying a singular noun ⟹ **book**

        • This is **his** car.

Possessive determiner↵- qualifying a singular noun ⟹ **car**

     • That house is **our** property.

      ⇑

Possessive determiner <u>**our**</u> qualifying a noun ⟹ **property**

       ⇑

    plural form of the possessive determiner

     • This is **her** handbag.

    ⇑

Possessive determiner qualifying a singular noun ⟹ **handbag**

• Where is **your** horse?

Possessive determiner qualifying a singular noun ⟹**horse**

• It is **their** homeland.

Possessive determiner *their* qualifies a singular noun ⟹**horse**

• <u>Indefinite determiners</u>

Indefinite determiners function as determiners if they modify a noun. The following sentences exemplify their use.

• **All** things work well here.

indefinite determiner ↵ – qualifying ⟹ **things** ⟹ a plural noun

• Can he be **another** Ali in boxing?

indefinite determiner ↵ – qualifying a noun ⟹ **Ali**

• He doesn't eat **any** meat.

⇑ meat - an unaccountable noun

indefinite determiner – qualifying⟹ **meat**

• <u>The determiner **any** is usually used with negative sentences.</u>

• **Both** students are brilliant.

indefinite determiner ↵ – qualifying ⟹ **students** ⟹ a plural noun

<u>Strictly speaking, the word **'both'** functions as adjective, adverb</u> and pronoun.

* **Each** article is priced.

⇑ – qualifying ⟹ **article** ⟹ a plural noun
indefinite determiner

* **Either** place is suitable for our purpose.

----

indefinite determiner ↵ – qualifying ⟹ **place** ⟹ a singular noun

* You can take a seat on **either** side of the table.

----

indefinite determiner↵ qualifying a noun **- side**

* Note that **either** is also a pronoun and an adverb. It is often
  used with **or** as **either …or** to indicate a choice between two
  alternatives.

* I have recorded **every** item I found.

* **Several** men refused to show their passes.

* **Few** players have shown an interest in this tour.

------

qualifying ⟹ **players** ⟹ a plural noun

The word **few** (= not many). It also functions as an adjective and pronoun. Its attributes are fewer and fewest. See ⟹ pronouns

• <u>Demonstrative determiners</u>

Demonstrative determiners are sometime called **demonstrative adjectives**. A demonstrative pronoun becomes a demonstrative determiner
<u>only if it precedes a noun</u>. You can leave out a noun, if you think that a
sentence makes clear sense. The following examples illustrate how a
possessive word becomes a demonstrative determiner:

• Please come to my office to see **this** invoice from the wine suppliers.

-----

demonstrative determiner precedes ⟹**invoice** ⟹ noun

This indicates that the invoice is near the speaker. *These* is the plural form of '**this**'. Its use is exemplified below:

• **These bags** are full of bank notes.

----

demonstrative determiner↵ - precedes bags ⟹ a plural noun

On the other hand, **that** and **those** imply that a person(s) or thing (s) are not so near but further away:

• **That** man looks suspicious.

----

precedes man ↵ - a singular noun

• **Those** eggs were hardly boiled.

----

precedes eggs ⟹ a plural noun

• <u>Demonstrative determiners can also be used to imply space of time in terms of:</u>

• **now** = near in space of time indicated by ⟹ **this** and **these**

• **then** = further away in space of time indicated by ⟹ **that** and **those** These are exemplified below:

• I will be in France **this** month.

----

this precedes month ⟹ a singular noun **this** = now at present

****

- The only thing I do in my spare time **these** days is reading.

----

precedes days $\Rightarrow$ a plural noun

- During 1999, I lived far from here. I travelled to work by car in **those** days.

In this example, **these** precedes days $\Rightarrow$ a plural noun

- When you telephoned me **that** time, I was having a shower.

----

that/ those = **then** $\Rightarrow$ some time elapsed.

 Those is used with a plural noun, e.g. those students.

. <u>Interrogative determiners</u>

What, which and **whose** function as interrogative determiners if they precede a noun. Interrogative determiners are **wh-words** or question words. For this reason, sometimes these are called **wh-determiners**. Their use is exemplified below.

- <u>The word **that** as an interrogative determiner is used when one wants to ask someone to specify something from an indefinite number of possibilities.</u> For instance:

  - **What** time is it?

   - question word $\Rightarrow$ what

interrogative determiner preceded the noun $\Rightarrow$ **time**

  - **What** politician did you see at Harrods of Knightsbridge?

  ------

interrogative determiner preceded the noun $\Rightarrow$ **politician**

- The word **which** as an interrogative determiner is used when one wants to ask someone to specify or identify something from a limited number of possibilities. This is illustrated below:

    - **Which** lecturer did you see in our department?

      Interrogative determiner preceded the noun ⇒ **lecturer**

    - **Which** library do you often visit in this area?
      ----

      interrogative determiner preceded the noun ⇒ **library**

- **Whose** is an interrogative determiner of whom when it comes before a noun. Here are some examples:

    - **Whose** book is this?
      ----

interrogative determiner preceded the noun ⇒ **book**

    - **Whose** car is parked in my place?
      ----

interrogative determiner preceded the noun ⇒ **car**

    - **Whose** idea is this ?
      ----

interrogative determiner preceded the noun ⇒ **idea**

. Numeral determiners:

Numeral determiners are best understood as cardinal, ordinal and fraction numbers. These are discussed below under these headings.

* **Cardinal numbers** show quantity but not order in a set of numbers. Here are some examples:

  1 one   2 two   3 three   4 four   20 twenty

  100 hundred   400 hundred   1000 thousand etc.

The following examples show how cardinal numbers are written in words and numbers:

  * I have ordered **ten** bottles of quality French red wine.

  * They have bought **two** new cars in the last **12** months for their family.

  * *5 million* people voted for our party at the last local election.

  * In **1999**, I met her in London.

* The following phrases illustrate the **use of commas** in cardinal numbers:

  * **3,580** full-time students and **500** part-time students.
    ----

  three thousand five hundred and eighty

  * **1,000,000**   read it as ⟹ a million or one million.

  * **123,000,590** people.

Read it as: one hundred and twenty three million five hundred and ninety people.

* You can make phrases with cardinal numbers: For instance:

  * **Three** of us together. ⟸ cardinal number is used in this phrase

  * **approximately** two thirds full.
    ----

  approximately modifying the number - about 2/3 full not exactly 2/3

****

- **Over** 100 guests.

- - - - - - - - -

over modifying the number – meaning ⟹ more than 100

- **Ordinal numbers** show the position of something in a series.
For instance:

1st first   2nd second   12th twelfth   20th twentieth
100th   hundredth etc.

Their use is exemplified below:

- On my **60th** birthday, I invited my parents for a meal
  at the Bombay Restaurant.

- **1st and 2nd** prizes were won by two brothers.

- She came **second** in her class test.

- **Fraction** - a fraction is a part of a number. For instance:

- quarter, half, third, fourth, two and a third, etc.

- If the number is less than one, the noun phrase is preceded by **of**.
For instance:

- **One third of** our products is for export. ⟸ 1/3 = one third

- It is only **four fifths** full.   ⟸ 4/5 = four fifths

- It should be **four and three quarter** metres long.

- The length of this stick is only **three quarters of** a metre.

- She was *an hour and a half* late.   **OR alternatively:**

- She was **one and a half hours** late.

In summary, the most common determiners are the definite and the indefinite articles. Determiners are always before a head noun. Sometimes, an element such as an adjective is between the head noun and the determiner. List 1 is a summary of determiners.

A list of determiners

Definite Determiners	Indefinite Determiners
Definite article: the	**Indefinite articles:** a, an
Possessive determiners: my, your, his, her, their, our - when qualifying nouns	**Indefinite determiners:** all, almost, another, any, both, each, either, enough, every, few, fewer, fewest, little, less, least, many, more, most, much, no, neither, other, several, some
Demonstrative determiners: this, that, these, those	**Interrogative determiners:** what, which, whose These are also known as **wh- determiners**
Numerals: - **cardinal:** one, three, ten,... - **ordinal:** third, fourth seventh ... - **fraction:** a quarter of, a seventh of...	

List 1

• See ⟹ adjectives   • See ⟹ pronouns

• <u>Interjections (Exclamations!)</u>

Interjections are considered as a minor class of words. These are exclamations. Interjections are useful for expressing feelings such as excitement, surprise, etc. They are not essential for the construction of sentences. Some of these are listed below:

> Aha! Alas! Blast! Damn! Gosh! Good gracious! Good grief! Goodness me! Hey! Honestly! Ooh! Ouch! Phew! Ugh! Whoops! Wow! Yuck!

Here are some examples:

> • *Oh!* How is he now?
> ------
>

Here it is used to show someone's reaction to something that has been said. It also indicates that one did not know it before.

> • **Phew**, it is stuffy in here.
> -------
>

It shows disapproval as the place is warm in an unpleasant way and without enough fresh air.

• <u>Some of the most commonly used exclamatory phrases are</u>
<u>as follows</u>:

> • Good heavens!   • Oh dear!   • Marvellous!   • Great!

• <u>You can see from the above examples that some interjections are</u>
made <u>from other words. There are some interjections in which verb</u>
<u>forms are used.</u> For instance:

- • Watch out!   • Cheers!
- • Look out!   • Shut up!
- • What lovely flowers !   • How warm it is today!
- • Thanks a lot! ⇐ sarcastic remark ⇐ opposite to what you mean

• **An exclamation mark(!) is also discussed under punctuation.**

In summary, interjections are words that express something emphatically. They are used to show your reactions to something or an event.

Over to You

1. The use of both definite and indefinite articles in the following sentences requires correction. Correct these sentences.

a) We all know that the bicycle does not run on petrol.

b) You should get a parcel on Friday as it is a special delivery.

c) There is a lot to show the visitor.

d) She was a only woman I loved.

e) He is a right person for this job.

f) We invited some friends for a lunch. Luckily sun was brilliantly bright in the afternoon.

g) In the dark, I was searching for switch button of my radio.

h) Suddenly, the car in front of us stopped and a driver of this car ran fast to escape arrest by the police.

i) A night Mary was taken ill.

j) Our new car is as big as a jeep we saw the other day.

2. The following sentences contain determiners, and pronouns. Distinguish these and list them separately.

a) One of the police officers shouted, 'Give me that instrument!'

b) One of the police officers asked gently, 'Please give that to me.'

c) This gentleman is a colleague of mine.

198   **Determiners & Interjections**

****

d) I can prove to the police that it is my car.

e) What about those books which we reserved this afternoon

f) What about this?

g) Those students who joined the class yesterday should show their registration cards.

h) Which is the most expensive car at this car show?

i) Which car is the most expensive car in this at this car show?

j) She said smilingly, ' There is enough room for you.'

3. Find possessive, indefinite and interrogative determiners in the following statements.

a) You can use my desk as I will be away today.

b) Whose place is this?

c) Has Anne received her parcel from Russia?

d) My students are busy in the library working on their project.

e) You can buy some flowers for your wife.

f) This is another book that I bought today.

g) In fact, you can park on either side of the street.

h) I'm afraid I do not appreciate their decision to walk out of the meeting.

i) Which way is the wind blowing ?

J) Mike, Kevin, Kim and two other new members joined our team.

4. Your task is to make meaningful statements in order to demonstrate the usage of the following interjections/exclamations:

dear me, oh blast, good grief, good heavens, goodness me,
nice,   ow,   surprise,   whoops,   yuck.

```
┌─────────────────────────────────────────────────┐
│                                                 │
│              Chapter 10                         │
│                                                 │
│              Conjunctions                       │
│                                                 │
└─────────────────────────────────────────────────┘
```

• Introduction

A word that joins other words, phrases, clauses or sentences is called a conjunction. For instance:

> • She is called Mary **and** she is my student.
> ```
>    ----------------------  -----  ------------------------
>            ⇑               ⇑            ⇑
>        clause 1       conjunction  clause 2
> ```

Commas are omitted between short main clauses.

In this case, **and** joins two main clauses or two simple sentences into a compound sentence. This is a simple conjunction. It has no other function except to combine parts of a sentence. In this example, clause 1 and clause 2 can exchange places without altering the meaning of this sentence. We can classify conjunctions into the following two classes:

> • coordinating conjunctions or coordinators
>
> • subordinating conjunctions or subordinators

• Coordinating conjunctions or coordinators

There are only the following coordinators: **and, but, or, so, nor**.

Nor is the negative counterpart of _or_ coordinator. It is less used than other coordinators. A coordinating conjunction is a linking element.

For this reason, it comes between two clauses. It cannot be placed anywhere in the sentence. It performs the following functions:

- <u>To join two or more clauses of equal status in a sentence. The use of the coordinator generates a compound sentence in which clauses are independent.</u> This is illustrated below:

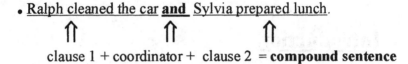

- <u>Ralph cleaned the car **and** Sylvia prepared lunch</u>.

clause 1 + coordinator + clause 2 = **compound sentence**

This is a compound sentence. It consists of two main clauses joined together by the **and** coordinator. The clause on the left of the coordinator **and** is of the same status. We can analyse clauses in this sentence as shown below:

Clause 1	Clause 2
Ralph $\Rightarrow$ subject $\Rightarrow$ s	Syliva $\Rightarrow$ subject $\Rightarrow$ s
cleaned $\Rightarrow$ verb $\Rightarrow$ v	prepared $\Rightarrow$ verb $\Rightarrow$ v
the car $\Rightarrow$ object $\Rightarrow$ o	lunch $\Rightarrow$ object $\Rightarrow$ o

svo (clause 1) = svo (clause 2)

⇑

Both clauses have an equal grammatical status.

We can reverse the order of clauses in this sentence without changing their meaning or the meaning of the whole sentence. Thus, the sentence becomes:

- Sylvia prepared lunch **and** Ralph cleaned the car.

coordinator is still between the two clauses ↵

It should be noted that **and** does not add any new information to the meaning, except that it tells us that there are two parts in the sentence. The sentence consists of two independent clauses. <u>Since it is not a long sentence, the use of a comma between the clauses is unnecessary.</u>

If you prefer to place a comma, in accordance with the rules of punctuation for a main clause, you can do so. See ⟹ punctuation

- Anne did the gardening **and** cooked a meal.

                   ----

             coordinator↵

In this sentence, both clauses have the same subject *Anne*.

The following two examples illustrate the use of the coordinator **but**:

- Barbara likes to travel abroad (/Barbara/she)* **but** hates flying.

                               -----

          coordinator /coordinating conjunction ↵

 – same subject in both clauses ⟹ **Barbara**

- She was in the car (she)* **but** was unhurt.

                   -----

         coordinator ↵ - same subject in both clauses

( )* - <u>When two clauses have the same subject ( ) as above, there is no need to repeat the subject in the second clause.</u> No comma is required when the linked clauses are short. The coordinator **but** suggests that there is an obvious contrast between the meaning of clauses on both sides of it.

- The shop was closed **so** I could not buy anything.

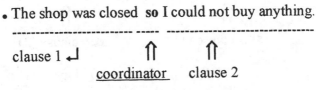

        clause 1 ↵   ⇑   ⇑

                <u>coordinator</u>   clause 2

in this context **so** means **'therefore'**↵

- I was tired last night **so** I went to bed early.

clause 1 ⤶   ⇑   ⇑

coordinator   clause 2

here **so** means '**therefore**'⤶

So as a conjunction is used to indicate a reason or result of something. In these two examples, it is pointing to the reason given in clause 1 and the result in clause 2. In fact, it is coordinating the verb in clause 1 with the verb in clause 2. Both clauses are units of equal grammatical status ⟹ **svo**clause (1) = **svo**clause (2)

The word **so** also functions as an **adverb** and **noun**.

The coordinator **or** introduces an alternative to the meaning conveyed by the first main clause. For instance:

- You mustn't stay **so** near the fire **or** your trousers will catch fire.

⇑   ⇑

1*   coordinator

1* (**so***) is functioning here as an adverb of degree.

See ⟹ adverbs. See ⟹phrases

Both clauses are of the same/similar grammatical status and thus **svo**clause (1) = **svo**clause (2).

Another example of the use of **or** :

- You can collect it tonight **or** your son can collect it now.

⇑   ⇑

svo clause (1)   **svo** clause (2)

SVO clause (1) = SVO clause (2)

****

- **<u>Correlative conjunctions or coordinators operate in pairs. These are used to join:</u>**

  - units of equal status – clauses in compound sentences

  - words and phrases.

<u>Some common correlative coordinators</u>

both ... and, but ... also, either ... or, neither ... nor, whether ... or

The use of correlative coordinators is exemplified below.

- **Either** you will drive the car to London <u>or</u> we will travel by coach.

main clause 1   main clause 2
first word in a compound   implies an alternative to the first
sentence   suggestion in main clause 1

Another example of the use of *either ---- or* is given below:

- **Either** you do the gardening this week **or** we ask our
  local nursery to do it.

These last two examples illustrate that **either** comes at the start of the first clause in a compound sentence. It is also shown that the pair of **either...or** joins clauses of similar status in a compound sentence.

- **<u>In order to render negative meaning, we can use neither ...nor in phrases.</u>** For instance:

  - **Neither** <u>the public library</u> **nor** <u>the main post office</u> were open.

                    noun phrase   noun phrase

  - Due to heavy snowfall, we could turn **<u>neither</u> north **nor** <u>south</u>.

                    noun phrase↵   noun phrase↵

- <u>**Examples of coordinators joining words of equal status:**</u>

- Slow **and** steady.

coordinator ⏎ - ⟹ joins two words together

- fast **or** slow.

⇑

coordinator ⟹ joins two words together

- The room was <u>narrow</u> **yet** <u>long</u>.

⇑

<u>coordinator joins two words</u>

equal status⏎ - <u>adjective</u> with <u>adjective</u>

- **Both** Jack **and** Jill are likely to be present at the wedding.

1⏎   +   2⏎ - correlative pair of coordinators

This pair of correlative coordinators demonstrates a mutual relationship between two nouns ⟹ **Jack** and **Jill** of equal grammatical importance.

- <u>**The correlative pair of *but ... also* shows a mutual relationship**</u>
  For instance:

- He was a great <u>Prime Minister</u>, **but also** <u>the winner of the Nobel</u>

           Phrase 1⏎   <u>Prize for Peace</u>.

                            Phrase 2 ⏎

- <u>**Or** has its negative counterpart **nor**. One can use **nor** to coordinate clauses providing the first clause in a compound sentence relates to a negative idea or thought. It can also coordinate words as well as phrases.</u> For instance:

- She can't dance **nor** can she sing.

coordinates negative clauses⏎

. The car could not move backwards **or** forwards.

       coordinates words/phrases↵

- **The pair *neither ... nor* does not join clauses but phrases**

  For instance:

        . Unfortunately, he **neither** hears **nor** speaks.

        . She is **neither** rich **nor** poor.

. Subordinating conjunctions or subordinators

Like the coordinators, subordinating conjunctions also join parts of a
sentence. They perform the following functions:

- to link two clauses of unequal status in complex sentences

- to introduce subordinate clauses (often adverbial clauses)

- to indicate the relationship between a subordinate clause
  and a main clause

- to link sentences - many subordinators can do so

. Complex sentences

Complex sentences have clauses of unequal status. Subordinating conjunctions such as **when, although, *if*, until, etc.** join subordinate
clauses to a main clause in compound sentences. Thus, they link
unequal grammatical units in compound sentences.

Sometimes, a subordinator can add meaning of its own to the overall
meaning of a subordinate clause. A subordinating conjunction introduces a subordinate clause, which is a less important component of a
compound sentence than its main clause. There are many subordinat-

ing conjunctions. See ⇒ Clause See ⇒ Sentences

There are also **multi-word subordinators**. These include: **so that, as
long as, in order that, etc**. Some of these are listed below.

<u>Some subordinating conjunctions</u>
⇓

> after, although, as long as, as quickly as, as soon as, as if, as though, as to, assuming that, because, before, even if, even though, except, except that, excepting that, if, in case, in order to, lest, more … than, rather … than, provided that, since, so that, sooner than, such, such as, till, unless, until, when, whenever, where, whereas, wherever, whether ,while.

● **<u>Coordinating conjunctions and, but and so can also be used as subordinators</u>.**

The following examples illustrate the use of some main subordinators:

- Our train arrived **after** the other train had left the platform.
  ------------------- ----- --

  main clause↵   ⇑   ⇑
                   subordinator   subordinate clause introduced
                   -------------- by the subordinator
          indicating time↵

Here the clause introduced by the subordinator is an **adverbial clause of time**. See ⇒clauses

 The use of the subordinator has linked two clauses in this compound sentence. Furthermore, it has established a relationship between these clauses which helps us to understand the meaning of the whole sentence. Without the subordinator, the meaning of the sentence would not be clear. The subordinator *after* has preciously enhanced the intended meaning of this sentence by indicating the time factor between the arrival of one train and the departure of the other train.

- You must have lunch with us **before** you leave.
              --------- -------------

      subordinator indicating time ↵   ⇑
                    subordinate adverbial clause introduced by
              the subordinator ⇒ **before**

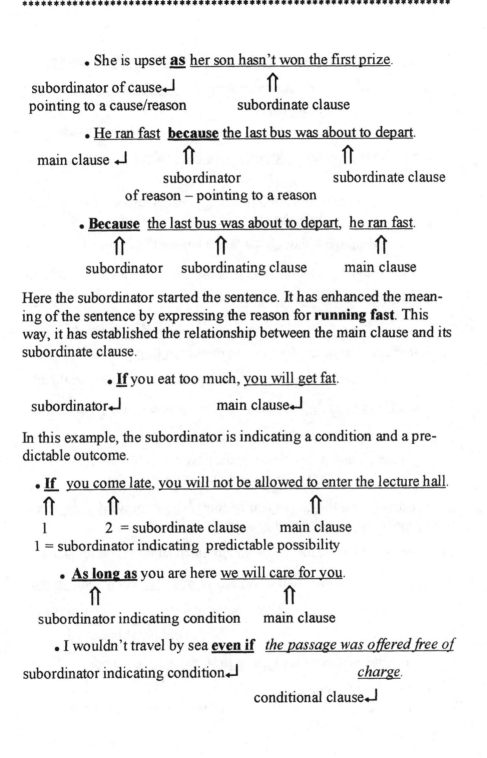

• She is upset **as** her son hasn't won the first prize.

subordinator of cause⏎
pointing to a cause/reason   subordinate clause

• He ran fast **because** the last bus was about to depart.

main clause ⏎

subordinator   subordinate clause
of reason – pointing to a reason

• **Because** the last bus was about to depart, he ran fast.

subordinator   subordinating clause   main clause

Here the subordinator started the sentence. It has enhanced the meaning of the sentence by expressing the reason for **running fast**. This way, it has established the relationship between the main clause and its subordinate clause.

• **If** you eat too much, you will get fat.

subordinator⏎   main clause⏎

In this example, the subordinator is indicating a condition and a predictable outcome.

• **If** you come late, you will not be allowed to enter the lecture hall.

1   2 = subordinate clause   main clause
1 = subordinator indicating predictable possibility

• **As long as** you are here we will care for you.

subordinator indicating condition   main clause

• I wouldn't travel by sea **even if** *the passage was offered free of*

subordinator indicating condition⏎   *charge.*

conditional clause⏎

- He spends his small inherited fortune ***as if it was a large fortune***

main clause↵ subordinator indicating↵ ***which could last forever***.

        comparison   ⇑

                                    subordinate clause

- He says he is penniless, **although** we know about his bank savings.

                     ⇑   ⇑

               subordinator indicating   main clause – it states fact
               comparison/contrast

           although = though ⟹ here it implies **but** or **yet**

- He works seven days a week **so that** *he can save enough for his trip*

subordinator indicating purpose↵   *to China*.

                                  subordinate clause ↵

- He teaches youngsters the game of cricket **so that** they can play for

             subordinator indicating result/purpose ↵   the local club.

- He ran fast **lest** he might be recognised by the policeman.

       ⇑   ⇑

     main clause subordinator indicating result ⟹for fear
             that ... (negative outcome)

lest is usually used to express fear of something or prevent something from happening. Here is another example:

- He was afraid **lest** he had revealed too much about his secret plans.

- I have written to some friends in Paris **in order to** invite them to the

         subordinator indicating purpose ↵   wedding.

                               subordinate clause ↵

- Our television works **except that** the picture is poor.

subordinator indicating exception ↵   ⇑

                        subordinate noun clause

• She would visit the hospital **except** she has little time to spare.

subordinator indicating exception ↵

    • I'd prefer to walk to my hotel **rather than** travel in his car.

    subordinator indicating preference ↵

• You should find out **where** the car was stolen.

⇑

subordinator indicating place

• He travels by car **wherever** he goes for his business in Europe.

⇑

subordinator indicating place

• We will decide tomorrow **whether** we can place an order for

⇑   a new car.

subordinator indicating possibility

• I don't know **whether** I will be able to fly from Humberside Air

    subordinator ↵   port to Berlin.

  - indicating possibility/alternative

• Our sales will decline **unless** we advertise our products.

⇑

subordinator indicating negative possibility

• Their house doesn't have a back garden **unless** you call a

main statement ↵   subordinator adding↵   backyard a back
                    an afterthought to   garden.

                    the main statement   ⇑

                                   *afterthought stated

---

* Note that **afterthought** is a noun – it means a thought that is added
later, and is often not carefully planned or thought out.

• You can send it by e-mail **so that** they can receive this message now.

   sentence 1⤶   ⇑   ⇑

            subordinator   sentence 2

                  ⇑

        linking two sentences

• Can we have lunch together? **If** you wait until my lunch hour starts.

   sentence 1 ⤶   ⇑   sentence 2 ⤶

      subordinator linking two sentences

• **Some subordinating conjunctions also function as prepositions and adverbs.** This is illustrated below:

    • I haven't seen you **since** last December.

                ⇑

      functioning as preposition of time

    • I haven't seen you **since** you moved away .

                ⇑

    functioning as subordinating conjunction

    • You have moved away and I haven't seen you **since**.

                 functioning as adverb⤶

    • You should have asked for it **before**.

        functioning as adverb⤶

    • The matter was brought **before** the tribunal.

    functioning as preposition⤶

    • You must do it **before** you forget.

             ⇑

    functioning as subordinating conjunction

In summary, conjunctions are widely used in phrases, clauses and sentences. There are numerous examples of their usage in this book.

• See ⇒ phrases • See ⇒ Clauses • See ⇒ Sentences

Over to You

1. Construct sentences to illustrate the use of the following:
when, before, if , just in case, because, provided that,
once, as if, as though, neither, while, as soon as, although, since,
whether ---or not.

2. Complete the following sentences. Name the type of each
conjunction inserted in the appropriate place in each statement.

a) The traffic lights changed to amber ------I approached.

b) It is possible ------Yvonne has not received our letter.

c) Our tutor said ---- we can leave ------ we answered the question.

d) My wife went to the Chelsea Flower Show ----she enjoyed her visit.

e) Our tutor was unhappy ------- we came fifteen minutes late.

f) She was very kind to us, ---- ------ she hurried us.

g) Milk ----- sugar.

h) Our roof leaked --------- it rained last year.

i) We can finish early ---- ---- -----get ready for the dinner and
dance tonight.

j) He is working very hard ---- --- the report can be submitted in time.

k) I liked her very much, ---- ----- I did not have much chance to
to meet her after work.

l) Hurry up , ----- you'll be late for work.

m) I have no car , ---- I'll hire one just for tomorrow.

n) She is not a racist ------ a feminist.

o) Some of the overseas students are very hard working -----
others aren't. **More exercises under phrases and sentences.**

Chapter 11

Phrases

• Introduction

A phrase consists of a small number of words and functions as a grammatical unit. In fact, a word may be considered as a phrase*. On the other hand, a clause may be a distinct component of a sentence, or a separate group of words with a subject, verb and any compulsory elements. The following examples illustrate the difference between these two groups of words, namely phrases and clauses:

> • your book
> -----------

phrase ↵ - it contains no finite verb

> • My book **is written** by my friend.
> ---

clause↵ - it contains a verb which is **highlighted**

> • in the car
> -----------

phrase ↵ - it contains no finite verb

> • He **bought** this car in London.
> ---------------------------------------

clause↵ - it contains a verb which is **highlighted**

> • fine wine
> ----------

phrase ↵ - it contains no finite verb

> * Strictly speaking, in grammar, a phrase may consist of one word or a group of words. However, the word phrase means to most people, a group of words.

- You **like** that red wine from Wiesbaden in Germany.

  ----

  clause⤶ - it contains a finite verb

- a white pure silk scarf

  ----

  phrase ⤶ - it contains no finite verb

- He **bought** a white pure silk scarf.

  ----

  clause⤶ - it contains a finite verb

- all these overseas students in my class

  ----

  phrase ⤶ - it contains no finite verb

- All these overseas students in my class **are** clever.

  ----

  clause⤶ - it contains a finite verb

- The main difference between **phrases** and **clauses** is that a phrase consists of a small group of words without a tense. On the other hand, a clause has a subject and predicate (verb and what follows it).

- It is important to understand the idea of **headword** or **keyword** in a phrase. The reason is that it gives the most important information. If you eliminate the headword from the phrase, its meaning will change. Furthermore, the structure of the phrase will be incomplete.

For example, in the phrase '**in the house**', without the headword '**in**', the phrase does not mean what it should do and because of its removal the phrase is incomplete structurally. Often, a headword comes at the end of the phrase. However, it is not always the case, as in '**in the house**'.

. <u>Types of phrases</u>

A phrase has an internal structure. This is illustrated below:

- my <u>**book**</u>

key word in this phrase is **book** ⟹ **noun** known as **headword**

- very <u>**old**</u>

headword ⟹ **old** ⟹ **adjective**

- may have <u>**gone**</u>

headword ⟹ **gone** ⟹ **verb**

- very <u>**slowly**</u>

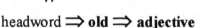

headword ⟹**slowly** ⟹ **adverb**

- <u>**in**</u> the house

headword ⟹ in ⟹ preposition

The above examples illustrate five different types of internal phrase structures. In each example, the internal structure is analysed in terms of its headword and its modifier. Let's consider another example:

- <u>certainly</u> <u>**nobody**</u>

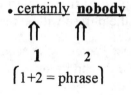

      1   2

⌈1+2 = phrase⌉

1 = adverb used to modify the pronoun nobody

2 = The headword $\Rightarrow$ nobody $\Rightarrow$ **pronoun**

- In these examples, each headword is either a noun or pronoun. Because of this noun or pronoun, each phrase is identified as a **noun phrase**.

In fact, there are the following five main types of phrases:

> (1) • **Noun phrase**
>
> (2) • **Verb phrase**
>
> (3) • **Adverb phrase**
>
> (4) • **Adjective phrase**
>
> (5) • **Prepositional phrase**

• How can you identify the type of phrase?

As shown above, the headword is a key word, which enables us to identify the phrase type. If you know the class of the headword, you can identify any of the above types of phrases. Indeed, there are some exceptions to this rule. One exception to this rule is that a noun phrase does not always have a noun as a headword. This exception is exemplified by the last two examples above.

The other exceptions are discussed with examples at the appropriate place in this chapter. The following examples show each type of phrase first.

> • Joan likes <u>James as a doctor</u>.

> noun phrase – noun $\Rightarrow$ **James** (another noun doctor)

You can identify a phrase in a sentence. A sentence may have more than one phrase.

- Our journey <u>has finished</u>.

verb phrase - verb $\Rightarrow$ **has finished**

- He returned <u>quickly from the office</u>.

adverb phrase - adverb $\Rightarrow$ **quickly**

- I am <u>very pleased to see you</u>.

adjective phrase - pleased $\Rightarrow$ **adjective**

Very is an adverb of degree qualifying the adjective '**pleased**' (placing a greater emphasis on the adjective)

- I have been thinking <u>of you all day</u>.

prepositional phrase - preposition $\Rightarrow$ **of**

. <u>Noun phrases</u>

Let's consider the following examples:

- She was a <u>**teacher here**</u>.

noun phrase $\Rightarrow$ headword $\Rightarrow$ **teacher**

The headword is preceded by a determiner $\Rightarrow$ **a**

This example has only one noun.

- She was a <u>**school** **teacher**</u>.

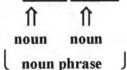

In this example, the first noun **school** is acting as a modifier. It is modifying the second noun ⟹ **teacher** ⟹ **headword**

The phrase is a noun phrase because the **headword** is a noun.

- She should do <u>**something now**</u>.

noun phrase ⟹ **something** ⟹ headword

This phrase is also a noun phrase due to the fact that the headword is a pronoun.

- <u>A noun phrase will include **one headword** which may be a noun or pronoun as demonstrated above.</u>

- Sometimes, a noun phrase has only one word, e.g. **flowers**. One noun or pronoun by itself is enough to make a noun phrase.

- In addition to this headword (noun or pronoun), a noun phrase may include:

  - **a determiner** before the headword, e.g., **a** book, the map, **an** apple, **this** computer, **that** hat, **these** chairs, **those** ladies, **my** coat.

    Determiners occur at the beginning of a noun phrase <u>only</u>.

    See ⟹ determiners

  - **a modifier (qualifier)** before the headword is used to modify/qualify the noun. A modifier may be another noun, an adjective, a verb used adjectivally (in 'kitchen knife' the word kitchen is used adjectivally) or a participle (a word formed from a verb, ending **in –ing**, e.g.

    seeing ⟹ participle). Here are some examples:

    - the <u>**beautiful**</u> women

    adjective used as ⟹ **pre-modifier**

- When a modifier comes before the headword, it is a **pre-modifier**. It is possible to have more than one modifier as illustrated below:

  - a **delicious** **hot** meal

  pre-modifier adjective 1 ⏎   ⇑

                  pre-modifier adjective 2

In this example, the headword **meal** is pre-modified by both adjectives ⇒delicious and hot

  - a **British** **insurance** company

  pre-modifier adjective ⏎   ⇑

                 pre-modifier noun

The headword company is pre-modified by:

an adjective ⇒ British and a noun ⇒ insurance

- It is important to note that when the headword is pre-modified by more than one type of modifier, the pre-modifying noun comes near to the headword/noun. Therefore, 'an insurance British company' would be <u>incorrect</u>.

  - a **really** **workable** plan

  pre-modifier adverb ⏎   ⇑

                pre-modifier adjective

In this case, there are two pre-modifiers before the headword **plan** (noun). Here, the noun is pre-modified by the adverb and the adjective.

- These examples demonstrate that you can have more than one adjective to pre-modify the headword. It is also possible to have an adverb and a noun to pre-modify the headword. For instance:

  - **Indeed** a **police** station

  pre-modifier adverb ⏎   ⇑

                pre-modifier noun

• How many adjectives are permissible before the headword?

There is no restriction on the number of adjectives which can come before the headword. However, if you use too many adjectives, their meanings may become blurred due to adjectives contrasting with each other. It is best to avoid using more than three adjectives before the headword. For instance:

    • a brave, dangerous, ruthless **incursion**

    ⇑   ⇑   ⇑   ⇑

    adjective adjective adjective headword/noun

Here, the head noun is pre-modified by three adjectives.

• A participle can pre-modify the headword:

    • a **running** total

    ⇑

    pre-modifier ⟹ **participle**

<u>Note that running is also an adjective and a noun.</u>

The phrase **running total** means a total of expenses or whatever which includes each item as it occurs.

• The headword may be **post-modified**. Post-modifiers come after the headword. These may prove to be more complex than pre-modifiers are. The reason for this complexity is that a variety of elements can function as a post-modifier. This is illustrated below:

    • a new bookshop **in our shopping precinct**

    ⇑ ⇑ ⇑   ⇑

    1 + 2 + 3   post-modifier/qualifier

    ⌊ **noun phrase** ⌋

    prepositional phrase⏎ **in** is a preposition of place

220   **Phrases**

****

1 = determiner   **2** = pre-modifier - adjective   **3** = headword/noun

After the headword/noun, a prepositional phrase is added to qualify or pre-modify the headword. <u>There can be more than one pre-modifier. This is illustrated below:</u>

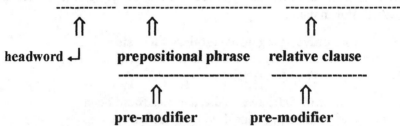

In this example, the headword is pre-modified by a prepositional phrase and by a relative clause.

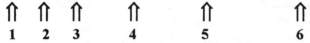

1 = pre-determiner
2 = pre-modifier- adjective modifying the noun ⟹ *shop*
3 = headword - *shop*
4 = adverb phrase modifying the noun ⟹ *shop*
5 = prepositional phrase of place modifying the noun ⟹ *shop*
6 = clause modifying the noun ⟹ *shop*

- This example shows that the headword can be post-modified by both phrases and clauses. In addition, it illustrates that several phrases can be joined together. This example has three phrases put together to make one long phrase.

• How big can a phrase be?

The size of a phrase is not restricted. The idea is not to make it too long. If you do so, your reader or listener may not receive it well. It is worth mentioning here that the largest unit of construction is a sentence.

The second largest unit of construction is a clause. As a unit of construction, then, the smallest unit of construction is the phrase. The fact is that phrases are formed from words and clauses are formed from phrases. Therefore, the clause as a unit of construction is larger than the phrase. Phrases constitute clauses. All three constructions are units of syntactic (connected with grammatical rules and structures) constructions.

- Possessive pronouns both proper and common can also be used as pre-modifiers:

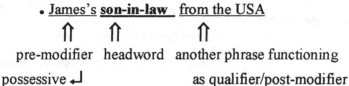

- James's **son-in-law** from the USA

   ⇑   ⇑   ⇑

pre-modifier headword another phrase functioning

possessive ↵   as qualifier/post-modifier
proper noun

- the **children's** birthday party

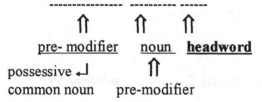

   ⇑   ⇑   ⇑

   pre- modifier   noun **headword**

possessive ↵   ⇑
common noun   pre-modifier

- **Note: not childrens but the children's.**

- Noun phrases can function as the subject and the object of a sentence:

- The policeman arrested the suspect.
  ----

noun phrase ↵ - functioning as the **subject** of this sentence

- I asked **the traffic warden**.

Noun phrase functioning as the **object** of a sentence

* A **complement** is an adjective or a noun which comes after a **linking** or **copula** or **copular verb**. A linking, a copula and a copular verb all mean the same.

  See ⟹ copular verb

* A noun phrase can function as a complement that is as an object. For instance:

  * He seemed **to be** an expert in mathematics.
      ------ ------------------------------

  copula verb ⏎   ⇑

                          describing the subject

                  noun phrase functioning as ⟹ **object**

When the complement is a noun phrase, and the copula is 'seem' or 'look', use **to be** in order to describe or identify the subject:

  * He looks to be **a perpetrator**.

                  ⇑

      noun phrase functioning as ⟹ **object**

One can leave out '**to be**', if the noun phrase gives some other kinds of information instead of identifying the subject.

* A noun phrase may be followed by another noun phrase. In such cases, the purpose of a second noun phrase is to give explanatory information about the headword. The second phrase is termed as '**an apposition**' to the first phrase. Here are two examples:

* **The city of York, in north-east England**, is visited by 3 million tourists a
  ⇑   ⇑
                                                              a year.
  first phrase   second phrase

- Gamal Abdel Nasser, once president of Egypt, nationalised the Suez Canal.

------------------------------   ---------------------------

⇑   ⇑

first phrase   second phrase

• <u>Verb phrases</u>

The headword of a verb phrase is a verb. A verb phrase may have only one base verb. Here are two verb phrases. Each has only one word, which is the base/basic form of the verb given in a dictionary:

- Go   - See

----   ----

⇑   ⇑

headword ⇒ base verb form   headword ⇒ base verb form

- The headword (main verb) of a verb phrase may be one of the following forms:

- **the base form** – arise, catch, know, show:

- I **arise** at 6 am.

- They **know** me well.

- *the present 's' form* – writes, talks, sees, goes, loves, washes:

- Anna **writes** to me regularly.

- She **loves** both her children.

- **present participle –ing form** - dancing, running, singing, talking, writing walking:

- We **are talking** about your success.

- She **is singing** her own song.

- **Past participle -ed form** (both regular and irregular verbs) –

driven, felt, ran, sung, striven,
talked, torn, understood, written:

- I **have written** to her today.

- She **has understood** you.

. Adverb phrases

An adverb phrase may consist of only a headword, which is an adverb. It may be a group of words, in which the headword is an adverb. It does not contain a finite verb. On the contrary, an adverb clause contains a finite verb. See ⟹ Clauses

An adverb phrase contains an adverb, and can modify an adjective or adverb. Let's examine some examples:

- She walks **slowly**.
      ⁻⁻⁻⁻⁻⁻⁻⁻

adverb phrase of manner **headword** ⟹ **slowly**
- describes how she walks

Here, the adverb phrase consists of only the headword. <u>The headword or the main word is an adverb</u>.

- You can enter the main library **through this doorway**.
                                   ⁻⁻⁻⁻⁻⁻⁻⁻⁻⁻⁻⁻⁻⁻⁻⁻⁻⁻⁻⁻⁻⁻⁻⁻⁻⁻⁻⁻

adverb phrase of place consists of three words ↲ through ⟹**adverb**

- He left our home **fairly quickly**.
              ⁻⁻⁻⁻ ⁻⁻⁻⁻⁻⁻⁻⁻⁻⁻⁻

adverb phrase of place consists of three words ↲

- adverb phrase of time consists of two adverbs ⟹ **fairly** and **quickly** The adverb **fairly** is pre-modifying the other adverb **quickly** by intensifying its meaning. See ⟹ **Intensifiers**

• We found travelling by buses in that country **incredibly slow**.

----

adverb phrase of time↵

The **adverb incredibly** is pre-modifying the adjective slow. Thus, the
pre-modifier **incredibly** intensifies the meaning of the **adjective slow**.
In this case, it functions as an intensifier.

• This reason is not **really sufficient** to secure a loan.

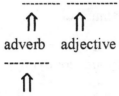

adverb   adjective

⇑

adverb is modifying the adjective

This is an example of an adverb phrase of **degree.** An adverb of degree
can be used before some adverbs and adjectives. By degree, we mean
an extent, or a measure of something. In this case, the adverb really is
used to express the actual fact or truth about something. Here, it is
about the reason to secure a loan. The adverb **really** is pre-modifying
the adjective sufficient.

• The cake is **quite tasty**.

----

adverb phrase of degree ↵

In this context, the adverb quite means somewhat, to some extent, not
very or fairly. The **adjective tasty** is pre-modified by the adverb quite.
In fact, quite intensifies the meaning of the adjective tasty. It attaches
to this cake's quality a medium degree(a measure of taste).The word
delicious is another adjective. When quite is used with delicious, it expresses a different meaning. For instance:

• The cake is **quite delicious**.

----

adverb phrase of degree ↵

In this example, the **adverb quite** is pre-modifying the **adjective delicious**. Depending on the meaning of the **adjective delicious**, the adverb quite means completely to the full extent.

- My son speaks German **fluently**.
  ----

  adverb of manner ↵

- You must take action **quickly**.
  ----

  adverb of manner ↵

- An adverb of manner modifies a verb - in the last two examples, adverbs **fluently** and **quickly** are modifying verbs **speaks** and **must take** respectively.

Most adverbs of manner are formed from adjectives. Often they end with *-ly*. Of course, there are a few adverbs of manner without *-ly* endings (e.g. fast, loud). The following two examples show the use of adverbs of manner without *-ly* endings: See ⟹ Adverbs

- You should do your best to do it **right** next time.
  ----

  adverb of manner ↵

- It answers the **question - how?**

  - She often arrives **late** by train.
    -----

    adverb of manner ↵

- it answers the question - **when ?** late or how? - by train

- **It is unusual to post-modify the head adverb with an another adverb.**

• Indeed I visit them **sometimes**.

----

adverb of time ↵

sometimes ⟹ adverb post-modified by another adverb ⟹ **indeed**
The pre-modifier adverb **indeed** intensifies the meaning of the adverb **sometimes**. This is rather formal. pre-modifiers⟹
and for

• <u>Adjective phrases</u>

An adjective phrase may consist of only a headword, which is an adjective. It may be a group of words in which the headword is an adjective. <u>An adjective phrase does not contain a finite verb</u>. It has an adjective. These phrases are similar to adverb phrases. Like adverb phrases, adjective phrases can also be modified. Like an adverb phrase, sometimes, it has an adverb of degree. Here are some examples:

• He is **brave**.

----

adjective phrase

headword ⟹ **adjective** ⟹ **brave** - just a single word

• It is **easy** to carry it.

-----

adjective phrase headword ⟹ adjective ⟹ **easy**

• He is **very brave**.

----

adjective phrase↵ - **very**

-----

adverb of degree before an adjective ↵

This adjective phrase consists of one adjective and one adverb.

headword $\Rightarrow$ **adjective** $\Rightarrow$ *brave* is pre-modified by the adverb **very**

• When **very** is used before an adjective, it is an adverb.

> • This is **good enough** for me.
> -----------------
>
> adjective phrase ↵

headword$\Rightarrow$**adverb enough** is pre-modified by the adjective **good**

> • We went to see a film, but the cinema was **almost empty**.
> ---------------------
>
> adjective phrase ↵

headword$\Rightarrow$adjective **empty** is pre-modified by the adverb **almost**

• **Almost, nearly** and **practically** are adverbs of degree with similar meanings. For instance:

> • The hall is **practically/nearly/almost full** with the audience.
> --------------------------------------
>
> adjective phrase ↵

headword $\Rightarrow$adjective **full** is pre-modified by the adverb
----

> **practically/nearly /almost** ↵

• He was finding living without a job **so difficult**
that he sold his car.   ----------------

> adjective phrase ↵

headword $\Rightarrow$*adjective* **difficult** is pre-modified by the *adverb* $\Rightarrow$**so**

• It was **extremely noisy** when the police arrived at the party.
----

adjective phrase ↵

headword $\Rightarrow$ adjective **noisy** is pre-modified by the adverb of degree
----

extremely ↵

. Prepositional phrases

What you have seen so far is that all four types of phrases have one thing in common, which is a headword. Indeed, in these types of phrases the headword can stand alone. In prepositional phrases, the headword cannot stand alone. **Why is it so?**

The headword, in a prepositional phrase, is a preposition. The head-word and the prepositional complement together form the prepositional phrase. Without the prepositional complement, the prepositional phrase is incomplete. Thus, the headword in a prepositional phrase cannot stand alone. Usually, the **prepositional complement** is a noun phrase. The typical structure of a prepositional phrase may be represented as:

> **Prepositional phrase = headword + prepositional complement**

- A prepositional phrase may be complemented by certain types
  of clauses. See $\Rightarrow$ Clauses

- A preposition can be a single word or a group of words.

  See $\Rightarrow$ Prepositions

Here are some examples of prepositional phrases:

- Pamela sat next to her husband Robin.
  ------- -------------------------
    ⇑   ⇑
  headword/group preposition   prepositional component
  consists of two words   noun phrase
        ⇑
  meaning in a place right beside her husband Robin

In fact, the preposition **next to** is complemented by the noun phrase <u>her husband Robin</u>. In this example, according to:

prepositional phrase =
               preposition (headword) + <u>prepositional component</u>

                                noun or noun phrase ↵

the prepositional phrase **=** next to her husband Robin

- You can walk **<u>along</u> <u>the footpath</u>**.

                Preposition + noun phrase = prepositional phrase

In this case, the preposition **along** is complemented by the <u>noun phrase</u>

                                                  the <u>footpath</u>↵

- Rachel was walking **<u>towards</u> <u>Tesco supermarket</u>**.

                Preposition + noun phrase = prepositional phrase

- Everything must be ready **<u>before</u> <u>this evening's seminar</u>**.

                Preposition + noun phrase = prepositional
                                        phrase

Some more prepositional phrases are highlighted in the following examples:

- She looks nothing <u>like her sister</u>.   (**like** means similar)

- Our house is situated <u>behind the church</u>.

- He has been my best friend <u>since* my childhood</u>.

- I want to go out <u>for ten minutes</u>.

Note: * The word **since** also functions as a conjunction and an adverb.

- **A prepositional phrase can function as the complement of a verb or adjective:** For instance:

  - She is **in a rush**.

  Prepositional phrase ⇒complement of **is** ⇒ verb

  - It is big **for my family**.

  Prepositional phrase ⇒complement of adjective ⇒**big**

Here are some more examples:

  - You do not have to be sorry **for us**.

  - We have spent a lot **of money**.

  - He was singing **on the stage**.

  - They were running **towards a bus stop**.

- **A prepositional phrase can function as a post-modifier:**

  - He is a **heavyweight boxer of great achievement**.
    --------------------- --------------------------

    noun phrase   preposition phrase

The headword of noun phrase ⇒ *boxer* is pre-modified by an adjec-

tive⇒**heavyweight** and post-modified by the prepositional phrase
      ----

of great achievement ⤶
In this sentence, 'of great achievement' cannot be placed in a different
place in this sentence.

• There is *a nice girl* **in a red uniform**.

⇑   ⇑

noun phrase   preposition phrase

The headword/noun of noun phrase ⟹**girl** is pre-modified by an

adjective ⟹ **nice** and post-modified by the prepositional phrase

in a red uniform ↵

• Prepositional phrases can occur in clusters in extended sentences :
  This is exemplified here:

  • There is **a girl** in a red uniform **with her mother**.

  ⇑   ⇑   ⇑

  noun   prepositional   prepositional
  phrase   phrase   phrase

• She lives in **a cottage** with her mother **in a village** near Stuttgart

1   2   3   4

in south Germany.

5

1 ⟹ noun phrase 2 ⟹ prepositional phrase 3⟹ prepositional phrase
4 ⟹ prepositional phrase 5 ⟹ prepositional phrase

• I saw [a herd of reindeer with long antlers on a country road in Finland].

⇑ ⇑ ⇑   ⇑   ⇑   ⇑   ⇑

1 2   3   4   5   6   7

We can analyse the above sentence as follows:

1 ⟹ noun phrase 2 ⟹ verb(verb phrase)

3 $\Rightarrow$ [noun phrase]. <u>In this complex noun phrase: the following</u>
<u>prepositional phrases occur:</u>

4 of reindeer = preposition+ noun phrase $\Rightarrow$ prepositional phrase

5 with long antlers = preposition + noun phrase $\Rightarrow$ prepositional
phrase

6 on a country road = preposition + noun phrase $\Rightarrow$ prepositional
phrase

7 in Finland = preposition + noun phrase $\Rightarrow$ Prepositional phrase
In prepositional phrases marked 4 to 7, you cannot change the position
of any of these prepositions in their respective phrases because each
preposition is the integral part of the prepositional phrase.

- <u>Sometimes, you can change the position of phrases or a phrase within</u>
<u>the sentence without altering the meaning.</u> For instance, we can re-
write the last example as follows:

  - On a country road, in Finland, I saw a herd of reindeer with long
    antlers.

  - In Finland, on a country road, I saw a herd of reindeer with long
    antlers.

- **Phrases can be embedded in another**.

A complex phrase contains within itself a number of phrases. These
phrases are embedded within each other in such a way that the highest
level phrase contains all low levels of phrases. The lowest level phrase
is embedded within the next higher level and the pattern is repeated
until all the phrases are embedded in the highest level phrase. This
repetition process is called **recursion**. For example:

- Mark was waiting [**in** a bus shelter **opposite** a bakery **for** my wife].

⇑	⇑	⇑	⇑	⇑
noun	verb	Prepositional	Prepositional	Prepositional
p	p	p	p	p

Here: p = phrase and [ ] above contain a complex phrase

The following analysis of this complex phrase in [ ] shows how phrases are embedded in one another in recursion manner. The head-word in each phrase is **highlighted**.

[*in* a bus shelter *opposite* a bakery *for* my wife] ⟹prepositional phrase

[a bus **shelter** *opposite* a bakery *for* my wife] ⟹ noun phrase

[*opposite* a bakery *for* my wife] ⟹ prepositional phrase

[a **bakery** *for* my wife] ⟹ noun phrase

[*for* my wife] ⟹ prepositional phrase

[*my* **wife**] ⟹ noun phrase

- You must telephone John after lunch about the meeting with Simon in my office.

In this sentence:

[**John after** lunch **about** the meeting **with** Simon **in** my office]

⟰

noun phrase but complex as several phrases in it

The headword in each phrase is **highlighted**.

[**John** after lunch about the meeting with Simon in my office] ⟹**noun phrase**

[**after** lunch about the meeting with Simon in my office] ⟹ **prepositional phrase**

[**lunch** about the meeting with Simon in my office] ⟹ **noun phrase**

[**about** the meeting with **Simon** in my office] ⟹ **prepositional phrase**

[the **meeting** with Simon in my office] ⟹ **noun phrase**

[**with** Simon in my office] ⟹ **prepositional phrase**

[**Simon** in my office] ⟹ **noun phrase**

[in my office] $\Rightarrow$ **prepositional phrase**

[my office] $\Rightarrow$ **noun phrase**

. Phrases in apposition

When in a sentence or clause, two **noun phrases** come one after the other and both refer to the same thing, then phrases are in apposition. In the following examples, phrases in apposition are shown in **bold**.

- Most tourists in London visit <u>Buckingham Palace</u>, **the London Office of the Queen**.

- She has shown me a letter from her <u>English tutor</u>, **a** <u>university lecturer</u>.

• **Sometimes, the second phrase is used to place emphasis on the adjacent noun phrase.** For instance:

- You must visit Windsor Castle, **The Queen's residence near London**.

   placing an emphasis on the adjacent noun phrase ↵

- **Nelson Mandela, the most famous African leader**, was
   --- imprisoned

emphasizing the meaning of the first phrase ↵   for 27 years.

In these examples, each second phrase is giving additional information about its adjacent noun phrase. <u>In these cases, a comma is needed to separate adjacent phrases.</u>

• <u>When the purpose of the second noun phrase is to identify the first one, there is no need for a comma to separate them</u>. Here are two examples:

- Mr. John Smith from London has arrived.
   --------------------- ------------------
           ⇑   ⇑
   first noun phrase second noun phrase

• What today's newspapers have revealed about **Mr John Major a famous politician** is disgusting. In this example, the purpose of the second phrase is identifying Mr Major. <u>Sometimes, the uses of</u> a comma in such phrases is debatable.

•<u>Coordination of phrases</u>

Coordinating and subordinating conjunctions are discussed in the last chapter. In grammar, coordination means joining together two elements of the same status. These two elements can be phrases or clauses. The coordination is achieved by using coordinating conjunctions. Let us examine the following sentences:

• We visited Frankfurt city **and** Stuttgart city on the same day.

    -------------------- ------ -----------------

    noun phrase⏘   ⇑   ⇑

            coordinating   noun phrase
            conjunction

• She likes to eat soup made from fresh cauliflower **and** fresh cabbage.

• Anne can write in German *or* in English.

• He cleaned **and** polished his shoes.

    ----

verb phrases coordinated ⏎ - coordinating conjunction ⇒**and**

• <u>**You can join other types of phrases as well.**</u>
  Here are some examples:

    • We drove in heavy snowfall **slowly and safely**.

        ----

            adverb phrases coordinated ⏎

    • He was **successful and happy**.

        ----

adjective phrases coordinated ⏎

****

- He was sitting **in the waiting room in Thomas Hospital.**

----

prepositional phrases coordinated ↵

Both coordination and apposition help us in explaining the meaning by merging words, that is using fewer words. For instance: the above example without the apposition might have been written or uttered as: **He was sitting in the waiting room and he was in Thomas Hospital.**

In summary, words are the smallest unit of language. The next category in the hierarchy of units is phrases. We can analyse a phrase in terms of the headword and its modifier(s). Phrases form both clauses and sentences. The next classification in the hierarchy of linguistic units is clauses. These are discussed in the next chapter.

Over to You

1. In the following sentence some phrases are underlined. Recognize the type of each phrase:

a) We travelled by <u>a double-decker bus</u>.

b) You <u>can leave</u>.

c) Will it be <u>a big party</u>?

d) <u>On Friday</u> I will be <u>at our home</u>.

e) Doreen writes <u>beautifully</u>.

f) John <u>run</u>!

g) Roger's car <u>has been stolen</u>.

h) I remembered that day was <u>very tiring</u>.

i) <u>For sometime,</u> we have been planning <u>to visit the Taj Mahal</u>.

j) I finished <u>that job today</u>.

k) Management seriously consider <u>staff suggestions</u>.

238   **Phrases**

****

l) She was <u>very happy</u> because of our visit.

m) <u>How long</u> have you been waiting?

n) This car is small <u>for me</u>.

o) Some candidates <u>are being interviewed</u> in the meeting room.

p) His story is <u>almost certainly</u> fabricated.

q) <u>We hardly ever</u> travel overseas.

r) I remember that place <u>vaguely</u>.

s) It is not <u>very difficult</u> work.

t) Carol is <u>twenty years old</u>.

u) The situation is <u>problematic</u>.

2. In what specific way does a prepositional phrase differ from a noun
   a verb, an adjective or an adverb phrase? Illustrate your answer
   with the aid of an example.

3. Phrases are embedded in one another. Show the recursion
   pattern – highest level to the lowest level of phrases in the
   following sentences:

a) Our sales are increasing since the publication of a new title.

b) Our town is crowded with holiday-makers during the summer every
   year.

c) Robin told us about his journey through the forest in Asian Siberia.
   South America.

d) Colin bought a beautiful fur coat for his wife from an expensive
   store in Moscow Russia.

4. Find phrases in apposition in the following sentences:

a) Victoria, the Queen of England, married a German Prince.
b) Mr. Bill Clinton, the US president, was an energetic person.
c) Sonia Gandhi, Italian born Indian politician, refused to become
   prime minister of India.
d) Marion Faithful, a housewife, is this month's First Prize winner.

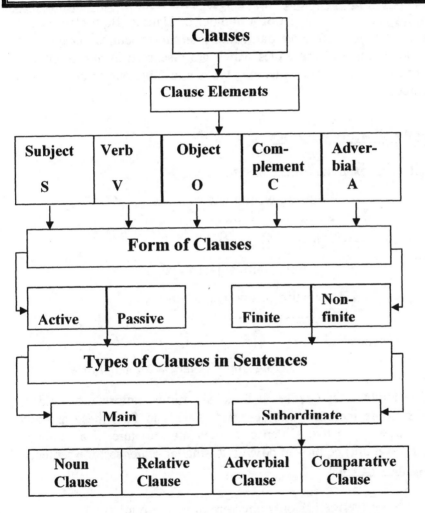

Chapter 12

Clauses

Clauses

Clause Elements

Subject S	Verb V	Object O	Com-plement C	Adver-bial A

Form of Clauses

Active	Passive		Finite	Non-finite

Types of Clauses in Sentences

Main		Subordinate

Noun Clause	Relative Clause	Adverbial Clause	Comparative Clause

Diagram 1   **Clause elements**

• <u>Introduction</u>

<u>A clause</u> consists of some words that include a subject and a verb. A clause in its own right is a sentence. It can also be a part of a sentence. <u>A sentence</u> may consist of just one clause, or it may have two or more clauses. A sentence may be a simple, compound or complex sentence. <u>A simple sentence</u> has at least one clause. <u>Compound and complex sentences</u> consist of a number of clauses. Both clauses and sentences have their own particular internal structures. Diagram 1 gives a summary of the topics which are discussed in this chapter in order to understand the structures, types and functions of clauses and sentences.

• <u>A clause or a sentence</u>

Let's first examine some clauses:

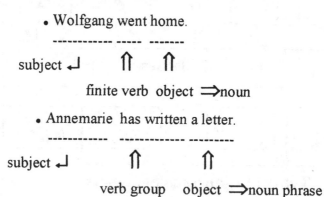

Both examples make sense without any further information added. Each example includes '**subject**' and '**verb**'. In fact, these are two clauses as well as two sentences. When the structure of a sentence cannot(= can not) be broken down into smaller sentences, the sentence is a <u>simple sentence</u>.

A <u>simple sentence</u> has only one verb or verb group.

Since the above two sentences cannot be broken down into smaller sentences, they are simple sentences. Both verbs in these examples are finite and active. The meaning or action (something changing or happening) of each verb is indicated by the noun phrase. These clauses do not require any further information to be grammatically complete. These clauses can stand alone. Any clause which can stand alone is <u>a</u> <u>**main clause**</u>.

As a main clause makes sense without the aid of any further information or clause, and is grammatically complete, it is also known as an <u>**independent clause**</u>. In terms of grammar, it makes syntactical sense on its own. Here are some more examples of main clauses. The verb/ verb group is **highlighted** in each clause:

- Karen **telephoned**.

- Mr. Taylor **will come**.

- The Prime Minister **has arrived**.

- Our guests **have left**.

- These are also examples of simple sentences as a simple sentence must have one subject element and one verb element. The structure of these examples based on the subject (abbreviated as **S**) followed by the verb (abbreviated as **V**). <u>SV is the minimum clause structure</u>. Clause structures and elements are discussed later.

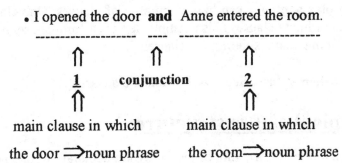

- This example consists of two main clauses joined together by a con junction **and** to form one sentence. We use **and, or, but** as **coordinating conjunctions** to join main clauses, which have the same status in a sentence.

- This is, in fact, a **compound sentence**. Unlike a simple sentence, a compound sentence can be broken down into smaller sentences or clauses. This example meets this criterion.

- In this sentence, both clauses can stand alone. It implies that the meaning of the verb in each clause is completed by its respective noun phrase. Thus, both clauses are main clauses.

- Let's change the last example to read as below:

  - When I opened the door, Anne entered the room.
    ------------------------------   ------------------------------
                 ⇑   ⇑
             clause 1   clause 2

This sentence still has two clauses.

Clause 1 begins with a **subordinating conjunction, when**. This clause is now dependent on clause 2 (⇒ main clause) in order to make syn-tactical(grammatical) sense. Therefore, any such clause is a **dependent clause**. The function of a dependent clause is to support the main clause as its subordinate. This is why it is also known as a **subordinate or sub clause**.

A **complex sentence** can have a number of clauses. One clause must be a subordinate clause. This example depicts a complex sentence, as it has both main and subordinate clauses.

. See ⇒Sentences . See ⇒subordinate clauses

. Typical clause structure

Now examine the structure of the following declarative statement:

****

- Robin Taylor **has made** a big profit.

  ⇈   ⇈   ⇈

 noun phrase verb phrase noun phrase

   ⇈   ⇈   ⇈

  subject   finite and verb complementation = **object**
         active verb

We can analyse this structure as:

- verb is preceded by the subject ⇒Robin Taylor

- the essence or the action of the verb is given by the verb

  complementation - noun phrase ⇒ a big profit

- this statement makes a declaration about the subject's action, that
  is giving information about the subject

- all three structural elements (subject phrase, verb phrase and verb
  complementation) are core or **obligatory elements**

- the removal of any of these obligatory elements would make this
  clause syntactically incomplete

This example typifies the structure of clauses. Since this structure relates to a declarative statement (declaring something), it is known as a
<u>declarative structure</u>.

In this example, the verb complementation is an object (abbreviated as
O), **a big profit**. <u>The object follows the <u>verb element</u></u>. The clause
structure displayed by this example is an **SVO.** It is widely used in
English.

- Indeed, you can add information to the **SVO** structure by adding
some non-obligatory items. For instance, we can re-write the above
example as:

- **Most certainly**, Robin Taylor has made a big profit **by selling shire horses**.

In this example, the adverbial information is **highlighted**. **The adverbial elements usually provide detailed information.** It is not essential as, without it, the clause is syntactically complete.

.Clause elements

Clauses are constructed by combining certain clause elements. There are five clause elements, each of which has a particular function and renders a specific meaning. These clause elements are listed below with their abbreviations pointed by arrows.

- **subject** $\Rightarrow$ **S**   • **verb** $\Rightarrow$ **V**
- **object** $\Rightarrow$ **O**   • **complement** $\Rightarrow$ **C**
- **adverbial** $\Rightarrow$ **A**

A clause may have some or all of these elements. All clauses contain subject and verb elements. Furthermore, the meaning of the verb has to be complete. For this reason, the verb element is followed by an object or complement. Usually, the object and complement elements follow the SV in a clause. There may be some adverbial elements.

. Subject element

The subject usually comes in the **subject position** which is usually before the verb element. The following examples illustrate the positions of the subject and other elements in clauses:

a)• Alison **likes flowers very much**.

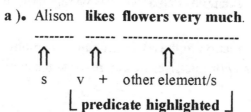

     s   v +   other element/s
          ⌊ **predicate highlighted** ⌋

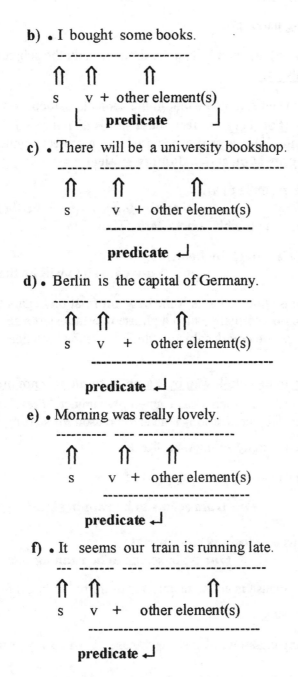

b) . I bought some books.

     s   v + other element(s)

       predicate

c) . There will be a university bookshop.

     s   v   + other element(s)

       predicate

d) . Berlin is the capital of Germany.

     s   v   +   other element(s)

       predicate

e) . Morning was really lovely.

     s   v   + other element(s)

       predicate

f) . It seems our train is running late.

     s   v   +   other element(s)

       predicate

. All the above examples show that the subject controls the verb in terms of singular or plural.

- Examples a), b), d) and e) illustrate that normally the subject element is a **noun phrase.**

- Examples c) and f) indicate that in the subject position, sometimes, there can be **it** or **there**. In fact, these words do not relate to any specific thing. When **it** or **there** is used in the subject position, it is called an **empty subject** or a **dummy subject**.

Let's re-write example c) as:
> **A university bookshop will be there**.
No doubt, this is a possible construction. Therefore:

There will be a university bookshop =
> **A university bookshop will be there**.

Usually, a phrase that contains some new information begins with *a* or *an* as in this case. Normally, such a phrase does not start a sentence. It is the dummy or the empty subject, which starts the sentence.

- When the verb **be** is followed by *some, a,* or *an,* it is not preceded by a real subject. In such a case, an empty subject "**there**" is placed in the subject position. This is the reason for starting the phrase with an empty subject $\Rightarrow$ **there**.

Similarly, we can re-write example (6) as:

> **Our train seems to be running late.**
Thus:
> **It seems our train is running late** =
> > **Our train seems to be running late**

The re-written clause is not so usual. It is preferred to begin the phrase with an empty subject $\Rightarrow$ **it**.

- The following examples also show the use of **an empty subject**:

- **It** was a cold night.

  --

an empty subject ↵ - (a cold night it was ⟹ unusual construction)

- **There** is a bank round the corner.

  ----

an empty subject ↵-   (a bank is round the corner ⟹ unusual)

- **The verb is controlled by the subject.** The following examples
  illustrate this rule:

- She is a cook.

  ---- ---

3rd person singular↵ ⇑
   subject   singular verb

- We are listening.

  ---- ---

1st person plural ↵ ⇑
   subject   plural verb

- They are at home.

  ------ ----

3rd person plural↵ ⇑
   subject   plural verb

- I am going to Austria.

  --- ----

1st person singular↵ ⇑
   subject   singular verb

- You are working very hard.

  ----- ----

2nd person singular↵ ⇑
   subject   plural verb

• You were wrong at that time.
       ---- ------

2nd person plural ⏎   ⇧
     subject   plural verb

Both second person singular and second person plural take the plural form of the verb.

• The subject of a clause is an important element. Indeed, it can be said that it is the subject which gives the clause its theme or topic.

• In examples a) to f), you can see that **V+ other element(s)** are marked as <u>predicate</u>. <u>The predicate is a traditional grammatical term</u> for the verb and any other element(s) that follow the verb. Traditionally, the clause was divided into two parts, namely the subject and the predicate. Here is another example:

• Denmark **is a small country**.
  ---------- --------------------

theme of this clause/ subject ⏎   ⇧

information about the theme/ subject ⇒**predicate**

> **In summary, the predicate includes all other elements except the subject element of a clause.**

•<u>Verb element</u>

The verb element is considered as the focal point of the clause. Let's first examine the following examples:

• A guest **has written** to the hotel manager.
  ----

verb element ⇒**verb phrase** (auxiliary verb + transitive verb)

- A guest ⟹subject - it is the topic because it is the guest who
                    has written

- **has written** to the hotel manager ⟹ this is the information about
the subject which the writer/speaker wants to say ⟹ **predicate**

> • She **walks**.
> --------

    verb element ↵ - **verb phrase**

Here the verb **walks** is intransitive, the predicate ends at walks.
thus the **predicate** ⟹ **walks**

> • Romania **is** a country in Europe.
> ----

    verb element ↵- verb phrase – copular/linking verb

Here, '*is* a country in Europe' ⟹<u>**predicate**</u>
                            ⇑

That is what the writer/speaker wants to say about Romania

If you remove the verb phrase, the clause will not make any sense.
Furthermore, it will be grammatically incomplete. As the subject sets
the theme, there must be something about it. It is the verb in the form
of a verb phrase which tells us about the action or the state relating to
the subject. It is suggested that you browse through the chapters on
verbs and phrases, where you can find more relevant information on
the verb element.

• Object element

The object element comes after the verb in a clause. Here are some examples:

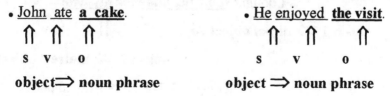

	• John ate **a cake**.			• He enjoyed **the visit**.	
⇑	⇑	⇑	⇑	⇑	⇑
S	V	O	S	V	O

object⟹ noun phrase   object ⟹ noun phrase

● In these examples verbs are transitive. The transitive verbs take an objective. Here are some more examples in which the verbs are also transitive:

● He likes **history books.**   ● Someone rang **the door bell.**

  ⇑⇑   ⇑   ⇑   ⇑   ⇑   ⇑

  S **V**   **O**   **S**   **V**   **O**

● **A clause can have two objects with some verbs as illustrated below:**

            ● Mary gave *[to]* Margaret some seeds.

object 1 ⇒ indirect object ↵   ⇑

                       object 2 ⇒ **direct object**

In this case, the action of the verb *gave [to]* directly affects *some seeds (primary effect)* as these were given to Margaret. Margaret is also indirectly affected *(secondary effect)* by the action of the verb as she received *some seeds*. Also note:

      Margaret ⇒ **noun** **some seeds** ⇒ noun phrase

           ● Alex has written <u>a letter</u> **to his mother-in-law.**

  object 1 ⇒ **direct object** ↵   ⇑

                 object 2 ⇒ **indirect object**

● It should be noted that both objects are **noun phrases** <u>but</u> to his mother-in-law is a

Prepositional phrase.(Remember a phrase can be just one word)

          ● I bought **some perfume** for <u>my wife.</u>

object 1 ⇒ direct object ↵   ⇑

               object 2 ⇒ **indirect object**

        for my wife ⇒ Prepositional phrase

****

Both objects are noun phrases.

The primary effect of the verb **bought** is on perfume. For this reason it is the first object. Of course, the second object is also affected to the extent that the perfume is for my wife. Thus, the secondary effect of the verb **bought** is on the second object.

- <u>**As shown above, the object is usually a noun phrase. Sometimes a clause functions as an object.**</u>

    - No one believed that <u>**he was alive**</u>.

        finite clause functioning as an object

    - We look forward to <u>**our weekend in Prague**</u>.

        non- finite clause functioning as an object

- In a clause, an object can be either **direct** or **indirect**. <u>**The difference between the direct and indirect object is that:**</u>

    - the primary effect of the verb is on the direct object

    - the secondary effect of the verb is on the indirect object

    - the indirect object can be preceded by **to** or **for** (by converting a noun phrase into a prepositional phrase as in examples 1-2)

. <u>Complement element</u>

A complement is a word or a group of words in a clause or a sentence. It is used after

- linking (copular) verbs and

- some transitive verbs, which take **an object** and **object complement**.

Often in constructing a clause or a sentence, a complement is an essential grammatical requirement. A complement which follows a linking verb is known as **subject complement**. A complement which comes after a transitive verb and an object is called **object complement**.

For instance:

- It <u>looks</u> <u>very pretty</u>.

copular verb↵   ⇑

       subject complement – tells us more about the subject ⇒**it**

- The head teacher **presented** <u>Jane</u> **with a medal**.

       transitive verb ↵   ⇑   ⇑

                    object   object complement

- **<u>A complement may be an adjective, noun or adverbial.</u>**

It is illustrated below:

- Adam seemed to be **<u>a very good person</u>**.

noun phrase - complement↵

- He is **<u>in a real mess</u>**.

complement ↵ - prepositional phrase

- Moris was **<u>angry</u>**.

adjective type complement

- Sara appears **<u>very patient</u>**.

complement - prepositional phrase   complement - adjective phrase

In the above examples, the complement refers to the subject of the clause (Adam, Morris, he and Sara). <u>Without the complement, the linking or copular verb cannot function in a clause.</u>

When the complement relates to the subject of the clause, it is also known as the **subject predicative**, which is the <u>**subject complement**</u> . The linking or copular verbs are useful for describing the subject's attributes such as **patient (attribute)** or *state* in which one finds oneself, i.e. **in a real mess**.

The weakness of linking verbs is that they cannot take an object and object complement. Furthermore, a clause containing a linking verb cannot be turned into a <u>passive clause</u>. However, the most used copula/copular verb **be** can be utilised to denote the association between the object and <u>**the object complement**</u>. The object complement is also known as <u>**the object predicative.**</u> This is exemplified below:

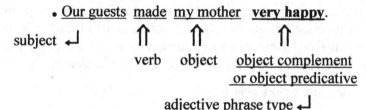

Since *very happy* is an adjective phrase, the object complement is considered as the adjective phrase type. In this case, the complement is <u>related to the object</u> instead of the subject. For this reason it is the <u>***object complement***</u> or <u>***object predicative***</u>. Here are some examples of object complement (object is in **bold**):

- The Student Union elected her <u>**treasurer**</u>.

           object complement - noun ↵

- The chairman has declared <u>**the meeting**</u> <u>***open***</u>.

      object complement – object ↵

- They consider <u>**their captain** *as the best team leader*</u>.

object complement = as + noun phrase ↵

- The Lottery money helped <u>**me** *to retire from work*</u>.

          object complement ↵
             - noun-finite clause with **to-infinitive**

- Our trainer kept **us** *practising for another hour*.

    object complement ↵
    noun-finite clause with *-ing* participle

- John helped Dolly **solve this puzzle**.

    object complement ↵
    - non-infinitive clause with **bare** infinitive

. Adverbial element

The adverbial element is often an adverb phrase or prepositional phrase. It functions as an adverb. A clause can also function as adverbial. An adverbial element can occur anywhere in a clause. The following examples illustrate the adverbial element in clauses:

- Anne works *very hard*.
      ----

    adverbial ↵-an adverb phrase functioning as adverbial

(1) . *Currently*, my boss is away in London.
      ----

adverbial ↵ - an adverb phrase functioning as adverbial

(2) . **At present**, he is having a shower.
      ----

    adverbial ↵ - prepositional phrase acting as adverbial

- My wife will not return from Russia *until* **tomorrow**.
                                      ----

                    adverbial ↵
    - prepositional phrase acting as adverbial

- I am not *against* his brilliant idea.
      ----

    adverbial ↵ - prepositional phrase acting as adverbial

- He talked slowly ***because of*** his recent illness.

----

adverbial - prepositional phrase functioning as adverbial

- Adverbial elements are often optional. For instance, examples (1) and (2) can still make sense without any adverbial element. These examples will also be grammatically complete without adverbs.

- **An adverbial element may not contain an adverb, but it still functions like an adverb.** For instance:

(3) • Adam is in London **to visit his sister**.

    non-finite verb phrase ↵ ⇒ to-infinitive

The above example answers the following adverbial questions:

- **Where** is Adam? Adam is in London?

adverb ↵

- **Why is** Adam in London? – to visit his sister

adverb ↵

Example (3) does not have any adverb. Since it answers adverbial questions, it contains an adverbial element. This is the reason for calling the adverbial element by this name.

There are four forms of clauses. These are summarised in List 1 towards the end of the chapter. Now we can discuss each form of clause.

• **Finite clauses**

Here are some examples of finite clauses:

- Daniel **works** for our company.

finite verb ↵ – present

****

- Adam **is walking** towards Hyde Park Corner.

finite verb – present continuous tense

- He is very pleased **that everything has worked well**.

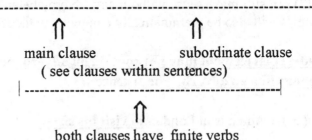

- You can see that all three above examples contain subjects . In fact, a finite clause can be without the subject as illustrated below:

  - **Sylvia and Ralf correspond with us** and **(they)** visit us regularly.

  main clause ↵   you can leave they out ↵
                            in this <u>finite clause</u>

  subordinate clause ↵

This sentence has two clauses: namely main and subordinate. These are discussed later. Both clauses have finite verbs. Here are two more examples of finite clauses *(in italic bold style)* <u>without subjects</u>:

- She is very busy at work and *cannot go out with you*.

- The weather was terrible and *caused some train cancellations*.

• <u>Non-finite clauses</u>

Here are some examples of non-finite clauses:

- **We went to Agra** _to see_ _the Taj Mahal._

   to-infinitive verb form⤶   ⇑

                         object

In the structure of this sentence, the main clause is shown in **bold style**. The subordinate clause has a _"to-infinitive verb"_, which is not marked for tense. Thus, it is a non-finite clause. It is without the subject.

- In this sentence, when you read the non-finite clause only, you can see that by itself it does not seem grammatically correct. For this reason, the non-finite clause is usually a part of a sentence which also has a finite clause. Here, "we went to Agra" is a finite clause, because it has a finite verb _went_ – past tense form of the verb _go_.

    - **The plan was** _to take a night train._

   to-infinitive verb form⤶   ⇑

                       object

The non-finite clause _(in italics)_ is without the subject.

    - He eats a variety of vegetables _**to reduce**_ _**his weight**._

subject of the non-finite clause⤶non-finite verb⤶   ⇑

                          object of the non-finite clause

Here the non-finite clause _(in italics)_ has a subject.

    - Antonia wanted _**Ivan**_ _**to marry**_ _**her.**_

subject of non-finite clause ⤶   ⇑   ⇑

                 non-finite   object of the

                 verb   non-finite clause

In the last two examples, each noun-finite clause _(in italics)_ has its subject.

    - Jane assisted _**John**_ _to develop_ _a CV._

subject of non-finite clause ⤶   ⇑   ⇑

                 to- infinitive   object of the

                       non-finite clause

* We wanted **_to eat_**   **_Indian food_**.

to- infinitive verb ⤶   ⇑

                    object of the non-finite clause

----

infinitive clause in **_bold italics_** ⤶

In this example, the non-finite clauses *(in italics)* are **without the subject**.

. <u>Active and passive clauses</u>

Here are some examples of **active clauses**:

(1). <u>Frank</u> **_is driving_** the car.

⇑   ⇑ - agent ⇒ driving ⇒ active verb

agent doing something/activity/action taken by the agent

<u>Therefore it is an **_active clause_** with present continuous tense.</u>

The active clause structure is considered as **the primary structure**. From it, the structure of the passive clause is derived as:

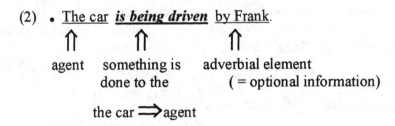

(2) . <u>The car</u> **_is being driven_** by <u>Frank</u>.

⇑   ⇑   ⇑

agent   something is   adverbial element
             done to the   (= optional information)

the car ⇒ agent

(3) . <u>The car</u> **_is being driven_**.

passive clause grammatically complete

* A comparison between Examples (1) and (2) reveals that the object in the first example is now in the subject position in the last example.

• The verb phrase, "*is driving*" in the first example has been modified
  to become, "*is being driven*" in the last example.

The reason for doing so is that the verb phrase in the active clause indicates the present continuous tense. The passive clause must also express the present continuous tense by using the passive verb form:

<u>**is being drive**</u>

present continuous form of the verb *be*↵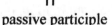

passive participle

• In the first example, the agent, **Frank** is preceded by the adverb *by*.
  Thus, *by Frank* is the adverbial element added to the passive clause.
  It is an optional piece of information.

• The adverbial element is not necessary as without it, the passive
  clause "The car *is being driven.*" is grammatically complete.
  See Example 3 above.

• In Examples 2 and 3, since the agent *(= the car)* is receiving the
  action *(=affected)*, it is a passive clause expressing the present
  continuous tense.

Here are some examples of both active and corresponding passive
  clauses:

> • She loved her children. ⇐ active clause

> • Her children were loved (by her). ⇐ passive clause

> • They ***should count*** the money. ⇐ active clause

> model + infinitive = active verb

> • The money ***should be counted***. ⇐ passive clause

> ⇑

> model+ infinitive = active verb

. We admire your sincere desire _**to help**_ the aged. ⇐ active clause

active to-infinitive

. Your sincere desire _**to help**_ the aged is admired (by us).

⇑ - passive clause

active to-infinitive converted to passive to- infinitive

. There is something _**to do**_ this afternoon. ⇐ active clause

⇑

active to-infinitive

. There is something _**to be done**_ this afternoon. ⇐ passive clause

⇑

active to-infinitive changed to passive infinitive

. They left without _**eating**_ their lunch. ⇐ active clause

⇑

active gerund

. They left without the lunch **being eaten**. ⇐ passive clause

----

active gerund converted to passive gerund

. <u>Subordinate clauses</u>

A subordinate clause supports the main clause. Subordinate clauses are categorized as:

- **Noun or Nominal Clauses**

- **Relative Clauses**

- **Adverbial Clauses**

- **Comparative Clauses**

This categorization is based on the function of clauses in relation to the main clause. When a subordinate clause is linked itself to the rest of the sentence, it performs its specific function as discussed here.

. <u>Noun or nominal clauses</u>

A noun clause can act as an object, subject or complement of the main clause. You will see that a noun clause functions in the same manner as a noun phrase does. Usually, a noun phrase commences with **that, if** or with a **wh-question** word such as **what**. It can also come after a <u>preposition,</u> <u>adjective</u> or a <u>noun</u>. The following examples illustrate their characteristics:

- <u>We believe</u> **that the business will grow.**

 ⇑ ⇑

 main clause   noun clause acting as an object

- <u>The teacher didn't think</u> *that she was an able girl.*

 ⇑ ⇑

 main clause   noun clause acting as an object

- Without **that** the above clauses will still convey the same meaning and are grammatically correct.

<u>Similarities between phrases and clauses</u>

The following comparison illustrates the similarities between noun phrases and noun clauses.

- the business ⇒ noun phrase   • the business will grow ⇒ noun clause

- she ⇒ noun phrase (grammatically: just one word can be a phrase)

- She was an able girl ⇒ noun clause

Here are some more examples of a noun clause acting as an object:

• We were thinking **whether you would come**.

noun clause acting as an object ↵

• I wonder **if you would stay with us.**

noun clause acting as an object ↵

• We told **the police** that we were strangers in London.

⇑   ⇑

direct object – noun phrase   indirect object – noun clause

It demonstrates that a noun clause can be an indirect object.

• **The following examples illustrate that a clause can function as a subject:**

• Whether I'll be able to attend a meeting depends on the transport.

⇑

noun clause acting as subject

• When a noun clause is the subject, it does not start with **if**.

• That my son returned from the war was the most memorable day.

⇑

noun clause acting as subject

• **_What you_** say is nonsense.

noun clause - subject ↵

• A **_wh-question_** word begins a question with any of the nine question words: _what, when, where, which, who, whom, whose, how_ and _why_. These are exemplified below:

• **Who** can come with me?

⇑

noun clause begin with wh-question word - **possible answer**:

* Someone can come with me

declarative statement/sentence↵

If the word order in an interrogative sentence is the same as in a declarative sentence/ statement as shown above then there is *no* **inversion** (change) of the normal word order in the wh-question.

* Here are some examples of noun clauses when a noun clause can **function as a complement of the main clause.**

    * Our problem is **how we are going to reach the airport on time by public transport**.

    noun clause acting as the complement of the main clause ↵

    * The fact is **that they are happily married**.

complement of the main clause *the fact is* ↵

* **The following examples illustrate that noun clauses can come after some adjectives and nouns:**

The following examples illustrate how this is achieved:

    * I am **afraid** that I shan't see you tonight.

    adjective ↵   ⇑
                        noun clause

    * I am **confident** that she will soon recover from her illness.

        adjective ↵   ⇑
                            noun clause

    * I am **glad** that Joan has returned home safely.

    adjective ↵   ⇑
                        noun clause

* **You can leave out *that* in the above examples and similar cases.**

****

- Your _**belief**_ that she is rich is only imagination.

noun ↵   noun clause ↵ - **do not leave out** ⇒ that

- What gave you the **idea** that Rachel is abroad?

noun ↵   noun clause↵- **do not leave out** ⇒ that

- The **news** that he is already married has shocked Monica.

noun ↵   noun clause ↵ - **do not leave out** ⇒ that

- **A noun clause can occur after a preposition as illustrated by the following examples:**

- Our jobs depend _**on**_ what management decide(s)* today.

preposition ↵   noun clause ↵

*The word management is a countable group noun. It can be singular or plural.

- We were amazed _(**at***_) how colourful and bright the

preposition ↵   Christmas lights were.

noun clause ↵

* You can also say **by** instead of **at** or no have preposition at all.

. Relative clauses

A clause introduced by any of the relative pronouns or a relative phrase, which refers to an earlier noun or a noun phrase, is a relative clause. It acts as a post-modifier of the noun or the noun phrase. For instance:

- The lady **who bought some tea bags** is my aunt.

relative clause ↵ - post-modifying the noun phras_e_ ⇒ the lady

- The word **who** is **a relative pronoun** which joins the relative clause to the **main clause** $\Longrightarrow$ the lady is my aunt.

The noun or the noun phrase which is post-modified (or refers back) is called the **antecedent of the relative clause**. Here, **the lady** is the **antecedent**.

- The cricket team **who were in red outfits** won the game.

  relative clause ↵

who $\Longrightarrow$ relative pronoun links relative clause to **main clause**

  the cricket team won the game ↵

You may think that the word team is not a person. It consists of persons. Is it?

It is a countable group noun, which can agree with a singular or plural verb.

- In these two examples , there is no need to place a comma before and after the relative clause.

The reason for omitting commas is that both relative clauses are acting as **identifying (restrictive) clauses**. The purpose of the information given by an identifying clause is to identify the earlier noun in the main clause. The following examples illustrate this rule as well:

- The footballer *who* **had short blonde hair** was not from Scandinavia.

  relative clause ↵ - **who** $\Longrightarrow$ relative pronoun (linkage)

Here, the head word *footballer* in the main clause is post-modified by a relative clause which begins with the relative pronoun **who**.

- The lady **who is wearing a white dress** is married to our mayor.

  relative clause ↵ - *who* $\Longrightarrow$ relative pronoun

- **The pronoun whose denotes possessive meaning.**

Let's consider the following examples:

- Our neighbours **whose daughter lives in Spain** have gone to Spain

                          relative clause↵   for a week.

functioning as identifying clause↵

- Some motorists *whose* **vehicles were damaged by the crowd**

complained to the police.   ⇑

                                   relative clause - identifying which motorists

- Wolfgang **whose car is a black BMW with an open roof** is a

German insurance expert.   ⇑

                                   relative clause

It tells us which Wolfgang is being talked about.

- When the relative clause functions as an identifying clause, the
  determiner **the** is usually used before the noun instead of any
  possessive pronoun **my, your, her** *etc*.

  For instance:

    - James is driving **the** car **that** he bought from me.

         determiner preferred↵   relative clause ↵

           that ⟹ relative pronoun refers to car

Here, the head word **car** in the main clause is post-modified by the
relative clause.

    - James is driving **his** car **that** he bought from me.

                     ⇑ relative clause ↵- *that* ⟹ relative pronoun
         possessive pronoun is unfit   refers to **car**

    - She liked **the** car that she bought last year.

           ⇑   ⇑

      determiner preferred   relative clause used as identifying clause
                              identifies which car

* She liked **her** car **that she bought last year**.

Possessive pronoun unsuited because it implies **which car**
The purpose is to identify the *car* - not refer to **which car**.

* I went to **the** cottage **that I inherited last year**.

determiner preferred ↵

            relative clause used as identifying clause

* I went to **my** cottage that I inherited last year.

Possessive pronoun unfit- as it refers to **which cottage** instead of identifying the cottage.

* The relative pronouns **who** and **that** are used to refer to both things
  and people as shown above. On the other hand, the relative pronouns
  which and **that** are usually used for things and ideas.

  Here are some examples:

* Flats **which/that** overlook the sea cost a great deal more.

      relative clause ↵ - you can use **which** or **that**

* She doesn't know much about the job **which/that has been offered to her**.

              relative clause ↵

         - **which/that** ⟹ relative pronouns

* It was a dream **which/ that** never came true.

        relative clause ↵

You can see that the pronoun *that* can be used with any noun.

* A relative clause also functions as **a classifying clause**. The idea of
  classifying is to describe the head noun in the main clause by its
  nature, types or class. Classifying clauses **do not** have commas
  around them. The following examples illustrate this rule:

- Annemarie does not want **customers** who waste her business time.

    head word/noun ↵   relative clause ↵

In this example, the purpose of the relative clause is to say what type of customers.

- They were asking for the **shopping centre** that has a car park

        head word/noun ↵   in front of it.

                                        relative clause↵

- We need some young persons **who** can do some community
                                        work once a week.

            relative clause ↵ - classifying the head noun

- Motorists **who have caused fatal accidents** should be banned

            relative clause↵   from driving.
- relative clause classifying and pointing to a particular type of driver

- **A relative clause can function as an adding (or identifying/non-restrictive)clause.**

An adding clause provides some additional information about the head word in the main clause. The relative clause is separated from the main clause by two commas. In fact, the punctuation rules regarding the use of commas with subordinate clauses are not universally the same rules. The following examples of relative clauses exemplify how they can function as adding clauses:

- **Buda**, **which** is a part of Budapest in Hungary, has many historical
  ⇑   relative adding clause ↵   buildings.
head noun   ⇑
                - giving additional information about the noun **Buda**

- **The gentleman,** who asked so many questions during the
                        meeting, **is my boss**.

    relative adding clause ↵ - additional information

The ⟹ article/determiner

gentleman ⟹ head noun of the main clause shown in **bold**

- All football hooligans, <u>**who have caused so much disturbance in London tonight,**</u>

should be expelled by their clubs.   ⇑
                                      <u>adding clause</u>

giving additional information↲about the noun⟹hooligan(s)

- Nobel, <u>**who was the captain of Test Cricket Team 2001,**</u>
                                   made 200 runs against Australia.

In this example:
                 the text underlined is the **relative clause**
           adding information about the noun ↲

- Some boxes, <u>**which had been missing for two months,**</u>

  were found hidden under the staircase. ⇑
                                         <u>relative clause</u>

  adding information about the noun ↲

- Margaret Thatcher, <u>**who was the first female British Prime Minister,**</u> was replaced by John Major in 1990.

                     . text in bold style ⟹ <u>relative clause</u>

functioning as an adding clause and giving extra↲
information about Margaret Thatcher

- In the above examples, if you leave out adding clauses, these sentences will still make sense. The information between the commas is not restricted. This is the reason for calling these types of clauses non-restrictive clauses.

* Usually, **whose** relates to people as shown above. Here are some more examples.

* Anne, **whose husband Wolfgang drives a Rolls-Royce,**

  is a businesswoman. ⇑

  relative clause

  acting as adding clause↵

* We wish to interview some students **whose overall performance is above B grade.**

  relative clause ↵ - acting as classifying clause

* Our neighbours **whose house was burgled last night**
  called the police.

  In this example:

  the text underlined is the **relative clause**

  relative clause ↵ identifying clause

  No commas needed to enclose an identifying clause - see punctuation

* Mahatma Gandhi, **whose courage I admire greatly**, was a pioneer
  and campaigner of a non-violent movement for freedom and justice.

  * whose courage I admire greatly ⟹ relative clause which is
    functioning as an adding clause

* **Whose** can also refer to an organisation or a country. For instance:

* Switzerland, **whose inhabitants speak four official languages**, is in

  West Europe.   relative clause↵ - giving extra information
                                            about the head noun

* IBM, whose ideas have been copied by many PC manufacturers, is a

  large company.   relative clause ↵
                    giving extra information about the head noun – IBM

Organisation$\Rightarrow$**group/collective noun** -considered as a singular noun
but it renders plural meaning

The relative pronoun *whose* indicates that something belongs to something (possessiveness). When it relates to things (entities), it is a group noun as in the last two examples. It can refer to people as shown below.

- We can use relative pronouns **which** and **that** for constructing identifying and classifying clauses. This is exemplified below.

- The city **which I have marked on this map** is a large place

            relative clause ↵   in Scotland.

- This schedule **which our supervisor submitted to the manager**

  has been rejected.   relative clause ↵

- These are imported garments **which can not be exhibited as made
  in England.**

        relative clause ↵

- A passage to India was her big ambition **that was fulfilled**.

           relative clause ↵

- It is a home-made cake **that is delicious**.

        relative clause ↵

- When should you use *which* or *that* as a relative pronoun?

In the last two examples, both **which** and **that** are possible relative pronouns in order to begin a relative clause. In these examples, you can replace **that** with **which** or **vice versa** without altering the meaning rendered in each case. The use of **that** is generally recommended with any noun, but **which** with ideas and things. For instance:

- Your silly plan **which/that has ruined our trip** should not have

        relative clause ↵   been accepted.

- I have developed a database system **that/which** generates my
  mail shot.

        relative clause ↵

* Some people consider the use of **which** as somewhat formal when it relates to only the head noun. On the other hand, when **which** relative pronoun refers to the whole clause instead of the head noun, **which** relative pronoun is used. This is illustrated below:

* The Indian touring cricket team drew the final test match, **which**
  ended the current test series in a draw.
  clause ↵ adding information

The main clause is referred by the relative clause. The main clause is:

'The Indian touring cricket team drew the final test match'

* Our coach driver suddenly felt a sharp pain in his chest, **which**
  caused this terrible accident.

  relative clause ↵ adding information
The main clause is referred by the relative clause.

* **In informal English, often the relative pronoun is omitted when it is not the subject of the relative clause.**

This is exemplified below:

* The book **I am reading** is really useful for my work.

  relative clause without which/that ⇒ relative pronoun

* The big man **my brother is talking to** is a well-known boxer.

  relative clause without whom/whom ⇒ relative pronoun

* The urgent letter **I posted to Anne last Friday** still hasn't
  ⇑
  reached her.
  relative clause without which ⇒ relative pronoun

- **When a relative pronoun is the subject of the relative clause, the relative pronoun cannot be discarded.** The following examples illustrate this rule:

- The lady **who was wearing a flowery hat** was his grandmother.

  ----

    relative clause ↵ - **who** ⇒ subject

- A student **who gave a talk on morality** lives in our area.

    relative clause ↵ - **who** ⇒ subject

- I have a number of software packages **that /which are used for administrative work**.

In this case, the relative clause is shown in **bold style**. The subject of this relative clause is either **that** or **which**.

- A relative clause can have either an active or a passive participle without a relative pronoun. Here are some examples:

- Some overseas students **taking part in the debate** tonight

                       relative clause ↵   are Asians.

  - who are (= relative pronoun + auxiliary) omitted

Note: **taking** is an active participle here as it relates to some overseas students and their on-going activity.

- Anne spotted the car **coming fast from the opposite side of the road**.

            relative clause ↵ - coming ⇒ active participle

  -   **which was** (= relative pronoun + auxiliary) omitted

- Projects **submitted today** will be assessed and returned to

  relative clause ↵   you by 30th June.

  - which were (= relative pronoun + auxiliary) omitted

Note: **submitted** is a passive participle here as it relates to projects given – the activity performed by other persons.

- Some sweets made in Bridlington **presented** *to the Kling family* were

                relative clause ↵   eaten up fast.

  - **which were** (= relative pronoun + auxiliary) omitted

  presented ⟹ **passive participle** - sweets were given by someone
                                    to the Kling family.

- <u>**Use of** *whom* **and** *which* **pronouns with prepositions**</u>

- <u>The relative pronoun **whom** is not used very often in spoken English.</u>
<u>Its use in the relative clause after a **preposition** is rather formal.</u>
For instance:

- The Plew family **with whom** *I stayed in Germany* is visiting us.

               relative clause ↵

- **with** ⟹ preposition comes before the pronoun

- We will telephone John Russell *to **whom** we supplied a red car*.

                    relative clause ↵

- *to* ⟹ preposition placed before the pronoun

- <u>In identifying and classifying relative clauses the relative pronoun</u>
<u>**whom** can be the object pronoun. In such cases, it is not usually</u>
<u>used. Instead of whom you can use *that* or *who*.</u>

Often, the relative pronoun is altogether omitted in identifying
and classifying relative <u>clauses.</u> For instance:

- John Smith **who/that** *I interviewed yesterday* has been appointed.

             relative clause ↵

- Robin Taylor **who/that** *I telephoned today* was pleased to accept

              relative clause ↵   our invitation.

- Yvonne **[who/that/whom]** *I met in France* will visit us soon.

        relative clause ↵
  - [the relative pronoun can be omitted]

- **In spoken English the use of *whom* is not common. It is preferred to use who and place the preposition at the end of the sentence.** For instance:

- You are not telling me **who** *you went out last night* **with**.

  relative clause ↵
- preposition *with* at the end of the sentence

- Please let me know *who you address the letter to*.

The relative clause is printed in *italic style*. Note that the

- preposition *to* at the end of the sentence is essential.

- **In adding clauses the relative pronoun who is often used instead of whom.** In such cases, you cannot leave out the relative pronoun as exemplified below:

- James Berg, **who we liked as a tutor,** is a science journalist for

  relative clause↵   "The Times."
  - adding extra information

- Our Russian colleague, **who** *we bought a wedding present for*, is a

  relative clause↵   father now.

- giving extra information about the colleague

Note that in the last two examples the use of **that** instead of **who** or **whom** is not allowed.

- Like **whom**, we can also put the preposition before the relative pronoun **which**. For instance:

- My long overseas trip **for which** *I saved for so many years*

was memorable .   ⇑

            relative clause - identifying trip

* The current upheaval **for which** *we are not prepared* is very harmful.

----

relative clause ↵ - identifying upheaval

In both examples, the preposition is put before the preposition ⇒ *for*

. Adverbial clauses

An adverbial clause in a complex sentence functions in the same way as an adverb in a simple sentence. It modifies the main clause by adding information about time, place, manner, cause, etc. An adverbial clause may be in the first position, in the middle position or in the end position in a sentence. So, it can occur anywhere in the sentence. The adverbial clause is joined to the main clause by a conjunction.

* A comma is inserted between the adverbial clause and the main clause when the adverbial clause is in the first position in a sentence.

The following examples illustrate adverbial clauses.

* They can visit us **if they wish**.

adverbial clause↵

- indicating a condition if ⇒ conjunction
Here, the adverbial clause modifies the main clause, *"They can visit us"* by giving additional information.

* **If she likes it**, she can have it as a present.

adverbial clause ↵ - relates to a condition if ⇒conjunction

* We'll go out for a walk by the sea **as soon as I finish my gardening**.

adverbial clause of time ↵ - **as soon as** ⇒conjunction

* **Since you are not coming with me**, I don't want to travel alone.

adverbial clause of reason - since ⇒conjunction

- **Where an Indian restaurant** is, there is a Chinese take-way at
  ⇑   at the corner.

  adverbial clause of place   - *where* ⇒conjunction

- I went to Paris **in order to attend an international book fair**.

         adverbial clause of purpose ↵

       - *in order to* ⇒*conjunction*

- **If we meet at Heathrow,** we can discuss the final draft.

  adverbial clause ↵ - if is used with the present simple for future time

- **As far as I can remember**, she was with her husband at that time.

       ⇑

     adverbial clause

       • expressing truth   - as far as ⇒conjunction

- How can she be happy **as though nothing had happened in her**
                                       family?

             adverbial clause of manner ↵

- as though ⇒conjunction

You can also say **as if** instead of **as though**. In passing, note as follows:

       instead   ⇒an adverb **but**   instead of ⇒ a preposition

- You should rest tomorrow **so that you can recover after your**
                              long journey.

  adverbial clause of purpose ↵ - so that ⇒conjunction

- We arrived *happily* **at the airport** *to* fly home   *for* **a wedding ceremony**.
      ⇑   ⇑   ⇑   ⇑

  adverbial   adverbial   adverbial   adverbial

     1   **2**   **3**   **4**

In the above example:

****

1 ⇒adverbial phrase   2⇒ prepositional phrase

3 ⇒ non-finite phrase   4 ⇒ verb phrase

- <u>There may be several adverbials in a clause as shown in the above example.</u>

Let's consider the following questions and answers in relation to the above example shown in a box:

- How did they arrive ? ⇒ happily

- Where did they arrive ? ⇒ at the airport

- Why did they arrive at the airport? ⇒ to fly home

- What was the purpose of flying home? ⇒ for a wedding ceremony

The above analysis shows that a clause can have a number of adverbials. Furthermore, it demonstrates that not all adverbials consist of adverbs, but adverbial phrases. Adverbial phrases do not always contain an adverb as illustrated by this example. <u>Types of adverbial clauses are discussed towards the end of this chapter.</u>

. <u>Comparative clauses</u>

These clauses express comparison. Some comparative clauses involve the use of the subordinating conjunction *than*. On the other hand, some comparative clauses introduce the second part of the comparison by means of correlative subordinators *as .... as*. Here are some examples of comparative clauses relating to different situations:

- <u>She is less interested in this job</u> **than** <u>I thought</u>.

        1   **2**

In the above example:

                1 = main clause   and
                2 = comparative clause

            than ⇒ subordinating conjunction or a subordinator

• The corner house looked more impressive **than I had expected**.

     main clause ⤶   comparative clause ⤶

• **He doesn't earn <u>as much money</u> <u>as</u> <u>James does</u>**.

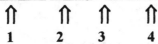

     1   **2**   **3**   **4**

Here: 1 = first correlative subordinator **2** = head word — noun
     3 = second correlative subordinator
     4 = comparative clause introduced by ⇒*as*

• You are <u>*as*</u> <u>*handsome*</u> <u>*as*</u> <u>*your father was some years ago*</u>.
        1   **2**   **3**   **4**
  1 = first correlative subordinator **2** = head word - adjective
  3 = second correlative subordinator
  4 = comparative clause introduced by the second

     correlative subordinator ⇒*as*

• She danced <u>**as**</u> <u>**elegantly**</u> <u>**as**</u> <u>**other winners did**</u>.
         1   **2**   **3**   **4**
  1 = first correlative subordinator **2** = head word - adjective
  3 = second correlative subordinator
  4 = comparative clause introduced by the second

     correlative subordinator ⇒*as*

• Colin replied *as* <u>**quickly**</u> *as* <u>Sylvia replied</u>.

     head word -adverb comparative clause

These examples illustrate that the comparative clause pre-modifies the head word. The head word may be a noun, pronoun, adverb or adjective.

• Forms of clauses

There are four different forms of clauses based on the verb used in each form of clause. These are discussed above. Their specific features are summarized in List 1, so that they can be compared at a glance.

****

Forms of clauses

Finite clause

. it has a finite verb

. the verb is marked for tense

. it has a subject which precedes the verb

. the subject may be left out to avoid repetition

Non-finite clause

. it has a non-finite verb

. the verb is to-infinitive or bare infinitive, present participle **–ing** form and past participle **–ed** form

. often it is a part of the finite clause

. by itself it does not seem grammatically correct

. it may not include a subject

. all verbs except modal auxiliaries have non-finite forms

Active clause

. it has an active verb form which shows the agent's activity

. doing something/ something happening

. agent is grammatically the subject

. it is extensively used as it is the typical voice

Active clause

. it has a passive verb form which indicates something is done to the agent/subject

. statements with the transitive verb can be converted to passive clauses form

. it sounds formal

List 1

Types of adverbial clauses

Adverbial clauses occur in sentences in order to express different situations. Broadly speaking, for the sake of understanding, we can classify these as shown below:

Adverbial clause	Example(underlined)
• **Adverbial clause of time** it refers to a period of or an event	• He went to Norway, <u>when he</u> <u>was a student.</u>
• **Adverbial clause of place** it relates to the location or position of something	• <u>Where our houses are now</u>, it was a farm land.
• **Adverbial clause of manner** it is used to say something about the way something is done or refers to someone's behaviour/attitude	• How can you enjoy yourself <u>as if nothing had happened</u>? • <u>Like last month</u>, it is raining.
• **Adverbial clause of purpose** it is used to indicate purpose	• Please come <u>so that we can</u> <u>travel together in my car</u>.
• **Adverbial clause of reason** to give a reason for something/ action	• Anne gave me this present, <u>because she is a kind person</u>.
• **Adverbial clause of exception** it is used for stating exceptions such as contrast, possibility...	• I used to play table tennis almost everyday <u>although</u> <u>I don't have much time for it.</u>
• **Adverbial clause of result** to indicate an outcome	• He sent us that letter <u>so that we</u> <u>can read it ourselves.</u>
• **Adverbial clause of condition** relates a condition and its outcome	• <u>If I could afford it</u> I would buy it right away.

This chapter begins with an introduction to clauses and sentences. Since a sentence consists of at least one clause, the idea of clauses is explained and exemplified in some depth. A sentence is the biggest unit of syntactic structure. For this reason, the next chapter is devoted to sentences. A classification of sentences is drawn for the purpose of understanding the meaning, types and structures of sentences.

Over to You

1. Separate phrases and clauses.

   a) A red sports car.
   b) Such a tall and friendly person.
   c) She is rich, kind and single.
   d) One day in our office.
   e) It is entirely your fault.
   f) The management decision is likely to upset our office staff.
   g) Kippers, toast, tea or coffee, cereals for breakfast.
   h) One of various types of grass.
   i) Remarkably fast, accurate and reliable machine in our office.
   j) We had no electricity.
   k) If I were a rich man
   l) Our guests have gone back home.

2. What is the shortest (minimum) structure of a clause? Exemplify it.

3. Illustrate with the help of an example the typical structure of a clause.

4. List five elements of a clause. How many of these elements can construct a grammatically correct clause?

5. Each of the following sentences consists of both main and subordinate clauses. Your task is to identify subordinate clauses and list them under adverbial clauses of time, place, manner, purpose, reason, exception, result and condition.

a) Jane's mother died in Sweden when Jane was one year old.

b) They haven't given us even a cup of tea since we arrived here.
c) I must wear my winter shoes in case it rains.
d) You should be well dressed in order to give a good impression.
e) Whenever we meet each other we don't greet ourselves.
f) He did not refuse to help us except that we had to ask him repeatedly.
g) Much as I liked this place, I would not like to return to it so soon.
h) Naive as it sounds, I did not suspect until now that you were spying on us.
i) Though he lived and worked in London for a long time, he did not visit the British Museum.
j) Please talk slowly so that I can understand you.
k) In Moscow, wherever I went, I saw many people walking.
l) We must pay an entrance fee like other visitors to this museum.
m) I do not know all the facts surrounding this event as you do.
n) If your car has broken down, we can't travel to Scotland.
o) We can go for a walk by the sea, if you like.
p) It was dark when we returned from Amsterdam.
q) If I met him in the town, we exchanged greetings.
r) If Joanne could afford the air fare to New York, she would travel.
s) She worried so often about everything back home that she returned home from overseas.
t) I don't know much about her opinions, since she is rather a quiet person.

6. Which of the following sentences consists of subordinate clauses namely **noun**, **relative**, **adverbial** and **comparative**?

a) I am looking for a young man **who** used to live in this house with his girlfriend.

b) I told you **that** it happened on a Christmas Day.

c) This new car is not as smooth to drive **as** the salesman told us.

d) When I rang this number, no one answered my call.

***

Chapter 13
Sentences

***

• **Introduction**

In the last chapter, the idea of sentences is introduced and discussed in relation to clauses. For the sake of understanding the structures, types and intended meaning conveyed by sentences, a classification of sentences is shown below. This forms the basis of our discussion in this chapter.

A classification of sentences

Meaning -   Positive, Negative, Active, Passive

Types - Declarative, Interrogative, Imperative, Exclamative

Structure - Simple, Compound, Complex

• **Positive and negative sentences**

A positive sentence expresses positive meaning. A negative sentence communicates a negative idea. A positive sentence can be converted to a negative sentence and vice versa. These are discussed below:

- Often a negative sentence is formed by using the word ***not*** or its short version **n't** after the auxiliary. If there is no auxiliary, the **dummy do or does** auxiliary is inserted. For instance:

- She **has** spoken to me about this matter. ⇐ positive statement/sentence

- She **has not** spoken to me about this matter. ⇐negative sentence

- Angelica **will** call you tomorrow evening. ⇐ positive sentence

- Angelica *won't* call you tomorrow evening. ⇐negative sentence

  the auxiliary **will** and **n't** (not) are written as one word ⇒ **won't**

- Frank likes a hot drink in bed. ⇐ positive sentence

- Frank *does not/ doesn't* like a hot drink in bed.

  ⇑ - negative sentence
  dummy auxiliary as the positive sentence is without
    the auxiliary in the previous example

- They were running in that direction. ⇐ positive sentence

- They **were not/ weren't** running in that direction.

negative sentence ↵

- You **should have** done this work.⇐ positive sentence

- You **should not have/shouldn't** have done this work.

         ⇑   ⇑

      not comes after   *n't* placed after first auxiliary
      the first auxiliary
      - negative statement/sentence

- The gold medal **had been** stolen. ⇐ positive statement/sentence

- The gold medal **had not/hadn't been** stolen. ⇐ negative
                                          statement/sentence

- Andrea **might have** told you about it. ⇐ positive statement/sentence

- Andrea **might not/ mightn't** have told you about it. ⇐ negative
                                          statement/sentence

• Ralf knew that I was visiting him. ⇐ positive statement/sentence

• Ralf **did not/didn't** know that I was visiting him.

⇑

negative statement/sentence

• You can include an appropriate *negative word* in a positive sentence to turn it into a negative sentence. There are many such words. A few are used in the following examples:

    • The teacher says *never* to do it again.
        ----

        negative word ↵ - means not ever

    • My parents allow **no** one to visit me after 20.00 hour.
        -----

        negative word ↵ - means not any person

    • She says *nothing* about her long holiday in Australia.
      ----

negative word ↵ - meaning not any thing

    • We tried hard but *nowhere* could we find him.
        ----

        negative word ↵ - means not anywhere

    • Our old house **no longer** exists.
        ----

        negative words ↵ - not any more/ not any longer

• Adverbial phrases with a **negative word** create negative sentences. The adverbial starts the sentence in order to emphasize the negative meaning. It also requires inversion of the subject and verb. Here are some examples:

• Before in my life, I have experienced such a terrifying road accident.

This is a positive sentence. Its negative form is:

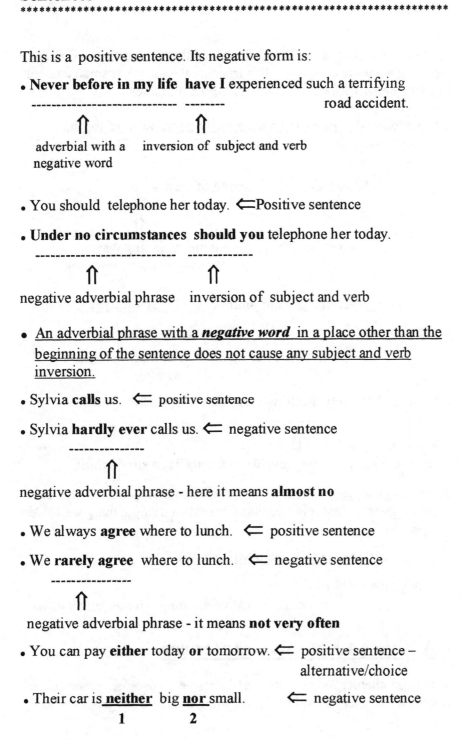

• **Never before in my life have I** experienced such a terrifying road accident.

⇑   ⇑

adverbial with a   inversion of subject and verb
negative word

• You should telephone her today. ⇐Positive sentence

• **Under no circumstances should you** telephone her today.

⇑   ⇑

negative adverbial phrase   inversion of subject and verb

• An adverbial phrase with a ***negative word*** in a place other than the beginning of the sentence does not cause any subject and verb inversion.

• Sylvia **calls** us. ⇐ positive sentence

• Sylvia **hardly ever** calls us. ⇐ negative sentence

⇑

negative adverbial phrase - here it means **almost no**

• We always **agree** where to lunch. ⇐ positive sentence

• We **rarely agree** where to lunch. ⇐ negative sentence

⇑

negative adverbial phrase - it means **not very often**

• You can pay **either** today **or** tomorrow. ⇐ positive sentence –
alternative/choice

• Their car is **neither** big **nor** small. ⇐ negative sentence
              1   **2**

In the last example, **1** and **2** together show that two attributes (big and small) of a car are compared. It is true that the car is not small and not big. The negative statement is true for both attributes.

- <u>An adverbial phrase can be used with a negative word for the emphatic negative.</u>

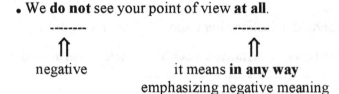

- We **do not** see your point of view **at all**.
       --------   --------
          ⇑   ⇑
      negative   it means **in any way**
                                    emphasizing negative meaning

- We **haven't** yet finished our journey, **not by any means /**
negative↵   **by no means**.
                    it means **not at all** ↵ - emphasizing negative
                                                    meaning

- There is **absolutely nothing** more we can do to help you.
         ------------ ----------
   emphasizing ↵   ⇑
   negative meaning   negative word means **not a single thing**

The word **absolutely** means something is completely true. In this example, it stresses that it is true that there is not a single thing we can do to help you.

- We are **not in the least** hungry.
   negative word ↵   ⇑
                    to underline negative meaning - it means *not at all*

. <u>Active and passive sentences</u>

In the last chapter, under active and passive clauses, a number of examples were given to explain the meaning of active and passive and their differences. Here are some more examples:

"The principal chaired the emergency staff meeting. At this meeting, the staff were addressed by the principal, who outlined current financial circumstances facing the college. The staff were also informed by the principal about the circular the college received from the Government concerning lower grants during the new financial year, which was to commence next month. The staff were told about the current unfilled vacancies and a cash shortage to pay wages. The staff, who were already under the stress of their workload, feared job threats, and greeted the announcement with dismay and anger."

The above paragraph contains five reported sentences. We can identify each sentence in terms of active and passive:

- The principal .... meeting. ⇐ active sentence

Because the principal (**subject**) which is the agent did something, that is chaired (**active verb**) the meeting. For this reason, it is an active sentence. As the verb element in this sentence is active, you can say it is **active voice**.

- At the meeting.........facing the college. ⇐ passive sentence

The action (**were addressed**) is a **passive verb** directed at the subject (**the staff**). We can say something was done to the staff. As the verb element in this sentence is passive, you can consider it as *passive voice*. By applying the same rules:

- The staff ----------next month. ⇐ passive sentence

- The staff --------- pay wages. ⇐ passive sentence

- The staff -------- and anger. ⇐ active sentence

- An active sentence has a topic and some new information which is of some interest. The topic of the sentence is the *agent*, which is at the front of the sentence. When a sentence contains a transitive verb, you can convert it into a passive sentence.

For instance:

- A young neighbour has ridden **our motorcycle.** ⇐ Active sentence
  ------------------------   ----------------------   with an agent

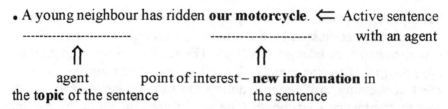

       ⇑   ⇑

       agent   point of interest – **new information** in
the **topic** of the sentence   the sentence

- **What has the agent done?** - has ridden our motorcycle. Thus, the
  active sentence contains some new information in relation to the
  topic of the sentence.

- You can convert this sentence into a passive sentence as shown below:

- Our motorcycle has been ridden **by a young neighbour.**⇐ Passive
  ------------------   ---------------------------- with an agent

    ⇑   ⇑

topic of the sentence   new information in the sentence
                                      of some interest

In the last example, the topic is what is the new information in the example last but one. It is also at the front of the last sentence. The **topic**
in the example last but one became *new information* in the last example. It is now a part of the phrase ⇒ **by a young neighbour.**

- You can have a passive sentence **without an agent.** The presence of
  an agent in a passive sentence is relevant only if it provides some
  new information about the topic. For instance:

- Motorcycles are ridden. ⇐ Passive without an agent.

- The car should be driven **carefully at all times.** ⇐ Passive
  --------   -------------------------- without an agent

   ⇑   ⇑

  topic   point of interest.

- WWW was invented in 1990's. ⇐ Passive without an agent

- Some games are played.   ⇐ Passive without an agent

- Mistakes have been made.   ⇐ Passive without an agent

- Roses are planted.   ⇐ Passive without an agent

- Nothing can be done now.   ⇐ Passive without an agent

- Here, new houses will be soon built.   ⇐ Passive without an agent

- <u>The following sentences cannot be in passive voice because each sentence has an intransitive verb element:</u>

    - I always **sleep** well.
           ------

intransitive verb ↵

    - It **happened**.
           ----

intransitive verb ↵

    - The hall has **<u>warmed</u>** up.

intransitive verb ↵

- <u>The passive voice is less common. It is considered as rather an impersonal and official style of writing. However, sometimes, you have to use it.</u>

Now is the time to discuss sentences by their types listed above.

. <u>Declarative sentences</u>

Declarative sentences are by far the most common sentences in the English language. In a declarative sentence, the subject is followed by the verb, and its complement.

The following examples illustrate this point further:

292   **Sentences**

****

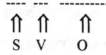

• Ari is a father.

```
----  ---  ----------
 ⇑   ⇑    ⇑
 S   V    O
```

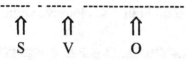

• Frank was a programmer.

```
------- - -----  -------------------
  ⇑      ⇑          ⇑
  S      V          O
```

In these two examples **SVO** elements are obligatory. If you remove any one of these elements, the sentence will **not** be grammatically correct. On the other hand, the good news is that you can expand this basic structure in order to convey a wide range of information. This is illustrated by the following examples:

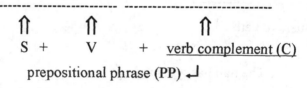

• *Joan has studied at London University.*

```
------- ------------------  -------------------------------
  ⇑          ⇑                      ⇑
  S  +       V        +      verb complement (C)
```
         prepositional phrase (PP) ↵

• This sentence has just one clause. This clause consists of *SVC* structural elements.

• The verb element in this clause **has studied** is **finite and active**.

• The absence of any of these structural elements will make this sentence grammatically incomplete.

• This sentence makes **a statement** which conveys some information. It is a typical example of a statement.

• In fact, this sentence or a clause will not render the desired meaning, if you remove any of **SVC** structural elements from the sentence. On the other hand, you can extend this sentence so that it can give additional information. For example:

Sentences   **293**

****

- *Joan has studied* **at** *London University* **for** *her PhD qualification.*

   ⇑   ⇑   ⇑

   S +   V   +   **<u>verb complement (C)</u>**

consists of two prepositional phrases (PP) ↵

- There are many different uses of declarative sentences for making statements. A statement may give just some information about something as illustrated above. Alternatively, it may give some information, which leads to an action or doing something. For instance:

- I will copy this document and send it to you by post today.

        indicating ⟹ action

- The following examples of declarative sentences demonstrate a variety of statements.

- I am ever so grateful for your help in this matter.

        thanking ⟹ someone

- Police ordered the crowd to clear the road immediately.

        giving ⟹ an order

- There were no injuries in this serious car crash.

        giving ⟹ an account of an accident

- Everything seems to be in order. ⟸ indicating approval

- One of the capital cities, in the European Union, on both sides of the River Thames, is London. ⟸describing a place

- I'm sorry to learn about floods, which have caused so much misery to your family. ⟸ conveying sympathy

- Please let me know your decision by tomorrow. ⟸ seeking information

- They'd like me to have lunch with them today. ⟸ giving invitation

<u>Each sentence is conveying some information in the form of a
statement or a declaration.</u>

. <u>Performative verbs</u>

Usually, a declarative sentence is constructed to make a statement as
illustrated above. Some verbs in the first person present tense and in a
declarative context indicate the action they perform. For instance:
'blame' in 'I blame you'. For this reason, these verbs are called performative verbs. The following are some examples of performative
verbs.

---

accept, accuse advise, agree, apologise, authorize, blame, challenge,
confess, congratulate, declare, defy, demand, forbid, forgive, guarantee, inform, insist, name, nominate, object, order, predict, promise,
pronounce, propose, protest, recommend, refuse, renounce, request,
resign, sentence, suggest, swear, thank, warn.

The following statements illustrate the use of some performative verbs.

- I promise to be there at the agreed time. ⇐ promising

- I swear to tell nothing but the truth. ⇐ **swearing**

- I thank you for the invitation. ⇐ thanking

- I can not predict the outcome of this General Election. ⇐ predicting

- <u>A modal verb or similar expression may be preceded by the
  performative verb in order to make it sound somewhat polite.</u>
  Here are some examples:

- I would require a guarantee in the form of a small deposit.

     indicating ⟹ guaranteeing

- I must confess my wrongdoing. ⇐ confessing

- I have to **declare** that you are no longer a member of this club.
  ----

  formal use ↵- pointing to ⟹ declaration

- Some performative verbs such as **declare**, *order* and **warn** are used in formal writing and speaking. The following examples show their use:

- I *warn (or I'm warning)* you for the last time, not to come late for
  ⇑   work any more.

both forms are possible

. Interrogative sentences

The basic use of interrogative sentences is to ask for information. The interrogative sentences or questions can generate answers in the forms of **yes/no or some specific information**.

- The interrogative sentences which lead to yes/no answers are known as *yes/no questions*. Examples of such questions are given below:

  - Have you seen John this morning?   **answer** ⟹ yes/no

  - Has your wife returned from her shopping trip? answer ⟹ yes/no

  - Have you ever had such an enjoyable outing to London?
    answer ⟹ yes/no

  - Do you sell fried chicken? **answer** ⟹ yes/no

It is possible that answers to any of the above questions in more detail than just *yes/no*. For instance, the answer to example (1) can be given as *Yes, I have seen him/John.* Even so, it is still a yes/no question.

- The interrogative sentences which generate some specific information information are known as *wh – questions.* The following examples illustrate this type of interrogative sentences and answers.

- Where were you yesterday at about 2 p.m.?

  answer ⇒ I was at home.

- When will we go for a long walk by the sea?

  answer ⇒ We will go now.

- Who can give me a lift by car to the station this afternoon?

  answer ⇒ I can.

- What's the matter with you? answer ⇒ I lost my hat.

- Why were you late this morning?

    answer ⇒ My car broke down on the way to work

- Whose is this car in my place? **answer** ⇒ *It is my car.*

- The structure of an interrogative sentence differs from the structure of a declarative sentence. The subject and the verb in an interrogative sentence do not occur in the same positions as in a declarative sentence. This is illustrated below:

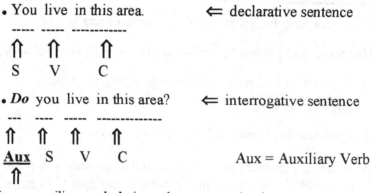

- You live in this area.   ⇐ declarative sentence

  ⇑   ⇑   ⇑
  S   V   C

- *Do* you live in this area?   ⇐ interrogative sentence

  ⇑   ⇑   ⇑   ⇑
  Aux S   V   C   Aux = Auxiliary Verb
  ⇑

  Primary auxiliary verb **do** is used to express simple present tense

- We worked all night to finalise the annual accounts. ⇐ declarative

  ⇑   ⇑   ⇑   sentence
  S   V   C

• Did we work all night to finalise the annual accounts? ⬅ interrogative
                                                                       sentence

⇑ ⇑ ⇑   ⇑
Aux S V   C
⇑

Primary auxiliary verb **did** expressing simple past tense

• In simple tenses the auxiliary **do** is used to form a question. It comes
before the subject.

If you compare the last four examples, you can see there is **inversion**
(changing word order) of the subject and auxiliary.

• In example (a), **be** is used on its own as an ordinary verb. This
example is converted to a question. This question is example (b).
This example shows an inversion of the **subject** and *be* as an
ordinary verb. Examples (c) and (d) also illustrate the same rule.

(a) • **She is** somewhere in the town centre now. ⬅ declarative
                                                            sentence/statement

⇑ ⇑   ⇑
S V   C

(b) • **Is she** somewhere in the town centre now? ⬅ interrogative
                                                  sentence

⇑ ⇑   ⇑
V S   C
⇑

be is used as an ordinary verb on its own

(c) • He was in Germany last week. ⬅ *declarative sentence/statement*

⇑ ⇑   ⇑
S V   C

(d) • Was he in Germany last week? ⇐ interrogative sentence

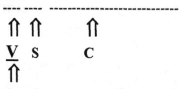

be functions here as an ordinary verb on its own

• If there is more than one auxiliary verb, then there is inversion of the first auxiliary verb and the subject. The next two examples illustrate this rule:

• I could have finished that job by now. ⇐declarative

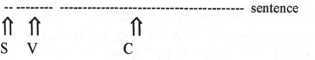

sentence

• Could I have finished that job by now? ⇐ interrogative

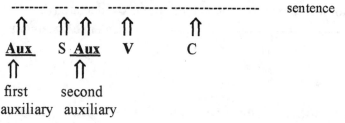

sentence

• There are the following nine **wh-question** words:

---

what, who, whom, which, whose, where, when, why, how

• **A question word may be the subject, object, complement or adverbial in a sentence as demonstrated below.**

• The next two examples demonstrate that the *wh-question* word generates the subject:

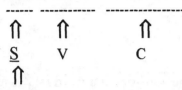

.Who will lunch with you today? ⇐ wh-question sentence

S   V   C

wh-question

This question generates the subject ⟹ **John Smith** in the declarative sentence without any inversion as shown below:

. John Smith will lunch with me today. ⇐ declarative

                                         sentence

S   V   C

• The next two examples show that the *wh-question* word generates the object **five boxes** in the declarative sentence.

    .What has John made? ⇐ interrogative sentence

     O   **Aux** S   V

wh-question↵

• Joan has made five boxes.   ⇐ declarative

                            sentence

S   Aux V   O

There is no inversion.

    . What will next month bring? ⇐ interrogative sentence

     O   Aux   S   V

wh-question↵

- **Next month will** bring some luck. ⇐ declarative sentence

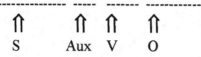

    S   Aux   V   O

- The last two examples exhibit that the **wh-question** word relates to the object **some luck** in the declarative sentence. There is inversion of the subject **next month** and the modal auxiliary **will**.

- The following examples exemplify that the **wh-question** word refers to the object **my car** in the declarative sentence. There is inversion of the subject and auxiliary verb.

- **Whose is** this car in this place? ⇐ interrogative sentence

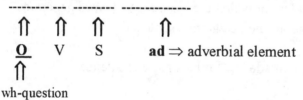

   O   V   S   **ad** ⇒ adverbial element

wh-question

- **This is** my car in this place. ⇐ declarative sentence

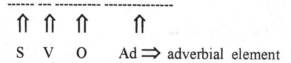

    S   V   O   Ad ⇒ adverbial element

In this case, the preposition **in** is before the noun **place**. Therefore, it is a prepositional phrase of place and an adverbial (or adverbial element).

See⇒ adverbial

- The next two examples clarify that the **wh-question** word refers to the adverbial element in the declarative sentence.

There is inversion of the subject *you* and modal auxiliary *will*.

Sentences **301**

****

- **When will** you come home? ⇐ interrogative sentence

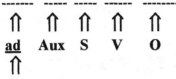

ad **Aux** **S** **V** **O**
⇑

wh-question

- **You will** come home at 11 p.m. tonight. ⇐ declarative sentence

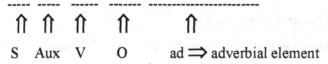

S Aux V O ad ⇒ adverbial element

- Finally, the last two examples make plain that the **_wh-question_** word refers to the object musical **play Cats** in the declarative sentence. <u>There is no inversion, except that the wh-question word is placed to the front in the last example.</u>

- Annemarie Kling likes a romantic short story most. ⇐ declarative

sentence

S V O ad ⇒ adverbial element

- Which short story does Annemarie Kling like most?

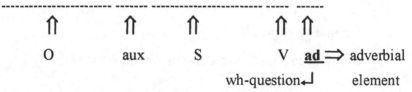

O aux S V **ad** ⇒ adverbial

wh-question↵ element

• <u>Interrogative sentences without inversion</u>

An interrogative sentence has the same word order as in a declarative sentence. This happens in informal conversation when the question follows on from what was said before. The following examples illustrate this rule:

- I may leave you. **You are leaving now?** ⇒ Not just yet

● I must visit my mother to see how she is now.

    Your mother is not well? ⇒ yes

● My friend met me at the airport.

    Colin Smith met you ? ⇒ yes, he did

● I bought a new house.

    The house is which type? ⇒ It is a semi-detached house

● I have not completed this task.

    You haven't completed this task yet? ⇒ no

● We had a nice holiday in France.

    You had a nice holiday in France? ⇒ Yes

● Rachel and Ari became parents.

    Rachel and Ari became parents? ⇒ Yes

Negative interrogative sentences are also exemplified below.

● You can include an appropriate ***negative word*** in an interrogative sentence. This is expounded below.

    ● Did he tell you **never** to do it again?
        ----

    negative word ↵

    ● Why does your father allow **no** one to visit you?
        ----

    negative word ↵

    ● Does she say **nothing** about her previous marriage?
        ----

    negative word ↵

● **Imperative sentences**

The imperative is the base form of the verb. A sentence with an imperative verb element is an imperative sentence. An imperative sentence enables us to make an earnest request, give an order or a command. In fact, you can use it to make someone act on your wishes whether it is under any prevailing condition or without any condition. You can also use the imperative to offer someone your good wishes. It is always in the present tense and refers to the second person, singular or plural form. Normally, an imperative does not have a subject. Here are some examples:

> • **Take** a seat, please. ⇐ an earnest request for an action
>
> \-\-\-\-\-\-   resulting in someone sitting down
>
> ⇑
>
> imperative form of the verb

It refers to the second person singular (= you). There may be several persons, but each person is requested to take a seat.

> • **Through** this entrance, please. ⇐ an instruction
>
> • **Be** careful. ⇐ an instruction/advice
>
> • **Do be** quiet. ⇐ strong order/more emphatic
>
> • **Do** sit down. ⇐ an order/more emphatic

In the last two examples, the auxiliary **do** helps to soften the effect of the imperative on the listener. In other words, the use of **do** sounds less authoritative.

> • **Don't** talk so loudly. ⇐ an order

In this example, the auxiliary **do** is essential in order to construct the negative imperative.

> • **Stop**. ⇐ an order – remember traffic/road sign
>
> • **Don't** talk. ⇐ *an order*
>
> • **Don't be** absurd. ⇐ *emphatic*

- **Come** in. ⇐ permission **But** the following:

- **Do** come in. ⇐more emphatic

- **Go** away! ⇐ an order – rather impolite

- **Shut** the door at once! ⇐ a strong command/order

- **Get out** of here! ⇐ an order - sounds rude

- If you can't afford to pay, **don't** come. ⇐ conditional instruction

- If you *are coming* late, **take** your keys. ⇐ conditional instruction

- If you drive to London, **don't drink** for a day. ⇐ conditional order

- **Enjoy** your meal.   ⇐ offering of good wish

- **Let's** have lunch. ⇐ a suggestion to perform an action together

     ----

    ⇑

     imperative form of the verb ⇒ **let + us = let's**

It implies that the speaker and the listener perform the action together. It is in the plural form.

- **Let's not** keep arguing about it. ⇐ negative form of the order

- You can also construct the negative imperative with **do let's**.

- **Don't let's** lose any of our clients. ⇐ negative form of the order
                                               (informal)

- When there are two persons, *you* can be the subject

     - **You be gentle** when she meets you. ⇐ an emphatic advice
       -----

subject ↵

- **You watch** the traffic, I climb the ladder. ⇐ an emphatic instruction

. <u>Exclamative sentences</u>

The purpose of exclamative sentences is to express a variety of feelings. These can be joy, sorrow, anger, shock, surprise or any other emotional feeling. The construction of exclamative sentences is based on **how** and **what** wh-words. An exclamation mark is placed at the end of the sentence instead of a full stop. Exclamative sentences are not as flexible as other types of sentences. We use them for the sole purpose of expressing emotions. The following examples demonstrate their construction and usage:

- How **intelligent** your son is!

It means that your son is very intelligent. It expresses the writer's or speaker's feelings about the degree of intelligence.

- <u>The following examples show that the wh-word can be followed by</u> <u>an adjective. The adjective can be with an article **a** or **an**</u>:

- How **wonderful** the scene is!

- How **lucky** you were!

- How **kind** those people are!

- What **a lovely** person your wife is!

- What **a simple** style it is!

- What **a memorable** show we watched!

- What **an enjoyable** weekend we had!

- <u>The following examples make clear that an exclamative can be</u> <u>a phrase. The phrase can also be just a short phrase – one word</u>:

- How **generous**!

****

- How **foolish**!

- What **a charming** evening!

- What **a mess** !   • What **fun**!

- **Oh!**   • **Look out**!

- **Excellent**!   • **Well done**!

- The following two examples show how the **wh-word** can be followed by an adverb/adverbial:

    - How **slowly** Elena talks!

    - How **carefully** Yvonne handled the glass!

- The following two examples show how the **wh-word** can modify the verb:

    - How they **run**!

    - How the girls **giggled**!

• Simple sentences

In the last chapter, a distinction between simple, compound and complex sentences is made. In this section, we examine each type of sentence in detail. Some points made in the last chapter are repeated here in order to develop each topic further.

- **A simple sentence has at least one clause**. Here are some examples:

    - Margaret enjoyed her meal.

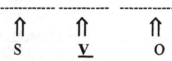

    ⇑   ⇑   ⇑
    S   **V**   O

    transitive verb type↵

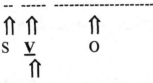

• It was a warm afternoon.

transitive verb type

• the structure of each sentence is stated in terms of SVO

• each sentence has a finite form of the verb

• each sentence cannot be broken into smaller sentences because each sentence has just one verb

• each sentence has just one clause

• each sentence is grammatically complete

Each sentence is a **simple sentence**. It can be said that each sentence has a **main clause** with a **finite verb** in each sentence. Now consider the following examples:

• She laughs.   • Susan comes.

S   V   S   V

In these examples:

• each sentence has an **SV** structure

• each has an intransitive verb – can not take an object

• each sentence can not be broken into smaller sentences because each has one verb element

• each sentence is grammatically complete irrespective of its size

308   **Sentences**

****

Each sentence is a **simple sentence**. It can be said that each sentence has a **main clause** with a **finite** form of the **verb**.

- **A structure may have a clause but it is still not a simple sentence.**

For example:

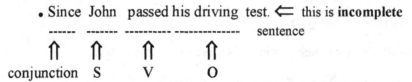

- Since John passed his driving test. ⬅ this is **incomplete** sentence

conjunction   S   V   O

This sentence contains a clause, but it is not a simple sentence. It begins with a conjunction, which requires further information. Thus, this is not a simple sentence as it is grammatically incomplete. If we can remove the adverbial *since* from this sentence, it will become a simple sentence containing a main clause as shown below.

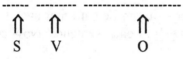

- John passed his driving test.

S   V   O

- It has been very cold all day. ⬅ simple sentence

.**Compound sentences**

This above sentence has only one verb. It can not be split into smaller sentences. It is a clause as well as a simple sentence. See clauses. We can re-write this sentence and add to it some other structural parts as shown below:

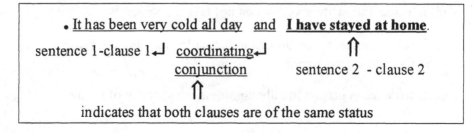

- It has been very cold all day   and   **I have stayed at home**.

sentence 1-clause 1⤶   coordinating⤶   ⇑

                 conjunction   sentence 2 - clause 2

             ⇑

indicates that both clauses are of the same status

The above example consists of two shorter sentences or clauses joined together with a conjunction **and**. In this example, each clause can stand on its own. In other words, grammatically, these clauses are of **equal status**. For this reason, this sentence is a compound sentence. A compound sentence can have two or more clauses of equal status. In fact, each clause is a main clause in its own right, and thus can stand alone. In order to form compound sentences by linking clauses, we use the following conjunctions at the appropriate place:

- **coordinating conjunctions/ coordinators: and, or** and **but** are mainly used to form compound sentences as illustrated below: The conjunction **for** is seldom used.

- **coordinating coordinator or with *not*: n*or*** can be used with the negative first clause. These are also exemplified below.

- **correlative coordinators:** *either* --- *or* are used for emphasizing an alternative course of action. Some examples are given later.

- Conjunctions **and,** *or* and ***but*** must be placed between the two clause (short sentences). In fact, you cannot place them anywhere except between the clauses.

Here are some practical examples of compound sentences:

- Jane wants to work in England, **but** she doesn't like to be away

    ⇑   ⇑   from home.

   clause 1   **coordinating**   ⇑

                conjunction   **clause 2**

Note that both clauses are of equal status.

- I like fried chicken **but** my wife likes grilled chicken.

- They went out to go swimming **and** we walked to the local shopping precinct.

- I wanted to travel to Paris ***but*** there is no direct train to
  Paris from here.

- The <u>coordinating coordinator</u> **but** <u>cannot join more than two main</u>
  <u>clauses.</u> The reason is that it is used only when two main clauses
  are expressing contrasting meaning in a compound sentence.
  See the above examples.

- <u>When the subject is the same in both main clauses, we don't have to</u>
  repeat it in the <u>second clause.</u> <u>When an element of a clause is left</u>
  out, it is called an **<u>ellipsis</u>**.

  <u>The reason is that the left out element can be inferred from the</u>
  <u>meaning and grammatical context of the sentence.</u>

The following examples illustrate the use of ellipsis:

  - You can take a taxi to Heathrow **<u>or</u>** go by airbus from Victoria.

  - I may travel to France by car **<u>or</u>** may fly to Paris by Air France.

  - Police caught John breaking the speed limit on the M1
    <u>and</u> charged him.

- <u>A compound sentence can have more than two clauses. The</u>
  <u>coordinating coordinators **and** and **or** are used to link more than</u>
  <u>two main clauses in a compound sentence.</u> For instance:

  - You can borrow my umbrella **<u>or</u>** buy a new one
    or you don't care about it.

  - You asked for some money **<u>and</u>** I had no money
    <u>and</u> the bank was already closed.

- <u>Now we can examine the use of **for**</u> through the following
  examples:

  - We were dancing ***for*** the music was played.

    ```
    ------------------  -----  ---------------------------
          ⇑              ⇑                ⇑
    main clause 1   coordinator     main clause2
    ```

The coordinator occurs in the same position where **and** coordinator is placed in a compound sentence. Indeed, **for** coordinator functions just like **and** in a compound sentence.

- We couldn't hear very well **for** it was noisy.   ⇐ For = because

In all examples given above, the sentences are too short to place a comma between two main clauses.

- When the first clause in a compound sentence is conveying negative meaning, **nor** coordinator is used as the negative complement of **or** to link clause 1 to clause 2.

  - He could **not** understand the question, **nor** did the teacher
    ----- ----- repeat the question.
    ⇑ ⇑
    in clause 1   joining clauses 1 and 2

  - I **wasn't** able to turn left or right on the motorway, **nor** were other motorists.

- We can use **either — or** in a compound sentence to express an alternative. The coordinator **or** begins the second clause. Here **or** places emphasis on the alternative – second part of the compound sentence. This is illustrated below:

  - **Either** Team A bat first **or** Team B bowl first.
    -------- ----
    ⇑ ⇑
    starts first clause   joins second clause with the first clause

No comma is between these two clauses, as it is a short sentence.

Here are two more examples to confirm that **Either** can commence the first clause:

- **Either** you fix it as per our agreement, **or**
  we employ another joiner to do it.

. **Either** Frank will drive the car back home from the pub, **or**
Elina will drink wine.

Warning!

Two pairs of correlative coordinators *neither … nor* and *both … and* can grammatically link phrases but not clauses. Therefore, these can not form part of compound sentences.

.Complex sentences

Like the compound sentence, a complex sentence also has two or more clauses. The difference between the complex and the compound sentences is that in the complex sentence clauses are **not** of the same equal status (main clauses). In a complex sentence, one clause is a main clause with one or more subordinate clauses. For instance:

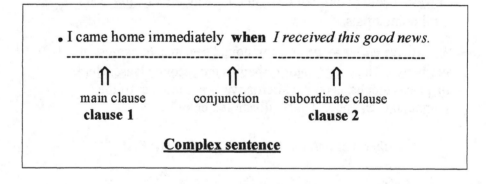

. I came home immediately **when** *I received this good news.*

main clause	conjunction	subordinate clause
clause 1		**clause 2**

Complex sentence

In this example , the main clause can stand alone. For this reason, it is also called an **independent clause**. It is not dependent on the subordinate clause, which begins with the adverbial element **when**.

Clause 2 cannot stand alone. Therefore, it is a **dependent clause**.

Dependent clauses are subordinate clauses. See ⇒ Clauses

• When Antonia visited us, **we made some Hungarian food.**
----------------------------------   ---
          ⇑   ⇑
subordinate/dependent clause   main /independent clause

begins with an adverbial ⇒ **when**

The presence of the subordinate clause makes this sentence complex.
Here are some more examples:

• Soon after we arrived home, <u>**our grandmother greeted us with a**</u>
-------------------------------- <u>**smile and kisses**</u>.
       adverbial.⌐   **main clause ⌐**

                   ⇑

 started subordinate clause

In this complex sentence, the subordinate clause begins with a multi-
word subordinator <u>**soon after**</u>, an adverbial element.

• *He found himself in a hospital bed* <u>because</u> he was involved in a
        main clause ⤶   adverbial element ⤶   <u>car accident.</u>

                                                   ⇑

                                       subordinate clause

As shown above, we can start a subordinate clause with **when** and
because. Similarly, *if* and some other adverbials can do the same.
See the last chapter on adverbial clauses.

• *He will help you* if you approach him gently.
---------------------- --- --------------------------------
          ⇑   ⇑   ⇑
     main clause   adverbial   subordinator clause begins with
                                   if ⇒ subordinator

- The following examples demonstrate that a complex sentence can have more than one main and subordinate clause.

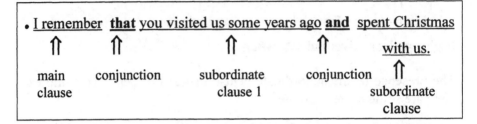

- I remember **that** you visited us some years ago **and** spent Christmas with us.

| main clause | conjunction | subordinate clause 1 | conjunction | subordinate clause |

In the above example **that** started a subordinate clause 1. Clause 2 started with **and**. In subordinate clauses 1 and 2, the subject (**you**) is the same. We can leave out the subject in clause 2.

In each of the next three examples, there is one main clause in **bold style** and two subordinate clauses.

- *Although* she was out of work, *she made a return trip to Switzerland because* her mother paid for it.

- *Liz Taylor was married to Richard Burton who* died some years ago *because of* his heart failure.

- *I went to Germany and* stayed with some family friends *because* it was interesting.

- *A thief,* who brandished a gun and raided a bank, got away with a lot of money.

In the last example:

- *A thief* got away with a lot of money ⟹ *main clause*

- who brandished a gun   ⟹ *subordinate clause -1*

- and raided a bank   ⟹ *subordinate clause -2*

- Ursula thought *that* Ralf was a millionaire **when** she saw him *coming* in a chauffeur driven Rolls Royce, *but* she was mistaken.

We can analyse this sentence into the following clauses:

• Ursula thought ⇒*main clause 1*

• that Ralf was a millionaire *subordinate clause 1* ⇒ noun clause

• when she saw him ⇒ *subordinate clause 2* ⇒adverbial clause

• coming in a chauffeur driven Rolls Royce ⇒*subordinate clause 3* ⇒ participle clause

• but she was mistaken ⇒*main clause 2 - but* joins two main clauses

This is how main clauses can be joined together, when there are two subordinate clauses between them.

• She was very tired when she returned from Poland, but went to work the next day, *where* she caught the flu, as it was a very stormy, cold, winter's day.

We can analyse this sentence as follows:

• She was very tired ⇒*main clause 1*

• when she returned from Poland ⇒*subordinate clause 1*

• but went to work the next day ⇒*main clause 2*

• where she caught the flu ⇒*subordinate clause 2*

• as it was a very stormy , cold, winter's day ⇒*subordinate clause 3*

• Here are two more examples of complex sentences with **non-finite** clauses:

• Sarah wishes to return home by car **because there is no train service tonight.**

     ⇑

  main clause

                     ⇑

                  subordinate clause

• I wanted to travel by air *but it was not possible* <u>**to fly from the**</u>

⇑   ⇑   <u>**nearest airport**</u>.

main clause 1   main clause 2   ⇑

subordinate clause

. <u>Direct and Indirect Speech</u>

The construction of sentences involving both direct and indirect speech is discussed in the next chapter. See ⟹ Quotation Marks

In summary, a sentence does not have to be short to be simple. What makes it simple is the presence of a single clause which is grammatically complete.

A compound sentence has two or more clauses of equal status. A complex sentence has at least one main and one subordinate or sub clause. Both compound and complex sentences can be broken down into smaller sentences or clauses. We often use the same tense in the main and subordinate clauses in both compound and complex sentences. Very long sentences should be avoided for the sake of clarity.

Over to You

---

1. Construct simple type sentence structure by using copular verbs:
   be, keep, seem, become, remain, prove, grow, be, sound
   and *taste*. Analyse the structure of these ten simple sentences.

2. Identify simple, compound and complex sentences. Give your reason(s) for your identification of each type.

   a) Rebecca is a shy young lady, but she knows her job well.
   b) How long is it since you left China for England?
   c) Peter is kind and friendly.
   d) Some people drive their own cars to work, but many people travel to work by public transport.

e) Although it was really hard work, I enjoyed it because it was a challenge.

f) I operate my business from a rented small premises.

g) Software business made John bankrupt.

h) We went to Scarborough and came across Colin Smith, who was with his family on a day trip to the seaside.

i) As soon as, our stores' gates were open, sales hunters(shoppers) rushed in and grabbed high quality merchandise at the lowest prices.

j) Visit our local store or phone or visit our website.

3. Convert the following declarative sentences into interrogative sentences.

a) They live in France in these days.

b) We were burgled while we were away on holiday.

c) London is the capital city of the United Kingdom.

d) Our company genuinely cares about staff.

e) She is a good mother and hardworking employee.

f) We walked up to the top of the hill.

g) In summer, there are a lot of holiday-makers from Germany in the Lake District.

h) We suffered many hardships during the transition between the old political system and the new one.

i) Doris contented herself with a small flat in Chelsea.

j) The customs officer found some drugs in her luggage.

4. Illustrate, with the help of five sentences, the prime function of performative verbs. Use in your illustration these performative verbs: **protest, nominate, renounce, forgive and confess.**

5. The following words are among the few negative words in English : *no, none, nothing, nobody, nowhere,* and *neither.* Build sentences with these words to express negative meaning.

6. Make a distinction between the exclamative and the imperative types of sentences. Give two examples of each type.

****

Chapter 14

Punctuation

• Introduction

Punctuation enables the writer to clarify the meaning of a piece of writing. Punctuation has a set of rules and corresponding marks. These marks are inserted in writing in accordance with these rules. Punctuation also denotes specific points of grammar in a piece of writing. The misuse of punctuation marks or the absence of punctuation can lead to misreading and ambiguity. The following punctuation marks with their rules of usage are discussed in this chapter:

• apostrophe	• dash	• paragraph
• asterisk	• ellipses /three dots	• question mark
• brackets	• exclamation mark	• quotation marks
• capital letters	• footnotes	• semicolon
• colon	• full stop	• slash/ bar/ diagonal/ oblique mark
• comma	• hyphen	• word-processing marks bullets, bolds, *italics*, underlining and arrows, etc.

• The above punctuation marks are not discussed in this chapter in a strict alphabetical order.

You may come across some other punctuation marks which are not listed above. On the other hand, you may find that some of these punctuation marks are not discussed in some other books. For instance, some people do not consider the paragraph formation and capitalisation as punctuation marks. In this book, these are considered as equally important punctuation marks and their application is outlined.

• <u>Apostrophe</u>

An apostrophe has the following two major functions:

- to indicate possession or genitive case ⟹ **Possessive Apostrophe**

- to mark contractions or show contractions or omissions of letters or syllables in the spelling of some words ⟹**Contraction Apostrophe**

  Each of these functions is exemplified below:

1. <u>**To indicate the possessive or genitive case or possession in the following ways:**</u>

   - <u>**When a noun is singular, an apostrophe and *s* are added to the noun.**</u>
     For instance:

     - The accountant's office
     - Robin's car
     - Anne's wedding dress
     - London's red buses
     - The company's management team
     - My friend's name is Plew who lives in Germany
     - It is **John's** chair.

   - <u>**An apostrophe and *s* is also added to indefinite pronouns that do not end in *s*.**</u>

     - This is **nobody's** fault.
       ----
       indefinite pronoun ↵- nobody = no one

****

- Someone's car is parked in my driveway.

----

indefinite pronoun $\Rightarrow$ someone = somebody or
a person unknown or not mentioned
by name

- We hope that this year **everyone's** dreams come true.

<u>**indefinite pronoun**</u>

everyone = all persons = everybody ↵

- <u>**An apostrophe is added to plural nouns ending in s.**</u>

This is demonstrated below:

- This is a **students'** computer laboratory.

- Our **doctors'** surgery hours are between 14 –18 hours on Fridays.

- Our **neighbours'** dog barked all night.

- Primary school **teachers'** trade unions help new teachers.

- Our car is parked in **Tesco's   customers'** car park.

----------- ------------

1 ↵   2 ↵

1 = 's with the singular proper noun to indicate possessive case
noun to show possession
2 = an apostrophe is added to a plural

- **The hostages'** release at Frankfurt Airport came unexpectedly.

- <u>**An apostrophe and _s_ are added to plural nouns that do _not_
end in _s_.**</u>

Here are some examples:

- There is the young *women's* hockey club.

- She reads *children's* short stories.

- I think *people's* opinions are important to politicians.

- No one other than parents is allowed in a *children's* playground.

- **An apostrophe can be used to show the possessive form without mentioning the noun to which a reference is made.** For instance:

- I met John outside the *barber's* (shop).

- Julie works for a local *optician's* (practice).

- We would like to have an Indian meal at *Taj's* (Restaurant).

You do not have to mention the nouns shown in brackets. Here are some more examples:

- I saw Janet at **Lyon's** *(sport club)*.
  ----
  omitted ⏎

- We have our current account at the **TSB-Lloyd's***(bank)*.
  ----
  omitted ⏎

- **An apostrophe is used with some units of measure to denote possession.** For instance:

- I think in a *week's* time she will arrive here.

- My father retired after *forty years'* service as a Civil Servant.

- Just imagine how you will look in *twenty years'* time.

- I must take a *fortnight's holiday* before 31 December.

- I don't think this shirt is *ten pounds'* worth.

- <u>**When a genitive (possessor) consists of more than one noun, the apostrophe is marked on the last noun. A genitive shows possession.**</u>

For instance:

- *The British Prime Minister's* country residence is not too far from London.

- *The Lord Chancellor's office* is in the Palace of Westminster.

- *The Duke of Edinburgh's* Award Scheme, to foster the leisure activities of young people, began in 1956.

- <u>**When possession is shared by more than one noun, the apostrophe and s are added to the last noun.**</u>

This is illustrated below:

- *Webster and Lancaster's* books can be seen on ADR web site.

- *Brinkman and Blaha's* Data Systems And Communications Dictionary is a well known book.

- <u>**When possession is not shared by more than one noun, the apostrophe and s are added to each noun.**</u>

This is exemplified below:

- *Earnest's* and *Klieg's* insurance training manuals are in our library.

- I have *Hornby's* and *Webster's* dictionaries.

- <u>**Use an apostrophe and s with personal names ending with s or z.**</u>

For instance:

- **Prince Charles's** ideas on the environment are serious.

- According to *Leibniz's Law*, if A is identical with B, then every property that A has B has, and vice versa.

- **An apostrophe and *s* are used with nouns which are preceded by the word – *sake*.**

For instance:

- *For God's sake*, you must not lie during the interview.

- *For pity's sake,* help your aged and sick parents.

- *For heaven's sake*, allow her a day off with pay.

In these examples, ***bold words (idiomatic expressions)*** are used to emphasize that it is important to do something. *God, pity* and *heaven* are **singular nouns**.

- **An apostrophe can be used with plural nouns which are preceded by the word sake.**

It is illustrated below:

- *For old times' sake*, Anne forgave him and invited him for a meal.

If you do something for *old times' sake (idiomatic expression),* you do it because it is connected with something good that happened to you in the past.

- **Use an apostrophe with abbreviations functioning as verbs.**

For example:

- I submitted my application for a day off and my boss *OK'd* it.

Ok'd =okayed ↵

- In the present tense ⇒OK!

In this context, it means my boss officially agreed to let me have a day off work. It is rather an informal expression.

● He was *KO'd* in the first round.

KO'd = knocked out ↵

In this example, it is connected with boxing.

● <u>Usually business names do not include an apostrophe in their business titles.</u>

For example:

● I work at *Sainsburys*. ⇒ *should be Sainsbury's*

● My wife used to work for *Browns*. ⇒ *should be Brown's*

● I bought this CD from *Victorias*. ⇒ *should be Victoria's*

Sainsbury, *Brown* and *Victoria* are business names in the UK.

● <u>In hyphenated compound words the apostrophe is added to the last word.</u>

For instance:

● My wife's *brother-in-law's* home is not far from our home.

● A *well-dressed lady's* car is parked in your place.

2 ● <u>To mark contractions or indicate omissions in spelling certain words.</u>

For instance:

● *We'll* see you soon.
    ----

we will = we'll ↵ also = we shall

● She *won't* go there today.
    ----

will not = won't ↵

- It is a lovely spring morning, *isn't* it?
                ----

                 is not = isn't ↵

- *I'd* love to come with you.

  ⇑

I would = I'd

- We arrived here at the beginning of Spring *'04*.

                     2004 = '04 ↵

- He left home at 8 *o'clock*.   ⇐ **omitting of the**
                  ----

of the clock = o'clock ↵ - use it only for telling the time
                            in an exact hour

It is **not** used with a.m. and p.m. It means that he left home at exactly 8 as shown or reckoned by the clock.

- **The following examples also show the use of an apostrophe with a pronoun + an auxiliary verb to contract them.**

For instance:

- I'm = I am   • We're = We are

- They're = They are   • She's = She is **or** She has

- **An apostrophe is also used with an *auxiliary verb + not* to contract them.**

Here are some examples:

- haven't = have not   • wouldn't = would not

- mightn't = might not   • couldn't = could not

- oughtn't = ought not   • needn't = need not

- who's = who is or who has

In addition to the above, you can find some more common contractions together with their meanings in Table 1.

Some most common contractions

Contraction	Meaning	Contraction	Meaning
aren't	are not	let's	let us
can't	cannot/can not	mustn't	must not
hasn't	has not	she'll	she will/she shall
he's	he is/ he has	there's	there is
he'll	he will/he shall	they'll	they will/they shall
I'd	I would/ I had	they've	they have
it's	it is/it has	weren't	were not
I've	I have	we've	we have
I'll	I will/I shall	you'll	you will/you shall
it's	it is/ it has	you're	you are
		you've	you have

Table 1

- <u>**An apostrophe is used to indicate the omission of figures in dates.**</u>

For example:

- They wanted to stay with us in _**'04**_.

    referring to the year 2004 ↵

- Thank you for your letter of 9th Jan. _**'04**_.

****

- **An apostrophe is not used with the possessive pronouns.**

  - *its*   - *ours*   - *yours*   - *theirs*

- **An apostrophe is not used when referring to wars, plans, projects and similar notions related to a specified length of time.**

This is exemplified below:

  - Six-Day War   - <u>Hundred Years' War</u>

this does not obey the rule – exception to the rule

  - Five –Year Plan   - Ten –Year Projected Savings

There are other exceptions to the above rule.

- **An apostrophe is not used with abbreviations and numbers which create plurals***:*

For instance:

  - the 1980s.

  - In the 1950s, she was very young and pretty.

<u>Some writers place it before adding 's', e.g.</u> $\Rightarrow$ In the 1950's.

<u>Indeed, there is some controversy surrounding it.</u>

- **An apostrophe is usually used with names of places, when possession is involved.**

This is illustrated below:

  - **12** St. James's Square London SW 11.

  - *St. John's Wood* Underground station is in London.

  - He was seen in the *Earls Court* area yesterday afternoon.

This rule is not always applicable as demonstrated by the last example. Sometimes the insertion or omission of an apostrophe is surrounded by uncertainty.

. Brackets

There are several types of brackets. In British English for writing purposes the round brackets ( ) which are known as parentheses are used. Square brackets [   ] are used in the USA. Of course, other types of brackets are used for mathematical and scientific work.

. Round brackets or parentheses ( )

Round brackets can perform the following functions:

- to enclose some additional or optional information without affecting the flow and meaning of a sentence, a paragraph or a piece of writing

- to show alternatives

- to include abbreviations and refer to something by figures or letters

The following example makes it clear:

(1) • Gandhi *(1869-1948)* was the foremost spiritual and political leader of the twentieth century. He was called the Mahatma *(Great Souls – in Sanskrit)*. Gandhi was a pacifist and a great champion of non-violence.

The removal of parentheses and their contents will not affect the flow and meaning of this paragraph. Here are some more examples:

(2) • Any *student(s)* who would like to join this trip must see me today.

(3) • Only 2 *(two)* delegates are allowed free of charge during the book fair.

(4) •

     (1) Introduction
     (2) Objectives
     (3) Who should attend

Sometimes, I number examples as (1) • (2) • etc. The purpose of this "." is to highlight each example for the ease of the reader. See above. I find parentheses ( ) very useful for this purpose.

• <u>Square brackets</u> [ ]

Square brackets are used to supplement or append to an original text some information which may be a correction, an explanation or some translation by a person other than the author.

The following examples explain their use:

     (1) • During the Second World War, the British Prime Minister
         [Churchill] made great and memorable speeches.
         ----

additional information appended by the editor

     (2) • In Germany, during the Second World War, the Führer
         [leader, Hitler] also made highly nationalistic speeches.
         ----

translation and additional information by another person

     (3) • The first woman party leader in British politics
         [Margaret Thatcher] became the longest serving
         20th century female Prime Minister in 1988.

In this case, **[Margaret Thatcher]** is added to the original text by the editor.

• <u>Capital letters</u>

The use of capital letters is governed by the following punctuation rules:

• <u>Use a capital letter at the beginning of a sentence.</u>

For instance:

> • **P**unctuation enables us to write clearly.

> • **U**se punctuation to improve your writing.

• <u>Use a capital letter after a colon.</u>

In the following examples, direct speech is within the inverted commas:

- The British Prime Minister, Margaret Thatcher, said: **'I am extraordinarily patient, provided I get my own way in the end.'** (The Observer 4 April 1989)

- Once Mahatma Gandhi said: **'There is enough for the needy but not for the greedy.'**

- Once Goethe (German poet, novelist, and dramatist) said: **'Boldness has genius, power and magic in it.'**

• <u>The pronoun I is written as a capital letter.</u>

For instance:

> • **I**'m pleased to meet you.

> • It's a pity **I** missed your birthday party.

• <u>Use a capital letter to begin a proper noun:</u>

This is exemplified below:

****

- **Mary** is here from **York**. ⇐ both names begin with capital letters

- **Mrs** Johnson has arrived. ⇐ both title and surname begin with
  capital letter

- **A title of a person and proper nouns begin with a capital letter.**

It is illustrated here:

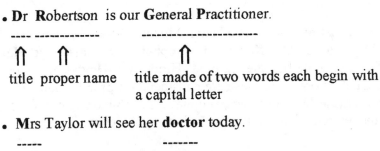

- **Dr** **Robertson** is our **General Practitioner.**

  title proper name   title made of two words each begin with
                      a capital letter

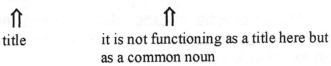

- **Mrs** Taylor will see her **doctor** today.

  title   it is not functioning as a title here but
                   as a common noun

- **Aunt** Kay lives in Nottingham.

⇑
title (Auntie or Aunty is informal for aunt)

- My **aunt** lives in Nottingham but **Uncle** Tom King died some

  ⇑   ⇑ years ago.
aunt is not a title but   it is the title of Tom King
a common noun

Words like doctor, aunt, grandfather are titles only when they are used
with proper nouns.

- **Nouns for religions, scriptural books and related titles begin with
  a capital letter.**

For example:

- Islam means submission to Allah. A Muslim is someone who has submitted to Allah, believing in Muhammad as a prophet of Allah. Allah is God in Islam. The Holy Qur'an (also known as the Koran) is the holy book of Islam.

- Christ, the Holy Bible, the Prophet Muhammad, Buddha, Judaism, the Talmud, Hindu and Hinduism are all connected with different religions.

In the last two examples, Islam, Muslim, Allah, Muhammad, God, the Holy Qur'an, the Koran, the Prophet Muhammad, the Holy Bible, Buddha, Judaism, the Talmud, Hindu and Hinduism all began with capital letters. Here these are considered as proper nouns. However, in the phrase 'as a prophet', prophet is a common noun, not a title. For this reason, it does not begin with a capital letter.

- **Capitals are used to begin the names of places, rivers, mountains, books, newspapers, plays, films, trains, ships, spacecraft, aircraft and other such things.**

The following examples make this rule clear:

- London, Berlin, Moscow and Paris are all capital cities in Europe.

- The longest span bridge in the world is Akashi-Kaiyo. It is in Japan. Its length is 1990 metres.

- The longest railway tunnel in the world is Seikan, Japan. It is 54 km long. The second longest railway tunnel in the world is the Channel Tunnel UK- France. It is 50 km long.

- The largest desert in the world is the Sahara in northern Africa.

- The highest mountain in the world is Everest in Asia.

- The longest river in the world is the River Nile in Africa.

- The largest country in the world by area is Russia.

- The largest city by population in the world is Tokyo, in Japan.

- The Himalayas are the highest mountain range on Earth. They are in Asia.

- The distance from the Earth to the Sun is about 150 million km.

- "The Times" is a daily newspaper for well-informed readers in the UK.

- "The Diamond Sūtra" is the oldest surviving printed book in the world. It is a Chinese translation of Buddhist scripture, printed in AD 868.

- The Orient Express is a famous train.

- Apollo 11 made the first lunar landing.

- The actress Elizabeth Taylor played the title role of the 1963 film "Cleopatra."

- "Java Simplified" is a computer programming book from ADR.

- **Capitals are used for abbreviations of names of some organisations and countries. These are formed from the first letter of each word in the name.**

Here are some examples to make this rule clear:

- **UN** is an abbreviation for the United Nations.

- **UK** is a short name for the United Kingdom.

- **EU** stands for the European Union.

- **BBC** is an abbreviation for the British Broadcasting Corporation

- **BP** is short for the British Petroleum company.

The correct use of both capital and small letters has been muddled by

the arrival of the Internet. Often proper nouns are written either in
capital or small letters and joined together. This practice is not recommended in this book.

. <u>A Word of warning</u>

- The Hilton Hotel. ⇒wrong   correct ⇒ Hilton Hotel

- a Hotel ⇒**wrong** – it should be ⇒ a hotel

- <u>**River**</u> Indus ⇒correct

River is the first part of this compound noun

- There are many **Rivers** in England.

        incorrect – it should be <u>**rivers**</u> ⇒ common plural noun

- Hyde Park is in London. ⇒correct

correct because it is the <u>second</u> part of this name

- There many **Parks** in London.

    incorrect ↵ - it should be <u>p</u>arks ⇒ common plural noun

. <u>Colon</u>

<u>A colon is used for the following functions:</u>

. <u>To introduce a list or a series of items.</u>

The following examples show the use of the colon:

- The following students must register their proposals today
  before 16.00 hours: James Walker, Joan Smith, Elizabeth
  Wood and John Baker.

- We can travel to London by any of the three means of travel: by car, by train or by coach.

- These are unused product code numbers: BA 00012C, CC 18919X and CC 18920 X.

- **To identify a speaker in direct speech and quotations.**
For instance:

  - Joy said: 'It was my handbag.'

  - Silvia shouted: 'Leave my home now!'

  - Tony Blair promised: 'Education, education, education.'

  - She asked me immediately: 'Who told you about my illness?'

- **Use a colon for introductory remarks.**
For example:

  - Ladies and gentlemen: allow me to present tonight's guest speaker.

- **To add information to a clause so that it is elaborated.**
This is exemplified below:

  - This group has students from six countries: Germany, Russia, India, China, Ireland and the United Kingdom.

  - We specialise in selling technical books: engineering, computing and physical sciences.

  - The inner city has been neglected by the authority: derelict buildings, dirty streets, lack of public transport, hardly any footpaths and ill-equipped hospitals are some of the things that local residents reported to the media.

- **To supplement information to a phrase so that it is expanded.**
For instance:

- Lots of books: computing, engineering, gardening, short stories, etc.

- **To start a clause which contains an explanation of the previous clause.**

  This is demonstrated below:

  - Today our town is very busy: there is an annual festival and a procession along the promenade.

  - Our train was full of overseas visitors: many passengers were travelling to London Heathrow Airport.

- **To introduce a subtitle.**

  This rule is illustrated below:

  - Essential English: <u>Grammar, Structure and Style of Good English.</u>

    subtitle ↵

  - C++ Simplified: <u>A practical C++ Programming Manual.</u>

    subtitle ↵

- **To form numerical ratios and other number systems.**

  Here are two examples to show you how to apply this rule:

  - Profit and expenditure ratio **4:1**

  - Our train left London Victoria at 15:30 sharp.

- **Another use of the colon is to refer to a document or correspondence or set the beginning of a letter etc.**

  For instance:

  - <u>From:</u> John Smith   <u>To:</u> James Taylor
    <u>Subject:</u> Delivery by car   <u>Dated:</u> 12.06.2004

- <u>Colons are also used in mathematical, scientific and engineering expressions.</u>

. Comma

The comma and full stop are the most common punctuation marks in the English language. The correct use of the comma is not a mystery. Its usage is fairly well documented and understood, yet there is a tendency either to use too many commas or to use too few commas in a piece of writing. Indeed, there is a wide variation in the use of commas. Sometimes, a comma as a separator is essential. There are occasions when the use of a comma may be considered as optional for the sake of clarity. The following discussion illustrates its use for some specific aims:

. List items

. To separate items in a list of three or more items. These item may be words, phrases or clauses.

Here are some examples:

- Anne, Wolfgang, Elena **, and** Frank went to Austria for a skiing holiday. ⇑

  a comma before a conjunction - see ⇒a comment below

- You can have one more portion of potatoes, peas**, or** cabbage.

  a comma before a conjunction ↵

  see ⇒a comment below

- John is energetic, ambitious**, and** rich.

  a comma before and ↵

In these examples, a comma is placed before the coordinating conjunction. These coordinating conjunctions come before the last item in each list. The placing of a comma before the coordinating conjunction indicates the start of the last item is often called the '**Oxford comma**'.

However, there is a growing trend towards the omission of the comma before the last coordinating conjunction. On the other hand, when the last item in the list has **and** in it, the comma is necessary to avoid ambiguity. Here are some examples:

- My children used to enjoy watching television game shows, children's programmes**, and** the **Little and Large** comedy show.

     essential comma compound noun -joined by **and**

      conjunction part of the compound noun ⏎

- He went to Fulham, Putney**, and** **Kensington and Chelsea** by bus.

  a comma is essential here ⏎ compound noun ⏎

- **If the list ends with such phrases as etc., and the like and so on, a comma is needed to indicate continuity of the same thing.**

It is demonstrated now:

- Gull, golden eagle, finch, duck, **and the like** creatures with feathers and two legs are birds.

- Tesco, Safeway, Morrison, **etc.** stores have been attracting customers of small corner shops to their own big retail outlets.

. <u>Main clauses</u>

. <u>To join main clauses if they are linked by the coordinating conjunction *and, but* or *so*.</u>

Here are some examples to show you how to put this rule into practice:

- Our staff room is situated on the first floor, and the students' room is on the third floor.

- You can attend our meeting today, but you must not come more than five minutes late.

- She has declined our invitation, but there is still plenty of time for her to accept it.

The comma can be omitted when the clauses are short. This is exemplified below:

- She cooks and I clean.

- We ran very fast but still missed the last bus.

- Susan is married yet she is known by her maiden name.

- **To separate a subordinate clause or phrase from the main clause, the use of a comma may be justified to avoid misunderstanding. The comma is more desirable and helpful, when the sentence is long.**

For example:

- After three hours of the skiing session, they returned to their hotel

       adverbial phrase↵   for a hot meal.

- At the end of the long working day, I didn't receive my wage.

       adverbial phrase↵

- As soon as they left home, we had to cook our evening meal.

subordinate clause ↵

- **The use of a comma is less common, when the subordinate clause follows the main clause. For this reason, the comma is enclosed within the [ ] to indicate that its use is optional.**

It is put into practice now:

- I did not travel with my wife to London [,] *because I had to attend an important meeting at work*.

      subordinate clause ↵

- She wrote short stories as well [,] so that she could support her family.

      subordinate clause ↵

****

- We left home in the morning **[,]** <u>soon after our breakfast.</u>

subordinate clause ↵

- ### Use commas to separate an adding /non-restrictive/ non-identifying clause from the main clause.

    For instance:

    - My son, <u>who was a soldier</u> , had left the army.

adding/non-restrictive/non-identifying clause

If you remove the adding/non-restrictive/non-identifying clause from the sentence, it will still make sense.

- Miss Jones, <u>who is our store manager</u>, grew up in a foster home.

adding clause↵

In these two examples, both relative non-adding clauses are qualifying the head noun.

- ### No commas are needed to separate identifying (restrictive) and classifying clauses from the main clause.

See ⇒ Clauses for examples.

- ### Use commas to separate the speaker from the direct speech.

Here are some examples to show you the application of this rule:

- The head teacher said, '<u>No one is allowed to use a mobile phone in class.</u>'

direct speech within single quotation marks ↵

- John Smith shouted, '<u>You are breaking speed limits. Reduce your speed now.</u>'

direct speech within single quotation marks ↵

- **Note the use of single quotation marks. Single quotation marks are often used to report direct speech. You can use double quotation marks.**

The use of double quotation marks is as follows:

- 'Ian, I don't agree with you,' he said angrily, 'you are not
thinking clearly.'

- Franklin D. Roosevelt said, 'The only thing we have to fear is
fear itself.'

- **Use commas to separate a question tag from the rest of the sentence:**

For example:

- This is your new car, isn't it?

- Your wife is a doctor, am I right?

- Your complaint was dealt with by me to your satisfaction, wasn't it?

- **Use commas with numbers in accordance with the following rules.**

- Write non-technical numbers, by placing a comma after every three units, commencing from the right of the number: For instance:

- 10,000   105, 111, 456   88,000,789

- The population of Bridlington is around 65,000.

- **Often a comma is not used in numbers smaller than 10,000.**

-    1,267   2,345   9,999   w

There is no need to place commas in these numbers - **_Reason:_** Commas
are used with numbers 10,000 and above.

- **When dealing with the British currency, the whole pounds should be written with the pound symbol £.**

    For instance:

    - £1   £5,349   £24   £1,009
                          --   --
    coma is essential here⤶   coma is essential here⤶

- **When the British currency involves both pounds and pence, write pence in numbers after the decimal point. The comma is also used if the number is £1,000 or greater.**

    For example:

    - £34 . 05   £467. 99   £ 9,789. 75
        ⇑   ⇑
    decimal point   two places after decimal point for pence

When the amount is in pounds and pence, do not use the symbol/abbreviation **p** for pence. Mixed currency is extended to two places after the decimal point as shown above. When the amount is less than the whole pound, it is written as:

- 66p, 99p, 5p Sometimes written ⟹ £0 .66, £0 .99, £0 .05 but
                                            it is the least preferred manner

Often people write currency in such a preferred way that makes them feel secure.

- **Large amounts involving a million or a billion or a trillion can also be written with their respective symbols/abbreviation or without it:**

For example:

    - **m**   is an abbreviation or a symbol for million
    - **bn** is an abbreviation or a symbol for billion
    - **trillion** is written as trillion

- 1,000,000 or 1 m   1,000,000,000 or 1 bn

- 178,000,000 or 178 m   1,500,000,000 or 1.5 bn

- <u>We say a, one, two or several billion or million. There is no need to say millions or billions. We say these without the final 's'.</u>

This is illustrated below:

- At the end of the first six months of this year, our sales reached between 2.6 m and 1 bn.

- <u>When there is no quantity or a number before million or billion, we say millions or billions.</u> It is clarified below:

- Millions/billions of pounds were invested in the London Dome.

  You can say:

  - Our government has wasted <u>**tens of millions**</u> on advertising their failed policies.   ⇑ – not a figure but a phrase
  plural number

  - His grandfather made his **millions** by selling whisky in the USA.

  - Have you finished your work? No. I have a million things to do.

- <u>Always use a plural verb with million or millions and billion or billions:</u>

The following examples demonstrate this rule:

  - One million <u>**pounds were**</u> spent on this building project.
plural forms of noun + verb ↵

  - Three million <u>**pounds have been**</u> deposited in his bank account.
plural forms of noun + verb ↵

  - Some gangsters **make their millions** by selling drugs and stolen goods.

• *Currency in the USA*

Money is written in the same way as pounds and pence in the UK, except with the dollar sign. For instance:

  • $ 5,567 $1.6m $ 10.66   50¢

• Use commas to separate parenthetic remarks from the rest of the sentence.

Sometimes it is desirable to give additional information by enclosing it in parenthesis by means of a pair of commas. In fact, you can do this by using brackets or dashes. The following examples show the use of parenthesis:

• John's business venture in the USA, **which almost cost him loss of his family home,** ended with the closure of his business in the USA.

• Last year, I attended a book fair, **Frankfurt International Book Fair,** in Frankfurt Germany.

• James Stewart, **secretary of our local social club,** speaks French fluently.

• Mikhail Gorbachev (1931 -), **president of the USSR,** was awarded the Nobel Peace Prize 1990.

• Is parenthetic use of commas is essential?

It is not always necessary. For instance:

• In the light of the above facts, we, **therefore,** very much appreciate your refund of our deposit . You can re-write it as:

• In the light of the above facts, we **therefore** very much appreciate your refund of our deposit .

• I assure you, sir, we will deliver the goods on the agreed date.

You can re-write it as:

• I assure you, sir we will deliver the goods on the agreed date.

You can use many parenthetic phrases such as **indeed**, **certainly**, **by chance,** and **incidentally** (adverbial elements) without parenthetic commas.

• Dash

The prime function of a dash is to separate a part of a sentence from the rest of a sentence. There may be one or more dashes in a sentence. The dash is used for a variety of aims. Some of these are exemplified here:

• **In the following examples, dashes have added some excitement and informality:**

    • Annabel loved Rex so much – and she left her husband.

    • Here is a bouquet of flowers – my sweetheart.

• **In the following examples the dash is used to place emphasis on a phrase towards the end of a sentence:**

    • He only has one thing on his mind – his girlfriend.

    • Their car is just six months old – and rather expensive.

• **Dashes are used to separate list items as illustrated below:**

    • All the team members – John, Carl, Carol, Barry, Derek, Elaine and Eva – left.

    • Today we have sold – 20 copies of C++, 20 copies of Java, 54 copies of XHTML – and taken orders for 45 copies of English Grammar – the forthcoming title.

• **A dash is used to comment on a phrase which preceded it:**

    • Frankfurt, Vienna and Budapest – **these cities are well served by fast trains throughout the year.**

- Just imagine his reaction – he will be furious to see this mess.

- Wait a minute – this isn't the right building for our meeting.

- **Dashes are used parenthetically - a pair of dashes must be used:**

  - The Himalayas – the highest mountains in the world –
    are the ultimate challenge.

  - Martin Luther King Jr – the US civil-rights campaigner, black
    leader, and Baptist minister – was awarded the Nobel
    Peace Prize in 1964.

  - Muhammad Ali – three times World Heavyweight Champion –
    was the most recognised person in the 20th century in the
    whole world.

In these examples, a pair of dashes is used instead of brackets in order
to enclose the information. This parenthetic use of dashes is equivalent
to brackets. For the parenthetic use, a pair of brackets is preferred as
information within the brackets stands out better and makes a stronger
impression on a reader. Therefore, it is suggested that you avoid using
a pair of dashes for brackets.

- **Dashes are used to separate the additional clause from the
  main clause:**

  - Berlin is smaller than London – **where underground trains are**

    main clause ↵   **too crowded during the rush hours.**

additional clause telling more about London/head noun ↵

  - Charlie Chaplin was a film actor and director – who made his

    main clause ↵   reputation as a
                                  tramp with a smudge moustache,
                                  bowler hat and twirling cane.

We usually separate the additional clause with commas.

• A dash is used to indicate different types of ranges:

The following examples show the use of dashes and ranges:

- World War I **1914 – 1918** caused the death of an estimated 10 million people.

- World War II **1939 – 45** caused the loss of an estimated 55 million lives

• When on both sides of the dash the dates are in the same decade, it is conventional to write only the last two digits on the right side of the dash.

- Queen Victoria 1819 – 1901

Here full dates are given on both sides of the dash because there is a change of century.

- See pp 210 – 220 **or** See pages 210 – 220

- A – K

- volumes I– V

Some writers use dashes to imitate spoken English, to place emphasis, to indicate a missing word or words (maybe a rude word or phrase), incompleteness or uncertainty. Comic writers and tabloid journalists use dashes frequently. In formal writing and in academic work, commas and round brackets (parentheses) for parenthetic use are generally preferred. It should be noted that after a dash, only a proper noun begins with a capital letter.

• Ellipses(dot dot dot)

Ellipses (singular ellipsis) are a series of usually three full stops, or points, or dots. In essence, ellipses indicate:

- omission of one or more words from a sentence

- a sentence or paragraph is missing from the writing

- withholding of something for whatever reason

These are exemplified below:

● They were thirsty, but also ... and penniless. ⇐ *a word (hungry) is*
                                                              omitted

● You must tell the panel nothing but ... ⇐ *a phrase (the truth)*
                                                          is omitted

In the last example, ellipses occurred at the end of the sentence. When ellipses are utilised at the end of a sentence, there is *no* need for the fourth dot or full stop.

● On the contrary, in the next example, the ellipses are used to separate two complete sentences. In this case, there is a need for the fourth dot. Here ellipses indicate that at least one complete sentence has been withheld. The missing or withheld sentence or further sentences should have been where ellipses are shown.

● I have never said that ... . I don't use that sort of language.

       1   ⇑   2

complete sentence   ellipses complete sentence

● They visited us in 1996,1997, 1998 ... ⇐ *omission of some*
                                                        subsequent years

● <u>Exclamation mark !</u>

The exclamation mark is represented by **!**. It is a terminator just like the full stop; but it is used for the following specific purposes.

● To indicate strong emotional feelings – anger, happiness, sorrow, surprise, etc.

Here are a few examples:

      ● What bloody awful weather! (to emphasize the nature
                                                          of the weather)

      ● How wonderful the party was!

- Didn't they cry!

- We won! Hurrah!

. **To mark emphatic phrases** - scorn, insult, swearing, irony, command , etc.

- She must be silly!

- You're a mess!

- Get out of my class! And wait outside until I call you back!

- Get lost!

- You have no money! And you buy a new BMW !

. **To mark the end of interjections**

- *Cheers!*

- *Blimey!*

- *Be quiet!*

- *Ow!*   *(Ow! That hurt me!)*

- *Ouch!*   *(Ouch! That hurt me!)* See ⇒ Interjections

. **To indicate the importance of a specific statement**

- What a difficult journey she faced!

- Didn't I call your name? Sorry!

- John is only twelve!

. **Some other uses of exclamation marks**

Sometimes people use multiple exclamation marks in order to make a piece of writing more interesting. Unless you are writing comic material or working for the tabloid press, try not to use them.

In mathematics, the exclamation stands for the factorial sign. e.g., five factorial = 5!. As a matter of interest, its value works out as: **5!** = (5x4x3x2x1) = 120.

There are other less common uses of the exclamation mark. For instance (!) and [!]. These are used in the publishing world.

. **Footnotes**

A footnote is written below the text at the bottom of the page. It may be an explanation, a comment, some additional information or a reference. The most common symbol used for footnotes is the Arabic numeral written as a superscript figure. A superscript number/figure is written above the normal line of writing. For instance:

- "Object Oriented Programming (OOP) is not new. What is new is the application of its concepts in modern programming languages such as C++ and Java."[1]

  1 Java Simplified, Adam Shaw, ADR, 1999.

Some people use some other symbols such as asterisks and oblique.

. **Full stop**

The full stop is the most commonly used punctuation mark. It is also known as **full point**. In the United States of America, it is called **period**. It is a terminator that is used for a variety of situations as exemplified below:

- Rose is engaged to Russell.   ⇐ full stop at the end of a sentence

- Would you kindly leave this room now? ⇐ at the end of a polite
                                          request

- What you should do is to listen to your mother. ⇐ at the end of a
                                          recommendation

- May I ask you to show me your current pass. ⇐ at the end of a
  polite request

Note that polite requests are not questions and thus a full stop is placed at the end of each statement.

- <u>**Use a full stop at the end of indirect speech that sounds like a question.**</u>

  For instance:

  - I would very much like to know where your manor in Yorkshire is.

  - The office manager wanted to find out why the monthly report was delayed.

- <u>**Many abbreviations end with a full stop.**</u>

  For example:

  - Joan Smith Ph.D.

  - Dr. A .Williams is away this week.

There is a tendency not to place full stops after initials. Some people do not use the full stop at the end of any abbreviation. For instance:

  - Jan ⇐ **January**

  - e.g. ⇐ **for example**

The abbreviation **e.g.** is derived from the Latin words *EXEMPLI GRATIA*. For instance: e.g. red colour.

  - et al. ⇐ and other people or things

The abbreviation **et al.** is derived from the Latin **'et alii or alia'** or **'aliae'** . It is usually used after names.

For instance: discovered by John Major et al., 2001

● etc. ⇐ for showing that in the list there are other items that could have been included.

It is an abbreviation **for *et cetera or et ceteri*** For instance: Colin, Robin, Jane, etc.

● www.adrlondon.ltd ⇐ in e-mail address *(known here as 'dot')*

●Mr and Mrs Blair have arrived. Or ⇐ Mr. and Mrs. Blair have
                                                                        arrived.

●The **UN** offices in the **UK** are in London. ⇐ the U.N. offices in the
                                                                        U.K. are in London.

● **Use full stops for both British and American currencies.**

● £45.<u>76</u> ⇐ pounds . pence   ● $ 45.<u>90</u> ⇐ dollars . cents
           ⇑   ⇑

      seventy-six pence   ninety cents

In both examples, the full stop is used as a **symbol for the decimal point.** In the UK, <u>less than a pound is usually written as a number with</u> <u>p. For instance: *96p*</u> (see ⇒currency)

● <u>No full stop is added to abbreviations for metric measurements, e.g.</u>

        cm ⇒ centimetre   mm ⇒ millimetre
        km ⇒ kilometre   mg ⇒milligram
        etc.

● **Full stops are used between days, months and years when dates** **are written in numbers.**

For example:

          ● 01.03. 03   ● 31.05.2001

● **A full stop is placed between the hours and minutes when time is** **written in the UK. There is a full stop after m in p.m.**

• 3.45 **a.m.**   • 8.15 **p.m.**

ante meridiem ↵ also am   post meridiem ↵ - also pm

• ante meridiem ⟹ before noon. It is from Latin⟹ *ante meridiem*

• post meridiem ⟹after noon. It is from Latin⟹ *post meridiem*

• **A full stop is placed at the end of a footnote irrespective of its grammatical status.**

For example:

• 1 pp. 12-33.   • 2 Adam Shaw in Java, pp. 10-12.

Note that **pp.** is an abbreviation for pages. It is written in lower-case letters followed by a full stop. A *lower-case* abbreviation cannot begin a sentence.

• Hyphen

It can be said that hyphens are used for two main functions:

• to join two words together

• to split the word at the end of a line of print

In British English, hyphens are more commonly used than in American English. The following examples illustrate some of the purposes for using hyphens.

• He went to see his **mother-in-law** in the Bahamas.

⇑compound noun containing a preposition
hyphen forming a compound noun

• **The following examples also demonstrate the use of the hyphen in forming compound words:**

• He is a **jack-of-all-trades** who takes on almost any work he is offered.

In this example, the compound noun is formed by including two prepositions **of** and **all**.

• You can travel by an *inter-city* train anywhere in France.

• His *ex-wife* is a hairdresser.

• She paid <u>**seventy-seven**</u> pounds for this beautiful dress.

hyphened ↵

<u>Compound numbers</u>

1. The hyphen is used in writing out numbers in words between twenty-one and ninety-nine.

2. Do not use hyphens when writing out numbers in words such as three hundred.
3. In compound numbers hundred, thousand, etc. <u>do not</u> end with –s.

• Your bill comes to *<u>two hundred</u>* and *<u>thirty-four</u>* pounds.

not hyphenated ↵   hyphenated ↵

• <u>**The following examples show that when a compound word is formed with a verb form, it is written with a hyphen:**</u>

• John couldn't think of a **put-down** fast enough.

a remark to make someone look /feel stupid ↵

• Natasha gave a *record-breaking* performance last night.

• It is a *well-thought-out* idea.

• Barbara is always *well-dressed*.

• <u>Some other compound words formed with **well, hyphen**</u> and **verb** forms are shown in List 1.

> ## Compound words = well + hyphen + verb form
>
> well-advised, well-aimed, well-behaved, well-born, well-built,
> well-connected, well-deserved, well-desired, well-documented,
> well-earned, well-founded, well-groomed, well-heeled,
> well-informed, well-intentioned, well-known, well-looking,
> well-made, well-off, well-preserved, well-respected, well-rounded,
> well-spoken, well-tempered, well-thought-of, well-tried, well-to-do,
> well-wished, well-won, well-worked-out.

List 1

The above list contains compound adjectives. The use of the hyphen in compound words is often debatable.

- The following examples illustrate that some nouns preceded by a letter are hyphenated:

    - On British motorways a *U-turn* is prohibited.

        compound noun ⏎

    - Our hospital is short of chest *X-ray* machines.

    - A *T-junction* is a place where one road joins another but does not cross it, so that joining roads form the shape of the letter T.

    - A bend in a pipe or road like the shape of the letter *s* is called an *S-bend*.

- **The following examples show that some compound nouns with adverbs or prepositions are usually written with or without hyphens:**

    - motorway *or* motor-way

    - phone *or* card phone-card

* **The following examples show that in some words with prefixes, hyphens are used to separate the prefix from the root word:**

  * Our home telephone number is ___ex___ - ___directory___.

       prefix ↵   ⇑

                                  root word

  * A *post-dated* cheque will be treated as payable immediately.

  * Please *re-enter* the office from the side entrance.

  * There is no *multi-storey* car park in our town.

  * At present, there are plenty of *semi-skilled* jobs in our area.

* **The following examples demonstrate that adjective compounds preceded by *self* are hyphenated:**

* The enclosed document is *self-explanatory*.

* In some Indian villages, *self-help* community projects have transformed villagers' lives.

* Last summer, we rented a *self-contained* flat in a small sea-side town in France.

* Don't be too *self-critical* because such an attitude can be *self-destructive*.

* Professor Burkhardt is a *self-styled* professor of the German language.

* He is a *self-taught* software designer.

* Kay always seems so calm and *self-possessed.*

* You shouldn't allow fear and *self-doubt* to rule your life.

Some other compound words formed with self + hyphen + root word are listed in List 2.

Compound words = self+ hyphen +root word

self-access, self-appointed, self-appraisal, self-assertive, self-assured, self-awareness, self-catering, self-centred, self-confessed, self-confident, self-congratulation, self-conscious, self-contradiction, self-control, self-criticism, self-deception, self-defeating, self-defence, self-denial, self-destruction, self-determination, self-discipline, self-drive, self-educated, self-employed, self-esteem, self-evident, self-examination, self-fulfilling, self-government, self-image, self-important, self-imposed, self-indulgent, self-inflicted, self-interest, self-made, self-opinionated, self-pity, self-preservation, self-reliant, self-respect, self-restraint, self-righteous, self-sacrifice, self-satisfied, self-seeking, self-service, self-serving, self-worth.

List 2

- **Hyphens are also used in double-barrelled family names as illustrated below:**

  - Mr. and Mrs. *Douglas-Home* are here.

  - Lord *Baden-Powell* founded the Boy Scout movement in 1908.

Note that the first letter in each double-barrelled name begins with a capital letter.

- **Some British names of places are also hyphenated.**

For instance:

  - *Southend-on-Sea* is in Essex near London.

  - *Stratford-upon-Avon* is where William Shakespeare was born in 1564.

The word after the preposition begins with a capital letter as illustrated above.

● **Hyphens at the end of a line (word division)**

We are in the age of Information Technology (IT). Typewriters have virtually been replaced by keyboards and word-processors. Generally speaking, word-processing software truncates a word at the end of a line in accordance with its own rule. Increasing numbers of books are created by using word-processing software. It is the word-processor which formats the document, hence inserts the hyphen at the point of a word division at the end of a line. This is shown below:

There are two subject areas, namely *etymology* and *phonetics*, which deserve mention here. *Etymology* is the study of word origin and *phonetics* is the study of speech and sounds. **Etymology** has a set of rules for dividing the word into syllables, prefixes and suffixes. Phonetics suggests the division of a word based on its sounds. If you are keen to explore word division, it is suggested that you pay a visit to your local library to consult reference books or search the Internet for further information on these topics.

● Paragraph

There are no hard-and-fast rules that regulate a paragraph's size and content. In any piece of writing, paragraphs enable the writer to lay the text in its most appropriate order so that the reader is at ease with the text. A paragraph contains a main theme. The main theme may have one or more related points. The whole idea is to place related points in a paragraph so that the reader is helped to grasp what is being written. Of course, the main theme may have several related paragraphs.

For instance, the main theme of the above section is the use of the hyphen. It has two related paragraphs. The first paragraph talks about the way words are divided by a word-processor these days. In the second paragraph, an example is given in order to demonstrate how the word-processor has divided the word *Etymology* at the end of a line (see above).

These paragraphs are short and concise. In fact, the length of a paragraph is dictated by the amount of the text in the main theme and related points. As in this example, the sizes of both paragraphs are based on the amount and flow of the text in each paragraph.

Some people write long paragraphs. For instance, a letter from a solicitor (lawyer) usually has long paragraphs. There are other experts such as philosophers who also construct longer paragraphs as longer paragraphs provide them with plenty of space to develop their ideas and argue their opinions. <u>Nowadays, the widespread tendency is to write shorter paragraphs</u>.

Paragraphs are also visual aids. Some writers prefer to leave at least one blank line between two paragraphs. This is the style of this book. Some writers have other preferences. For instance, they start a paragraph by indenting the first word by a number of letter spaces, usually 3 to 5. They do not allow a blank line between two paragraphs. Hardly ever, writers indent and allow a blank line space at the same time. If you are interested in fiction and poetry, consult some relevant reference materials for paragraphing techniques. <u>It is worth mentioning that publishers have their own house style for paragraphing.</u>

<u>Example of paragraphing by indenting the first word</u>

> This is an indented paragraph....
> you said that---------------
> ....
> This is the second indented paragraph.....

<u>Example of paragraphing with a blank line between two paragraphs</u>

> This is a paragraph...............
> ------------------------------------
> ------------------------------------
>
> This is the second paragraph --------

. <u>Question mark ?</u>

The question mark (**?**) is a terminator like the full stop. The main purposes for which it is used are exemplified below:

- **The following examples elucidate that what precedes the question mark is an interrogative sentence:**

    - Are you related to this woman?

    - What are you carrying in that heavy suitcase?

    - The policeman asked me first, 'Is this your car?'

    - I asked him, 'Where were you at the time of the accident?'

The purpose of the interrogative question is to get an answer from the respondent. An interrogative question or a **direct question** always ends with a question mark.

- **A Direct *'question-like'* statement ends with a question mark(question tag):**

For instance:

- It is a lovely morning, isn't it ?

- She looks very pretty in her wedding dress, doesn't she?

- They look disappointed, don't they?

- Joan's mother is always nagging her, isn't she?

- You are a footballer, aren't you?

- They are always **as busy as bees**, aren't they?
  idiomatic expression ↵ - it means very busy

- **The following example shows that instead of asking a full question, you can make it short. The short question also ends with a question mark:**

- What is your name? ⇒ short form ⇒ First name please?

- What is your surname? ⇒ short form ⇒ Surname please?

- What is your home telephone number? $\Rightarrow$ short form $\Rightarrow$ Home telephone please?

- What is your permanent address? $\Rightarrow$ short form $\Rightarrow$ Permanent address please?

The above example (it is just one example) illustrates that a short question can be a short phrase(a phrase may be just one word, e.g. run!).

- **When there is uncertainty about a fact, a question mark is usually used to point it :**

  - Socrates (?470 –399 BC) was a Greek philosopher.

  - Friedrich Engels (?1820-95) was a German philosopher who collaborated with Karl Marx on *The Communist Manifesto (?1848)*.

  - Albert Einstein was born in Berlin(?).

Often a date or place of birth is doubtful or unverified.

- **The question mark is not used with an indirect question:**

  - We would like to know what your thoughts are on capital punishment.

  - I was wondering if you could give my wife a lift to the town centre.

  - We would like to know what the cost is.

- **In chess, the question mark is used by itself and with other symbols.**

  Here are two examples:

  - ? means a bad move
  - ?? stands for a serious blunder

- **Some writers use two question marks (??) or a question mark with an exclamation mark (?!) to imply scepticism or strong feeling :**

- Do you really think he is telling us the truth??

- What made you believe her??

Some people repeat question marks several times with or without the exclamation mark.

- <u>The use of more than one question mark is not recommended for formal writing.</u>

- **<u>Nine question words listed together with examples of their use in List 3 always end with a question mark.</u>**

Question words exemplified

	Question word	**Example**
(1) •	What	What is your question?
(2) •	When	When did you order the goods?
(3) •	Where	Where is your mother?
(4) •	Which	Which is your desk?
(5) •	Who	Who won the election in our area?
(6) •	Whom	Whom did you invite?
(7) •	Why	Why were you late this morning?
(8) •	Whose	Whose book is this?
(9) •	How	How are you this morning?

<u>List 3</u>

. <u>Quotation marks</u>

Quotation marks are also known as inverted commas, speech marks and quotes. There are single quotation marks (' ') as well as double quotation marks (" "). In Britain, single quotes are preferred. The main purposes of using quotation marks are exemplified here.

. <u>Direct speech</u>

It is someone's exact spoken words. When direct speech is reported or quoted, the words actually spoken must be within quotation marks. The writer must also give the precise source of the words actually spoken. The reader should know to whom quoted words are attributed.

- **. <u>The following examples illustrate that quotation marks are used in order to enclose direct speech:</u>**

  - 'How do you like the flowers I sent you through Interflora?' Miss Stubbs asked Anne.

  - 'War is always a sign of failure,' said the President of France.

The rule is that the words within the quotes must be exactly those spoken.

  - 'We will always remember Jill as a kind person,' said Mrs. Jones. 'she was ever so friendly and generous to us.'

This example illustrates:

a) when a quoted speech is interrupted at the end of a sentence, instead of a full stop a comma is used to mark the end of the sentence, and

b) the word which resumes the quoted speech begins with a small letter.

- **. <u>When words *where, why, yes* and *no* are part of direct speech, these are enclosed within quotation marks (but not in reported speech):</u>**

Here are some examples to show the application of this rule:

- Veronica said to him, 'Yes!'

- 'Yes,' Tom replied, but Monica shouted, 'No! It is not for me.'

- Joyce asked, 'Where?'

- Gary said, 'Why?'

- When we asked him to come along with us, he replied, **'No**.'

                                                 direct speech ↵

• <u>Indirect speech</u>

When instead of reporting someone's exact words, the meaning of words is expressed in the third person form using the past tense. It is exemplified below:

- When we asked Derek to travel with us, he said **no**. ⇐ *indirect*

    in reported speech *no* is not within quotes ↵   *speech*

- She has just left home. She did not say where she was going.

• <u>When a quotation is within another quotation, double quotation marks are used to enclose the quotes within quotes:</u>

- 'What do you mean by **"late"**?' I asked him.

    a quote within a quote↵– enclosed within double quotation marks

- I asked the speaker, 'Could you please give an example of **"willy-nilly"**?'

In this last example, *willy-nilly* is a quote within a quote. It is an ad-verb (informal use). It means irrespective of whether someone wants to or not, e.g. we were forced willy-nilly by the policeman to turn left. It also means doing something carelessly without planning or thinking,

e.g.   • She spends her money willy-nilly.

- **When the direct quotation has several paragraphs, it is customary to start each paragraph with an opening quotation mark, and place the closing quotation mark at the end of the entire quotation:**

  - 'Tagore also believed in learning by doing. For this purpose, a garden and a handicraft shop were part of his school. He had great interest in ecological matters. He used to have tree planting ceremonies.

    'Tagore also founded a university. At his university, he established an international faculty in order to teach unity in diversity.'

    (Rabindranath Tagore – the first Asian to receive the Nobel Prize for Literature 1913)

- **When a phrase or a word is quoted, it is enclosed within quotation marks:**

  - Colin told me 'certainly no deal', which I conveyed to my boss.

  - My doctor declared my health was 'excellent'.

  - The hyphenated word 'willy-nilly' has two different meanings as explained above.

- **Titles of lectures, book chapters, articles, short stories and short poems, television and radio programmes and musical writing are shown in quotes:**

  - The title of our annual lecture is ' The Role of Neighbourhood Watch'.

  - 'Fruit Gathering' is one of Rabindranath Tagore's poems.

- **The following rules should be observed for quotes:**

a) • <u>Punctuation marks (comma, full stop, question mark, etc.) connected with quoted words are placed *inside the closing* quotation mark:</u> Here are two examples:

- 'I am fine. How is your wife?' he said to me.

- 'We have been trying to compromise for three days. Can someone suggest another idea which may appeal to all of us? Let's see who has a bright idea. First, let's have a drink!' the chairman remarked.

b) • <u>When a statement or a sentence finishes with a quotation that ends with a full stop, or a question mark, or an ellipsis, or an exclamation mark, the full stop to stop the entire statement is not required:</u>

For example:

- She said, 'I sent you my CV yesterday.'

- Sarah shouted, 'It's marvellous!'

- Alan said to his wife, ' I never agreed to your … '

- My teacher asked me, 'How long do you need to finish this essay?'

c) • <u>Punctuation marks (comma, full stop, question marks, etc.) connected with the entire sentence are placed outside the closing quotation marks:</u>

For instance:

- A few days ago, I read a book ' Napoleon Bonaparte – The French Emperor'.

- I wrote a letter to a friend and told her about 'White teeth by Zadie Smith'.

• <u>Semicolon</u>

A semicolon (;) indicates that there are two separate pieces of information in a sentence. It is used for the following purposes:

- **To join two related clauses:**

  - Alexander is a well-known local businessman; he is also mayor.

  - Anne went to Austria from Frankfurt; she stopped en route
    in Stuttgart for a few hours.

In these examples, clauses could have been joined by **and** ⇒ a coordinating conjunction.

You can also write each example as two separate short sentences, ending each with a full stop. A semicolon, like the full stop, indicates that these are separate but related short sentences.

- **To join clauses that are linked by a conjunction in order to place greater emphasis on the following clause:**

  The following examples make clear this rule:

  - All motor cars must be fitted with seatbelts; and both the
    driver and passengers must fasten their seatbelts correctly.

  - It is not true to say that poverty is man-made; but it is the result
    of many complicated and inter-related factors.

- **To separate groups within a list which may have a number of commas in each group:**

  For example:

  - We publish computer programming, Web design and
    information technology books; we represent American and
    Australian medical, engineering and science books publishers;
    we also supply technical, medical and IT periodicals through the
    post to our regular subscribers both at home and abroad.

  - You should demonstrate both written and spoken working
    knowledge of German and French; explain how European Union

laws are incorporated and implemented at governmental levels in France and Germany; and the way industry and commerce operate in these countries.

In these examples, semicolons have created groups within the list. The elements in each group are separated by commas. In essence, semicolons eliminate the overuse of coordinating conjunctions and refine long sentences by balancing them well.

- **To create a pause when preceded by an adverb or conjunction such as *nevertheless, moreover, hence, besides, also, consequently, that is to say*:**

  For instance:

  - In city centres car speed is limited; moreover, honking your car horn aimlessly is prohibited.

  - She is really self-motivated; hence, she always completes her task on time.

  - Elizabeth is friendly, rich and generous ; therefore she has many friends.

. Slash

A slash functions as a separator. It is also known as bar, diagonal, oblique mark, solidus, and stroke. Some of its uses are as follows:

- **To indicate alternatives:**

  - Tea/Coffee   ⇐ instead of *or* a slash is used

  - Dear Sir/Madam (may be ended with or without a comma)

  - We vote now/adjourn the meeting for lunch.

  - True/False

  - He/she can stand for the election of club secretary.

- **To indicate fiscal (connected with the government's financial year), academic, accounting and similar fixed periods of time:**

  - Tax Year 2003/04

  - Academic year 2003/04

  - Balance Sheet for the Period 2001/02

- **To form part of certain abbreviations:**

  - I/O   ⇐   Input – output in the computing world

  - A/C No. 1200   ⇐ Account = A/C

  - Send it to me c/o John Smith   ⇐   c/o = care of

    - We must **w/o** these long outstanding bad debts.

  w/o = write off ↵

- The slash is also used for some specific purposes in scientific, technical and Information Technology (IT) fields. It has two forms in IT. These are a forward slash (/) and a backslash(\). Personal Computers and Internet users deal with these types on a regular basis.

. Asterisk

The symbol for the **asterisk** is a star (*). It is used for the following purposes:

- **To indicate a reference, a footnote or an explanation given at the bottom of the text or elsewhere on the same page:**

  - First-degree burns affect the very top layer of the skin.*

    * Hazel Courtney with Gareth Zeal in
    500 of the Most Important Health Tips 2001.

Some people prefer to use superscript numbers instead of the asterisk.

- **To indicate omission of letters in taboo words:**

  - He is really a gentle person who rarely loses his temper.
    He was understandably annoyed and shouted, 'F *** off!'

- **To show the importance of a particular word or phrase:**

  - The items out of stock are marked with an asterisk and
    should be re-order by tomorrow:

       ISBN 19011 97808
       ISBN 1901197 883*
       ISBN 1901197 999
       ISBN 1901197 700*

It is also one of the symbols used in some dictionaries to indicate
important points.

- ## Word-processing symbols (or marks)
  (bullets, bolds, italics, underlining and arrows, etc.)

We are in the age of IT and increasingly using word-processors. There
are many symbols now that were not available on typewriters. These
symbols or marks should be used sensibly.

Bullets have been increasingly appearing in printed material. In this
book bullets are used in order:

- To begin a heading so that it can stand out as the start of another
  section.

- To form part of numbering system for examples.

- To show the importance of the text to follow.

- To summarise points made or show conclusions.

* To use bold, italics, underlining techniques, and arrows which can help the reader in the following ways:

<u>Bolds, italics, underlining and arrows are used for the following functions:</u>

* To highlight the importance of a word, phrase, or a larger piece of text by means of **bold,** *italics* and <u>underlining</u> tools.

* To pinpoint a particular word, phrase, or a clause in a sentence by means of an arrow (⇐ ↵ ⇓). In many places in this book, this technique is applied.

* To clarify the pinpointed text by giving further information on its nature and function. You can also make the pinpointed text larger so that it can stand out.

These techniques can only be applied if you use a word-processor. These are very useful tools when the writer wants the reader to easily comprehend the idea being introduced and discussed. These means of marking text are new and on the periphery of punctuation. With the passage of time, they will be well recognised and used, especially by science, technical, and text books writers. Use them if you think they will help you clarify the text.

In summary, punctuation marks enable us to join, separate, and manipulate words, phrases, clauses, and paragraphs. In addition, these marks can enhance the meaning of a piece of writing irrespective of its size.

Over to You

1. Punctuate the following passages:

a) The importance of language skills in a literate society can hardly be exaggerated. People are judged on how they speak, **and** nearly all academic teaching is done by means of language. so anyone who

has not achieved an average standard in literacy is likely to be
seen as deficient across a wide range of skills.

b) humour is a diffuse fuzzy sort of thing a matter of taste and
something you do not expect to find in even the most sophisticated
computer unless it has been programmed in by human beings

c) unlike space time as we understand has a direction there is
an asymmetry between the past fixed and the future yet to exist
times arrow is whatever gives time this direction

d) its my nature to be like i am she said I was fated to be
unhappy I believe you can learn to be happy and healthy
i replied

e) the man mr Joe Bloggs, was reported present when the morning
roll call was taken though officials are not sure now whether it was
he in fact who replied present

f) did people really speak this way of course they did but as with
many other aspects of the language the words and phrases which
people use change and change again as the years go by

g) this woman was still unemployed she had neither money nor
prospects even so her world was relatively good for she was
at peace with herself she was not eating away at her health her
resolve and stamina with angry self-defeating thoughts she was
not filling her mind with negative ideas positive thinking helped
her to take great strides she could sleep at night her stomach
was better and she didnt blow her top like she used to in
other words she was learning how to make the world a great
place to be with her positive attitude soon she found a new
job a well paid job in fact well done!

h) a week later I was thrilled to see Nancy open her eyes and gaze at
me with loving recognition from that day her recovery was swift
Although she regained her usual weight she bore one sad scar of her
nearly fatal illness her legs were paralyzed as both armies waited for
sunrise, a tempest arose and dawn was darkened by dust clouds so

that men could scarce behold one another evil were the omens blood dropped like rain out of heaven while jackals howled impatiently and kites and vultures screamed hungrily for human flesh.

i) It is necessary to return to those centuries which followed after the fall of the roman empire north of the alps in europe in the first centuries AD the romans crumbled under the repeated onslaughts of those tribes who were part of the great and still mysterious migration westwards from the asian steppes in the fifth century one of the most infamous tribal leaders attila king of huns made his base in the fertile plains of the middle Danube he gave the region the name by which it is still known to most of the world hungary attila c.406-53 Hunnish King 434/53 his dominion extended from rhine to the caspian sea chambers dictionary of world history 1994

J) The following members have won prizes sarah dean first prize £1000 one thousand pounds robert mcDonald second prize £200 two hundred pounds natasha robinson third prize £50 fifty pounds our annual membership fee in accordance with the cost of living index will rise to £55 fifty-five pounds from £50 from 1st January next year finally our revenue for the year just ended amount to £550 000

Over to You
Suggested Answers

Chapter 1

1. Your explanation should include:

- distinct sound – can be a combination of sounds

- intended meaning or definition of the word

- word's structure so that it can be recognised when written

- Use any English word to explain the above requirements for the recognition of a word – both spoken and written.

2. The following particles/adverbial particles are used in the question in the order listed below:

   up, about, ahead, off, down, away, in, back, over,
   out, together, on, apart, around, forward, by, fallen.

Each particle comes after the verb in each sentence. For instance:

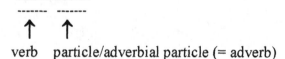

                  verb   particle/adverbial particle (= adverb)

<u>Remember:</u>

Verb + particle(adverbial particle) = Phrasal Verb

Chapter 2

1.

Proper Nouns:

John Smith, Jane Clarke, Epping Forest (a particular place),
Forest Hotel, London (also a particular place), British, England,
Ireland.

John Smith and Jane Clarke are proper names, because they refer to
distinct individuals. Of course, John, Jane, Smith and Clarke are also
proper nouns when these are names of specific individuals.

Common Nouns:

secretary, delegates, countries, hotel, bedroom/s, bathroom,
restaurant, cafeteria, hall, recreation, facilities, amenities,
adult, children, delegates, ideas, information, book, trade,
trading, conditions, requirements, pressure, multimedia,
publishers, products, booksellers, aims, discount, structures,
representatives, distributors, wholesalers, goods, ordering
(the way in which something is arranged or ordered), facilities,
accounts, president, persons, members.

Collective Nouns:

UK Branch, International Association of Booksellers,
conference, seminar, forum, Multimedia Book Forum,
Booksellers Clearing House.

aristocracy	club	crew	population
army	college	enemy	public (takes plural verb)
association	committee	family	police (takes plural verb)
board	community	majority	seminar
choir	company	management	team
class	council	media	university

Collective nouns refer to group of people, institutions, companies.

teams, animals and the like. Some collective nouns are listed above.

> The phrase **en suite** is not a noun. It may be used as an adjective or adverb. It is derived from French and used in standard English. It means a bathroom joined onto a bedroom and for use only by persons in that bedroom.

2.

Compound nouns:

alarm clock, credit card, human being, brother-in-law, letter-box, heart attack, passers-by, police constables, breakfast time, weekdays, address book.

3.

Concrete Nouns

computer, desk, bird, king, village, college, factory, bus, yoghurt, navy, sunglasses, committee, human being, guided missile, manager, central heating, chocolate.

Abstract Nouns

answer, hunger, relationship, allusion, allergy, beauty, admiration, love, remedy, sympathy, taste, contrast, dislike, desire, need, threat, human rights, dishonesty, aims.

4.

. An independent **team of** expert doctors gave their evidence.
. A **group of** international students will arrive from Paris.
. A **family of** eight persons were made homeless by this new law.
. He bought a **bunch of** fresh flowers for his wife.
. A **herd of** cattle will be transported to Holland.
. You can see a **flock of** sheep over there.
. The <u>**Government of**</u> India <u>**have/has**</u> increased travelling restrictions.

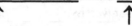

         countable noun   use either singular or plural verb form

In this example, it means a group of people who are controlling India.

It also has **uncountable meaning**(uncountable noun). In this case, it means a particular system or method of controlling a country. As an uncountable noun it takes a singular verb after it, e.g., the British Government **has** a new vision. Often **the** (determiner) precedes this noun.

5.

singular nouns together with their plural nouns

singular Noun	Plural Noun	Singular Noun	Plural Noun
activity	activities	army	armies
attempt	attempts	bonus	bonuses
authority	authorities	bridge	bridges
beer	beers	cloth	clothes
coupon	coupons	demand	demands
effect	effects	driver	drivers
experience	uncountable **	foot	feet
goose	geese	journey	journeys
knee	knees	kitchenware	uncountable **
lady-in- waiting	ladies-in waiting	manner	manners
neighbour	neighbours	ownership	uncountable **
a pair of * pyjamas	pyjamas – only plural form - it has two parts for two legs	query	queries
reef	reefs	meeting	meetings
a pair of * trousers	trousers – only plural form - it has two parts for two legs	sleeping bag	sleeping bags
tax	taxes	thought	thoughts
unemployment	uncountable **	weatherman	weathermen

* She wore a pair of blue trousers/pyjamas.
** these are uncountable nouns and have only one form.

Chapter 3

1. The following personal and possessive pronouns are inserted:

Personal Pronouns

a) •We sell most-------------. **They** are also printed outside London.

     subjective personal pronoun ↵
     as it is in the subject position

b) • My friends wrote ------------------I wrote to **them**.

             objective personal pronoun ↵
             as it is in the object place

c) • We have just received----------. **It** has 500 pages.

      subjective personal pronoun ↵

d) • He was here----- We were enjoying talking with **him.**

          objective personal pronoun ↵

e) • This job----- me. I have done **it** before.

     objective personal pronoun↵

Possessive Pronouns

f) •They telephoned us-----.I cannot guess **their** reason for doing so......

      possessive pronoun dependent form ↵
      because it is used with a noun ⇒ **reason**

g) • Certainly, this old car is not **mine**. I ....motorcycle.

        possessive pronoun↵
        independent form because it is used in place of a noun

h) . At last, we bought-------. It is **ours**.

           possessive pronoun↵

           independent form used in place of a noun

i) . My wife and------ guests. They were **our** old friends

           possessive pronoun ↵

dependent form as it is used with a noun phrase ⟹ old friends

j) . There is a big difference between our opinions and **theirs**.

           possessive pronoun↵

           independent form used in place of a noun

2. The following reflexive pronouns are inserted:
himself, ourselves, itself, yourself, herself, himself.

3.

a) It should be **yourself** ⟹ reflexive pronoun when referring to
one person **you**.

b) It should be **yourselves**⟹ reflexive pronoun when
referring more than one person – **you**.

c) Usually reflexive pronouns are not used with some action verbs if
the result of the action is on the person performing the action.
Therefore the correct sentence is: **I have not shaved since
last Monday**.

d) For the reason given in c) above, the correct sentence is:
She is dressing to go out with her friend.

e) In this sentence, the action verb **wash** is used with the reflexive
pronoun **himself** in order to emphasise that the grandfather, once
again, can perform the action of washing. The idea is to emphasise
that grandfather can do something (washing) that he was not able
to do before without some help.

f) In this statement the use of **myself** is justified on the ground that it is used here to indicate that the action of cooking was performed without any help by the person ⇒ **myself**.

g) She saw the burglar herself with her own eyes. Here, the use of the reflexive pronoun **herself** is to emphasise that the action 'saw' was performed by herself.

4.

The following pronouns are required to fill in the blank spaces:

a) . who   ⇒ relative pronoun

b) . who   ⇒ relative pronoun (you may prefer to use⇒ whom)

c) . who   ⇒ relative pronoun (you may prefer to use⇒ whom)

d) . who   ⇒ relative pronoun (you may prefer to use⇒ whom)

e) . which   ⇒ relative pronoun (refers to things)

f) . which   ⇒ relative pronoun (refers to things)

g) . which   ⇒ relative pronoun (refers to things)

h) . who   ⇒ interrogative pronoun

i) . whose   ⇒ interrogative pronoun

j) . which   ⇒ interrogative pronoun

k) . what   ⇒ interrogative pronoun

l) . which   ⇒ interrogative pronoun

m) . whom   ⇒ interrogative pronoun

n) . whom   ⇒ interrogative pronoun

o) . this   ⇒ demonstrative pronoun

p) . these   ⇒ demonstrative pronoun

q) . each other ⇒ reciprocal pronoun

r) . one another ⇒ reciprocal pronoun

s) . no one   ⇒ indefinite pronoun

t) . everyone or everybody ⇒ indefinite pronoun

Chapter 4

1.

A large number of verbs have grammatical endings. The vast majority of English verbs are regular. Their verb endings are formed by changing the bare infinitive, root form or stem of the verb. Thus the changing of the base form(root form/ infinitive form/stem) of the verb is called verb inflection. In accordance with the verb inflection (or just inflection), a regular verb can have an **s/es form**, **ed-form** or **ing-form**. The changed form of the verb is known as an **inflected verb**.

The following sentences are constructed by using inflected verbs:

• John is **singing** tonight at our party.   ⇐ **ing-form** from sing

• She was **living** in London for five years. ⇐ **ing-form** from live

• They **worked** very hard tonight. ⇐ **ed-form** from work

• I am **pleased** to see you again. ⇐ **ed-form** from please

• He plays cricket very well. ⇐ **s-form** from play

• Rita goes away now. ⇐ **es-form** from go

2.

Regular verbs change their forms in accordance with the rules as outlined above in answer 1. There are four forms of regular verbs as illustrated below. There are some regular verbs such as **try,** which also change their forms according to the rules but **y** becomes **ie** before adding –s(**try** ⇒ **tries** ⇒ **trying** ⇒ **tried**).

Irregular verbs are not as common as regular verbs. There are about 300 in total. They also change their forms but do not obey any set of rules. There are three forms of irregular verb as exemplified below.

★★

Two examples of regular verb forms

Base form	Present form -s/es -form	Participle form ing -form	Past participle form ed- form
laugh	laughs	laughing	laughed
push	pushes	pushing	pushed

Two examples of irregular verb forms

Base form	Past tense Form	Past participle form
do	did	done
throw	threw	thrown

3.

Transitive verbs	Intransitive verbs	Function as transitive and intransitive verbs
granted designed rejected	happened waiting	*arrested, talked, united, rush, cried, closed, cook, coughed, love,

* when it is used to mean that someone's heart stops beating, e.g.
He **arrested** in the car on the way to the hospital.

----

functioning as an **intransitive verb**

But in:

    e) it is functioning as ⟹ **transitive verb**

A transitive verb cannot stand alone and thus it takes an object in a sentence, e.g. I want **a cup of tea**.

                    ----

                object ↵

An intransitive verb can stand alone as well as can be followed by a prepositional phrase in a sentence, e.g.

I work **for a large company**.

      ----

prepositional phrase ↵

On the other hand in the sentence: **I work,** the verb work does not need an object or a prepositional phrase.

4.

Active voice	Passive voice
b)	a)
f)	c)
g)	d)
h)	e)

• If the subject performs the action, the voice is active.

• If the subject is the recipient of the action, the voice is passive.

5.

Infinitive	Participle	Gerund
a)		working
b) to-infinitive-**to post**	past participle/**got**	
c) to-infinitive-**to finish**	past participle/**asked**	
d) to-infinitive- **to do**		
e)		gardening
f) to-infinitive – **to finish**	past participle/ **ordered**	
g)		walking

Infinitive	Participle	Gerund
h)		going
i)	participle –ing form/**buying**	
j)		
j) bare infinitive/**mind**		waiting

- Bare infinitive is the base form of the verb.

- to-infinitive is when the bare infinitive is preceded by the word **to**.

- Participle endings are – **ing** or –**ed**

- Gerund has endings like the particle but it functions as a noun.

6. Blank spaces are filled in with words shown in **bold style**:

a) Can you **fix** up a meeting?

b) We were looking **at** the photo.

c) Their car's noise woke us **up**.

d) Please do not **throw** away these papers.

e) Mary **looks** after her sick mother.

f) Fame has crept **up** on him after just one television appearance.

g) Don't just fool **around/about**.

h) I do not wish to hang **about** here.

i) I cannot put **up** with this sort of behaviour.

h) You ought to get **out** of the house more.

i) She gave **away** one million pounds to charity.

j) We must set **up** a new system for dealing **with** so many claims.

k) He is so humble that he always talks **down** his own achievements.

7. Auxiliary verbs such as **be**, **do** and **have** are used with main verbs such as **run**, **smile**. etc. Auxiliaries are divided into primary and modal auxiliaries. Without the auxiliaries, you cannot express all kinds of meanings.

a) **have** ⇒ primary auxiliary verb used with the past participle to form present perfect

b) **could** ⇒ modal auxiliary verb used with the infinitive asking permission

c) **should** ⇒ modal auxiliary verb used with the infinitive indicating possibility or to predict the future

d) **must** ⇒ modal auxiliary verb used with the infinitive to emphasize necessity.

e) **ought to** ⇒ modal auxiliary verb pointing to an obligation in the form of advice

f) **might** ⇒ modal auxiliary verb used with the primary auxiliary **have** to indicate a possibility

g) **should** ⇒ modal auxiliary verb used with primary auxiliary **have** to imply an expectation

h) may ⇒ modal auxiliary verb used to give formal permission.

i) could ⇒ modal auxiliary verb used to request help - it indicates an appeal for help in the form of instructions

J) could ⇒ modal auxiliary verb indicating a possibility in the future

k) **will** ⇒ modal auxiliary verb indicating certainty

l) **shall** ⇒ modal auxiliary verb used with the primary auxiliary **be** in order to indicate a future outcome - certainty

m) **could** ⇒ modal auxiliary verb used to show ability

n) **will** ⇒ modal auxiliary verb used with the primary auxiliary **be** to express doing something - **ability**

o) **can** ⇒ modal auxiliary verb used to indicate negative certainty under unfavourable circumstances

p) **may** ⇒ modal auxiliary verb used here to offer help- it is less common now than can which is illustrated below

q) **can** ⇒ modal auxiliary verb used here to specify an offer of help

r) **shall** ⇒ modal auxiliary verb used here to make a suggestion

s) **will** ⇒ modal auxiliary verb its short form is **won't** - it is used to show one's unwillingness to do something.

t) **have** ⇒ primary auxiliary verb used here with the **to-infinitive verb** emphasizing the importance of the intended meaning.

Chapter 5

1.

Finite verb	**Non-finite verb**
a) leave	b) to remedy
b) took	d) to help
c) interrogated	e) to know
d) tried	g) to come
e) want	h) to be assured
f) denied	J) to telephone
g) wished	k) bleeding
h) wanted	l) to work
i) crowded	m) do deliver
j) trying	n) to do
K) found	o) having seen
l) reported	
m) prepared	
n) wondered	
o) recalled	

* Finite verb inflects for tense and agrees in number with the subject.

* Non-finite verb does not change its form for tense.

2. Highlighted words are inserted in blank spaces. Required tenses are indicated with the aid of arrows below:

a) I **am** happy. ⇐ simple present

b) They **are** going to the beach now. ⇐ present progressive

c) Two years ago, she **was** in England for three years. ⇐simple past

d) Recently, Harry **has** written to us from Cambridge.
   present perfect↵

e) On my arrival, I **will** write to you from Spain. ⇐simple future

f) Now we **are** watching a film. ⇐present progressive/continuous

g) Last week they **were** skiing in Switzerland.

   past progressive ↵

h) Not long ago, they **have** travelled to France. ⇐ present perfect

i) Last year, we **had** the Indian summer in the UK. ⇐ past perfect

j) She **had** never ridden a horse before she joined our club.
   ⇑
   past perfect

k) You must believe me I did not think that I **would** come First
   in London Marathon Race this year. ⇐simple future in the past

l) The Indian summer **has** returned today. ⇐ present perfect

m) We will **be** arriving at 14.000 hours at Victoria Coach
   Station. ⇐ future progressive

n) Most certainly, I **will** be staying at The Regents Hotel in Paris.
   future progressive ↵

o) By that time, we will **have** retired. ⇐ future perfect

p) The weatherman told us that it **was** going to rain all that day.
   past progressive ↵

q) He had **been** talking to me. ⇐ past perfect progressive

r) At that time our train will **have** been travelling through ⇐ future
   the tunnel.   perfect progressive

s) By that time, We **would** have returned to France.
   ⇑
   future perfect in the past

t) At the end of this year, we **would have** been living in this house
   for ten years. ⇐ future perfect progressive in the past

u) Indeed, she promised that she **would** be <u>writing</u> to me soon about our plans for the future. ⇑

        future progressive in the past

v) During our visit to Paris last year, you indicated that you **would have** been <u>moving</u> to another flat. ⇐ future perfect progressive in the past

w) We all knew Jane would **be** <u>working</u> at the post office. ⇑

        future progressive in the past

x) Your father told me that you **had** <u>served</u> your country in Bosnia. past perfect↵

y) I have **been** <u>showing</u> our learning resources to new colleagues. ⇑

present perfect

z) We **are** <u>having</u> torrential rain now. ⇑

present progressive

3.

    <u>**Answer is on the next page.**</u>

4.

    a) There **are** three reasons for not accepting their invitation.

simple present ↵ - tense . Subject and the verb should agree.

    b) If we had been requested for help in this matter, we **would have taken** all the necessary steps to protect her.

past perfect ↵ -tense . Past perfect tense is needed.

    c) She was disappointed that her daughter **would** not be travelling to England to see her mother. ⇐ future progress

    d) They asked her if she **would** be accepting this post. ⇐ future progress

3.

Table
A Summary of Tenses Passive Voice

Present Simple	Past Simple	Future Simple	Simple future in the Past
It is eaten	It was eaten	It will be eaten	It should/ would be eaten
Present Progressive	**Past Progressive**	**Future Progressive**	**Future Progressive in the Past**
It is being eaten	It was being eaten	It will be being eaten*	It should/ would be being eaten*
Present Perfect	**Past Perfect**	**Future Perfect**	**Future Perfect in the Past**
It has been eaten	It had been eaten	It will have been eaten	It should/ would have been eaten
Present Perfect Progressive	**Past Perfect Progressive**	**Future Perfect Progressive**	**Future Perfect Progressive in the Past**
It has been being eaten*	It had been being eaten*	It will have been being eaten*	It should/ would have been being eaten*

* these are seldom used.

Chapter 6

1.

a) **stronger = correct** because it is a comparison between two states

b) **loveliest = wrong**. No comparison - use lovely - positive form

c) **fuller = wrong**. It should be **full.** No comparison here

d) **fuller = correct** because it is used to compare normal clothes with clothes designed for larger people

e) **smaller = wrong**. No comparison intended. It should be **small**

f) **less = wrong**. Since we are comparing John's salary with the salary of everybody in the group, it is better to use **least**. It is the lower degree comparison and John 's salary is the lowest = least

g) **very ill = correct**. 'ill' is gradable adjective. Very is an adverb of degree which is used here to intensify the meaning

h) **most = incorrect**. It should be **more** to compare two boxers

i) **wiser = wrong**. It should be **wise** as no comparison intended.

j) **rather advisable =correct**. adverb **rather** is used to intensify the meaning of this adjective

k) **almost empty** = correct. No comparison made except to quantify the adjective empty

l) **tall and thinnest** = wrong. It should be **tall and thinner** comparative form is needed because it is a comparison of two physical states

m) **somewhat depressed** =correct. adverb somewhat is modifying the adjective depressed by reducing its effect/meaning

n) **confused** = correct because it is used here to describe the manner in which she was affected

o) **most clever = correct**. Also correct = **cleverest** ⇒ superlative

p) **extremely narrow = correct**. The meaning of the adjective is intensified by the adverb ⟹ extremely

q) **brighter = wrong**. It should be **bright**. The colour is specified by using a pre-modifier such as **bright, pale, light, dark** or **deep**.

r) **sufficient = correct**.

s) **most perfect = wrong**. It should be **perfect** because it has absolute meaning and is usually not used for comparison.

t) **British = correct** adjective. It is connected with the United Kingdom of great Britain and Northern Ireland.

2.   **Modifiers**   **Adjectives**

a) so ⟹ adverb   tired

b) absolutely ⟹ adverb

c) not at all ⟹ adverbial phrase   informative, interesting

d) really ⟹ adverb   nicest (superlative form)

e) by far ⟹ adverbial phrase   best   (superlative form)

f) no ⟹ it is adverb here   better (comparative form)

g) enough ⟹ adverb   warm

h) somewhat ⟹ adverb   crowded

i) pretty ⟹ adverb   sure

j) quite ⟹ adverb   enjoyed

3.

a) Warsaw has a **very interesting old town**.

adverb/intensifier⌐ ⇑   ⇑
               adjective   adjective

When two adjectives come before the noun, usually the adjective giving an opinion is placed before the adjective which is closely associated with the noun.

In this example, **old** is closely related to the noun **town** and **very interested** is expressing someone's opinion.

b) At the present time, our weather is **depressing**.
                                              ----

ing- adjective ↵

A large number of adjectives have **–ing** endings. They look like the present participles but they are words in their own right and listed as such in quality dictionaries.

c) His employers have sent him a **cautiously worded** letter.
                         ---------------- ------------

adverb ↵   ⇑
-ed adjective

Many adjectives have **–ed endings** and thus look like the past participle of a verb. There are many adjectives that are formed by adding **–ed** to a noun, such as worded formed from word.

- Note that here an adverb is necessary because **worded** is one of those adjectives which do not make complete sense without the adverb.

d) **Those nice** people came from Egypt for the conference.
   -------- -----

   1   2

1 = is a demonstrative adjective - modifying the noun ⇒ **people**
It is pointing out the noun and that is why it is called demonstrative

2 = is descriptive adjective but it tells us the quality of people ⇒ **nice**

e) **Which local** hotel are you booking for the party?
   -------- ------

   1   2

1= interrogative adjective – asking for information about the hotel
2 = descriptive adjective – qualifying the noun as local

Chapter 7

1. Adverb /adverbial	**Type of adverb**
a) softly modifying the verb ⇒ held	adverb of manner
b) regularly modifying the verb ⇒ telephone	adverb of frequency
c) too modifying the verb ⇒ expensive	adverb of degree
d) abruptly modifying the verb ⇒ ended	adverb of manner
e) certainly modifying the verb ⇒ made	adverb of truth
f) hardly modifying the verb ⇒ cover	adverb of truth/ telling how likely it is to be true
g) afterwards modifying the verb ⇒ took	adverb of time
h) even focusing on ⇒ Sundays	focus adverbial it focuses on a word/phrase it is a special use
i) below modifying the verb ⇒ took	adverb of place/position directing to a place
J) economically - modifying the adjective⇒ beneficial	adverb of focus/point of view
k) much modifying the comparative adjective⇒better	adverb of degree

Adverb /adverbial	Type of Adverb
l) where modifying ⟹ will meet	adverb of place
m) anti-clockwise modifying ⟹ drove	adverb of direction/place
n) most modifying another adverb ⟹ likely	adverb of attitude
o) intentionally	adverb of purpose

2.

Adjectives	Adverbs
alarming	alarmingly
brilliant	brilliantly
continual	continually
depressing	depressingly
extreme	extremely
elegant	elegantly
frightening	frighteningly
gross	gross
horrible	horribly
immense	immensely
independent	independently
light- hearted	light-heartedly
misleading	misleadingly
nationwide	nationwide
off-hand	offhandedly(no hyphen in it)
ragged	raggedly
sleepy	sleepily
underground	underground
worried	worriedly
wrongful	wrongfully

3.

- It is alarming news. ⇐ adjective

- This year prices have been rising alarmingly. ⇐ adverb

- It is a brilliant answer. ⇐ adjective

- Our plan worked brilliantly. ⇐ adverb

- Our children are a continual source of pleasure to us. ⇐ adjective

- Business software is continually being developed. ⇐ adverb

- I find this film very depressing in a variety of ways. ⇐ adjective

- He told us depressingly about his experience in Africa . ⇐ adverb

- I find his political views extreme. ⇐ adjective

- It is extremely difficult to get on with him. ⇐ adverb

- Elena is tall and elegant just like her mother. ⇐ adjective

- Anne is always elegantly dressed. ⇐ adverb

- It is frightening to think that it can happen to us all. ⇐ adjective

- He spoke frighteningly about his sad experience. ⇐ adverb

- Our gross profit is higher this year. ⇐ adjective

- I earn £30000 a year gross. ⇐ adverb

- I have got a horrible feeling we will not arrive on time.⇐ adjective

- His idea of renting a car went horribly wrong. ⇐ adverb

- The benefits of this new scheme are immense.⇐ adjective

- Once he was immensely popular on the radio. ⇐ adverb

- Mr. Brown is a man of independent means. ⇐ adjective

- It was the first time that I had travelled independently. ⇐ adverb

* It was a light-hearted party. ⇐ adjective

* The conference progressed light-heartedly. ⇐ adverb

* Please do not give us misleading information. ⇐ adjective

* Her eloquent speech misleadingly made us believe her. ⇐ adverb

* They have launched a nationwide campaign. ⇐ adjective

* Our bank has 200 branches nationwide in the UK. ⇐ adverb

* John was very offhand with Peter last night. ⇐ adjective

* I cannot tell you offhand when they placed the last order. ⇐ adverb

* Martin was wearing a ragged jacket. ⇐ adjective

* Mandy is raggedly dressed these days. ⇐ adverb

* I am afraid I am beginning to feel sleepy. ⇐ adjective

* He yawned sleepily. ⇐ adverb

* Our water authority is replacing underground pipes. ⇐ adjective

* The local gang leader went underground to avoid arrest. ⇐ adverb

* He always looks so worried. ⇐ adjective

* My mother worriedly said goodbye to me. ⇐ adverb

* It is a wrongful dismissal from his managerial post. ⇐ adjective

* He was wrongfully convicted ten years ago. ⇐ adverb

4.

a) Often one can buy fruit cheaper in the market.

An adverb of frequency usually is in the mid position in the sentence. Thus **often** is in the wrong place in this sentence.

* cheaper is an adjective ⇒ comparative form

- It is suggested to re-write it as:

    One can buy fruit **often** cheap(or cheaply) in the market.

b) Here the use of an adverb should be in the **comparative form**. It should be re-written with **more** as:

    She told the grocer that she could buy this **more** cheaply at a supermarket.

c) **On the left** – this is an adverbial phrase which is modifying the noun gentleman. It is in the wrong position as usually an adverb or adverbial phrase comes after the noun which it modifies.

It should be : The gentleman **on the left** is my uncle.

d) Usually is in the wrong place. An adverb of frequency **usually** goes in the mid position in the sentence. **It should be:** This car park usually is full.

e) In this sentence the position of the adverb **probably** is correct. An adverb can come after the subject and before the negative form of the verb phrase such as does not.

f) The position of the adverb such as **purposely**, **deliberately** and similar adverbs depend on what is the intended meaning. If the intended meaning is to say that he has chosen not to greet, then the position of the adverb purposely is **correct.**

    On the other hand, if the intending meaning is to say that he did not greet because of a mistake or did not get a chance to greet, then it should be re-written as:

    - He did not **purposely** greet avoiding his opponents.

g) **much** is an adverb of degree modified by the adverb of degree to intensified the meaning of the adverb **much**. As an adverb of degree it can be used at the end of a statement.

h) The use of adverbial phrase **even more rapidly** in the given order and position in the sentence is correct. The reason is that the adverb

even can be used before another adverb, if we wish to focus on it. This is a comparative use of the adverbial phrase.

Chapter 8

1. The required prepositions are **highlighted** below:

a) The lady who is sitting almost **at** the end of the second row.

b) When he was waiting **for** his wife outside the supermarket.

c) You must be ready **before** I arrive **at** 06 hours.

d) We drove **through** the Channel Tunnel **to** France.

e) My desk is **next to** Karen's desk **on** the third floor.

f) When I was going **up** the stairs and she was coming **down** the steps, we spoke to each other.

g) She wrote to my boss angrily **against** his cleaning rota schedule.

h) **At** that time, we went **to** the cinema **with** our French guests.

i) We were walking **along** the path, when we suddenly appeared.

j) During the tea break, he came **up** to me and introduced himself.

k) **After** winning the jackpot, she became famous overnight.

l) The intruder disguised himself **as** a policeman.

m) Silvia (Sylvia) is more intelligent **than** Clair.

n) She is a colleague **of** my wife.

o) Our government ought to do everything **within** their power to stop increasing gun related crimes.

p) You will find a package **by** the main gate.

q) I wandered **round** their beautiful garden.

r) Please take your hand **off** my shoulder.

s) I cannot copy it now as our machine is **out of order**.

---

idiomatic phrase using **out** and **of** prepositions↵

t) **On the way** to Scotland, we had lunch in the Lake District in
England. (idiomatic phrase using the preposition ⟹ **on**)

2.

a) • basic and applied ⟹ adjectives

   • some ⟹adverb   and • of ⟹preposition

b) • worldwide ⟹ adjective

   • still ⟹adverb

   • of and for ⟹ preposition

c) • distinct and • spontaneous ⟹ adjectives

   • quite, more, evenly, slowly, now, almost, just and
   certainly are all ⟹ adverbs

   • up ⟹adverb but it is used with **conjure** (verb) to form

   • conjure up ⟹ phrasal verb

   • **just now** - in this phrase both words are adverbs and
   forming an idiomatic phrase

   • from, for, by and without are all ⟹ prepositions

d) • constantly ⟹adverb

   • hard-working and healthy are ⟹ adjectives

   • with⟹ prepositions

e) • encouraging $\Rightarrow$ adjectives

     • just $\Rightarrow$ adverb and • for $\Rightarrow$ preposition

     • Since **than** is used before a noun to express a comparison, it is functioning here as a preposition.

3.

A) **In** the garden everything was very colourful.

b) Our plane landed **at** Frankfurt Airport on time.

c) This is my Hungarian friend whose home I stay **at**.

d) We are looking **into** what has to be ordered.

e) Has the medical nurse been sent **<u>for</u>**?

f) There is something strange **about** him.

g) My wife was very much worried **about** what to wear tonight.

h) I told the policeman that I did not have my driving licence **with** me.

i) To be successful **in** life, you must believe **in** yourself.

j) They cut **down** their tree a month ago.

    cut down $\Rightarrow$ prepositional phrase/phrasal verb

k) I have received some DVD's from a friend to listen **to**.
In this case, the preposition **to** is needed, as the verb phrase is **listen to** somebody/something.

l) I haven't met him **since** last Christmas.

m) We arrived **on** time **at** 23.00 hours.
     ------

     punctuality⏎

n) Our guests arrived **in** time for the evening meal.

to mean early enough↵

o) Could I please use this desk **instead of** the other desk?

a preposition is essential ↵ - group/compound preposition

p) **In** the course of our discussion, she became rather angry.

q) How long did you stay in Berlin? I stayed in Berlin **for a** week.

r) I was lucky **in that** I had a friend in Warsaw to call for help.

Here the preposition is forming an idiomatic expression and essential

---

Chapter 9

1.

a) We all know that **a** bicycle does not run on petrol.
   the indefinite article before the singular noun is needed
   Here we are referring to bicycles in general – not uniqueness

b) You should get **the** parcel on Friday as it is a special delivery.
   the definite article requires as you are referring to a particular
   parcel

c) There is a lot to show **a** visitor.
   a – the indefinite article is required – here visitor is not unique

d) She was **the** only woman I loved.
   the is used with **only** and superlative adjectives

e) He is **the** right person for this job.
   the is used with **right** and superlative adjectives

f) We invited some friends for lunch. Luckily **the** sun was brilliantly

bright in the afternoon. no determiner before ⇒ lunch
there is only one sun and thus **the** comes before ⇒ sun

g) In the dark, I was searching for **the** switch button of my radio.
radio has one switch button **the** switch button ⇒uniqueness

h) Suddenly, **a** car in front of us stopped and **the** driver of this
car ran fast to escape arrest by the police.
Here the indefinite article is required because **car** ⇒ not unique
When referring to its driver the definite article is needed
because now we are referring to a particular driver

i) **The** night Mary was taken ill. night ⇒ a particular event ⇒the

j) Our new car is as big as **the** jeep we saw the other day.
The definite article before jeep as you are referring to a specific jeep.

2.

a) **that** demonstrative determiner because it precedes a
noun ⇒instrument

b) **that** is used as a demonstrative pronoun
used instead of a noun

C) **this** ⇒ demonstrative determiner - noun before it ⇒gentleman
mine ⇒ possessive pronoun – showing a relationship

d) **my** ⇒ possessive determiner – qualifying a singular noun – car

e) **those** ⇒ demonstrative determiner as it is before a noun.

f) **this** ⇒ demonstrative pronoun as it is used instead of a noun

g) **those** ⇒ demonstrative determiner precedes a plural noun –students

h) **which** ⇒ demonstrative pronoun used instead of a noun

i) **which**⇒ demonstrative determiner qualifying the noun car

j) **enough** ⟹ demonstrative determiner qualifying the noun car

3.

  a) **you**⟹ possessive determiner

  b) **whose** ⟹ interrogative determiner

  c) **her** ⟹ possessive determiner

  d) **my** and **their** ⟹ possessive determiners
     (**their** ⟹ possessive form of they)

  e) **some** ⟹ indefinite determiner and **your** ⟹ possessive determiner

  f) **another** ⟹ indefinite determiner

  g) **either** ⟹ indefinite determiner

  h) **their** ⟹ possessive determiner

  i) **which** ⟹ interrogative determiner

  J) **other** ⟹indefinite determiner

4.

  a) **Dear me!** - what else can you do now? indicating ⟹ surprise

  b) **Oh blast!** We won't make it on time. showing ⟹ annoyance

  c) **Good grief!** What a disaster! expressing ⟹ shock

  d) **Good heavens!** What are you doing in my office without
     my permission?   showing ⟹ surprise and annoyance

  e) **Goodness me!** What a wonderful place! expressing ⟹ surprise

  f) How **nice** to see you!

g) What a pleasant **surprise**!

h) **Ow!** It hurts! pointing to ⟹ sudden pain

i) **Whoops!** You almost dropped it on my new carpet. Be careful!
   - giving a warning about ⟹ accident , bad thing to happen

j) **Yuck!** Let's get out of here. expressing ⟹ feeling

Chapter 10

1.

a) **When** our friends visited us, we went to Whitby by the sea.

b) Have some lunch **before** you start your long journey.

c) **If** I were you I 'd start looking for another suitable flat.

d) I am here **just in case** you need my help.

e) I couldn't disappoint him **because** he is a very gentle person.

f) **Provided that** you are 18 years old, you can vote.

g) **Once** I went to Finland for three weeks.

h) Kim behaves **as if** she were the business owner.

i) She loves children **as though** they were her own children.

j) We haven't got a new car. **Neither** have you.

k) Our house was burgled ten years ago **while we** were away abroad.

l) **As soon as** I paid my bill, I left the shop.

m) **Although** rich, she hardly had any quality furniture.

n) We have been living in this house **since** we were children.

o) I'm going to the cinema **whether** someone comes with me **or not**.

2.

a) The traffic lights changed to amber **as** I approached.
　　　　　　　　　　　subordinator ↵

b) It is possible **that** Yvonne has not received our letter.
　　subordinator ↵

c) Our tutor said **that** we can leave **as soon as** we answered the
　　subordinator 1↵　　subordinator 2↵　　　　　　　question.

d) My wife went to the Chelsea Flower Show **and** she enjoyed
　　　　　　　　　　　　　coordinator ↵　　her visit.
　- joining two clauses of equal status/important

e) Our tutor was unhappy **because** we came fifteen minutes late.
　　　　　subordinator ↵

f)　She was very kind to us, **and yet** she hurried us.
　　　　　　　　　　----------

　　　　　two coordinators↵ - units of equal status

g)　Milk **and** sugar.
　　　⇑

　　coordinator – two words ⟹ still units of equal status.

h)　Our roof leaked **whenever** it rained last year.
　　　　subordinator↵

i)　We can finish early **in order to** get ready for the dinner
　　　　subordinator↵　　　and dance tonight.

j)　He is working very hard **so that** the report can be submitted in time.
　　　　　subordinators↵

k)　I liked her very much, **even though** I did not have much chance to
　　　　subordinator↵　　　　　to meet her after work.

l) Hurry up , **or** you'll be late for work.

 coordinator↵ - used here with the imperative clause – hurry up
m) I have no car , **so** I'll hire one just for tomorrow.

        coordinator↵
n) She is not a racist **and** a feminist.

            coordinator↵ - these are clauses of equal status but
                        referring to the same person without

repeating the same subject ⇒ she and the same verb ⇒ is

o) Some of the overseas students are very hard working **whereas**

   others aren't.   subordinator used to compare/contrast↵

Chapter 11

1.

a) We travelled by **a double-decker bus**.

            noun phrase↵
b) You **can leave**.

 verb phrase↵

c) Will it be <u>a big party</u>?

adjective phrase↵

d) <u>On Friday</u> there will be a birthday party <u>at our home</u>.
   ⇑   ⇑

   prepositional phrase   prepositional phrase

e) Doreen writes <u>beautifully</u>.

        adverb phrase↵
f) John **run!**

     ⇑

   verb phrase - verb in the imperative

****

g) Roger's car <u>has been stolen</u>.

      verb phrase↵

h) I remembered that day was <u>very tiring</u>.

               adjective phrase↵

i) <u>For sometime</u>, we have been planning to visit <u>the Taj Mahal</u>.

  ⇑   ⇑

  prepositional phrase   noun phrase

j) I finished <u>that job today</u>.

    noun phrase↵

k) Management seriously consider <u>staff suggestions</u>.

                  noun phrase↵

l) She was <u>very happy</u> because of our visit.

adjective phrase↵

m) <u>How long</u> have you been waiting ?

    ⇑

  adverb phrase (how long = for how long)

n) This car is small <u>for me</u>.

        ⇑

    prepositional phrase

o) Some candidates <u>are being interviewed</u> in the meeting room.

        verb phrase↵

p) His story is <u>almost certainly</u> fabricated.

    adverb phrase↵ certainly with adverb of degree ⇒almost

q) We <u>hardly ever</u> travel overseas.

adverb phrase↵ ever with adverb of degree ⇒hardly

r) I remember that place <u>vaguely</u>.

      adverb phrase↵

s) It is not <u>very difficult</u> work.

  adjective phrase↵

t) Carol is <u>twenty years old</u>.

   adjective phrase↵

u) The situation is <u>problematic</u>.

   adjective phrase↵

2.

A prepositional phrase always has a prepositional complement which is a noun phrase. The reason is that a preposition cannot act alone as the headword of a phrase. For instance:

   • Maria will buy a present **<u>from us all</u>**.

      prepositional phrase ↵ - us all ⟹ **<u>complement</u>**

         noun phrase↵

You can see that the preposition **from** is not functioning alone but in association with its complement. Thus a preposition can be the headword of a phrase but it must be followed by a prepositional complement.

3.

a) Our sales are increasing since the publication of our new title.

Our sales are increasing [since the publication of a new title].

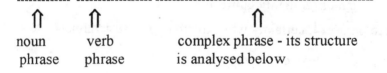

noun   verb   complex phrase - its structure
phrase   phrase   is analysed below

[**since** the publication of a new title] ⟹ prepositional phrase
   [**publication** of a new title] ⟹ noun phrase
      [**of** a new title] ⟹ prepositional phrase

[a new **title**] ⟹ noun phrase*

---

* [a new **title**] ⟹ noun phrase because the adjective **new** is
premodifying the noun – **title** ⟹ **headword Think!!!**

---

b) Our town is crowded [with holiday-makers during the summer
          ---------- ------------   every year].

  ⇑   ⇑

noun phrase verb phrase

[with holiday-makers during the summer every year] is the
complex phrase whose structure is analysed below:

[**with** holiday-makers during the summer every year]

----

          prepositional phrase ↵

[**holiday-makers** during the summer every year] ⟹ noun phrase

    [**during** the summer every year] ⟹ prepositional phrase

      [the **summer** every year] ⟹ noun phrase

        [every **year**] ⟹ noun phrase *

---

* Is [**every** year] ⟹ adjective phrase [**year**] ⟹ noun phrase
possible? Think in terms of the headword -----

---

c) Robin talked about his journey through the forest in Asian Siberia.

Complex phrase in this sentence:

[about his journey through the forest in Asian Siberia]

Its structure is analysed as:

[**about** his journey through the
                    forest in Asian Siberia] ⟹ prepositional phrase

[his **journey** through the forest in Asian Siberia] ⇒ noun phrase

   [**through** the forest in Asian Siberia] ⇒ prepositional phrase

      [the **forest** in Asian Siberia] ⇒ noun phrase

         [**in** Asian Siberia] ⇒ prepositional phrase

           [**Asian Siberia**] ⇒ noun phrase

d) Colin bought [a beautiful fur coat for his wife from an expensive
   ------ --------   store in Moscow Russia].

   ⇑ ⇑   --

noun   verb   ⇑

phrase phrase   complex phrase – it is analysed below

[a beautiful **fur coat** for his wife from an expensive
        store in Moscow Russia] ⇒ noun phrase
[**for** his wife from an expensive
        store in Moscow Russia] ⇒ prepositional phrase
  [his **wife** from an expensive store in Moscow Russia] ⇒ noun
                                phrase
[**from** an expensive store in Moscow Russia] ⇒ prepositional phrase
[an expensive **store** in Moscow Russia] ⇒ noun phrase*
   [**in** Moscow Russia] ⇒ prepositional phrase
     [**Moscow Russia**] ⇒ noun phras

---

* [an expensive **store** in Moscow Russia] ⇒ expensive is
   premodifying the noun **store** - headword.

You have to think in terms of the headword – Which one is the
headword store or expensive? Think!]

4.

       Phrase in apposition:

a) Victoria   ⇒ the Queen of England

b) Mr. Bill Clinton ⟹ the US president

c) Sonia Gandhi ⟹ Italian born Indian politician

d) Marion Faithful⟹ Housewife

Chapter 12

1.   **Phrases**   **Clauses**

        a)   c)
        b)   e)
        d)   f)
        g)   h)
        i)   j)
                k)
                l)

2.

The shortest (minimum) structure of a clause consists of two clause elements. These are subject (s) and verb(v). For example:

> • **She** **laughed.**
> ⇑   ⇑
> s   v

3. The typical structure of a clause consists of three clause elements namely, subject (s), verb (v) and object(o). This structure is illustrated below:

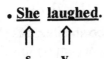

> • Margaret loves flowers.
> ⇑   ⇑ ⇑
> s   v   o

4.

  a) There are five clause elements: subject (s), verb (v), object (o), complement(c) and object(o). All elements may be combined or at least two of them to construct a clause.

b) In the active clause the subject(agent) performs the action. On the other hand, in the passive clause the subject is affected by the action indicated by the verb. For instance:

- I run this sweet shop. ⇐ active voice/active clause

- This sweet shop is run by me. ⇐ passive voice/passive clause

c) - A finite clause has a fine verb which is marked for tense. For example: She **giggles** for nothing.

⇑ - giggles ⇒ finite verb
finite clause (it is also a short sentence)

- A non-finite clause has a verb which is **not marked** for tense. The verb form is to-infinitive. Here is an example:

Sigrid wished **to remain single**.

non-finite clause⤶ - it is without the subject here

d) - A main clause can stand alone but a subordinate clause cannot stand alone. For example:

- I talk. ⇐ main clause as it makes complete sense

- **I came to see you** because I would like to talk to you.
⇑   ⇑
main clause   subordinate clause because it is
                       dependent on the clause

5.

Subordinate clauses	Adverbial clauses
a) when Jane was one year old	clause of time
b) since we arrived here	clause of time
c) in case it rains	clause of reason
d) in order to give a good impression	clause of purpose
e) Whenever we meet each	clause of time
f) except that we had to ask him repeatedly	clause of exception
g) Much as I liked this place	clause of exception

h) Naive as it sounds	clause of exception/ suspicion
i) Though he lived and worked in London for a long time	clause of exception/ contrast
j) so that I can understand you	clause of result
k) In Moscow, wherever I went	clause of place
l) like other visitors to this museum	clause of manner
m) as you do	clause of manner
n) If your car has broken down	clause of condition/ conditional clause
o) if you like	clause of condition/ conditional clause (suggestion)
p) when we returned from Amsterdam	clause of time
q) If I met him in the town	clause of condition/ conditional clause (possibility)
r) If Joanne could afford the air fare to New York	clause of condition/ conditional clause (wish)
s) that she returned home from overseas	clause of result
t) since she is rather a quiet person.	clause of reason

6.

a) I am looking for a young man **who** used to live in this house with his girlfriend.

relative clause ↵ identifying relative clause/ identifying a young man

No comma is needed between identifying and main clauses.

b) I told you **that** it happened on Christmas Day.

noun clause ↵ - it begins with **that**

c) This new car is not as smooth to drive as the salesman told us.

comparative clause ↵ - no comma needed
-began with **as** the second subordinator in this sentence.

d) <u>When I rang this number</u>, no one answered my call.

adverbial clause ↵ - it is an adverbial of time

Chapter 13

1.   <u>Subject</u>   <u>Verb</u>   <u>Complement</u>

a)   A passenger   was taken   ill.
b)   I   kept   some red wine for you.
c)   She   seemed   depressed recently.
d)   Windows software became   world famous quickly.
e)   They   remained   silent and composed during.
                                                       the meeting.

f)   It   proved   totally wrong.
g)   She   has grown   tall and beautiful.
h)   It   was   nice and quiet in that area.
i)   You   sound   a bit disappointed today.
j)   This yogurt   tastes   bitter.

2.

a) **<u>Compound sentence</u>** - it has two clauses of equal status
     joined together by ⟹ **but** ⟹ coordinating conjunction

b) **<u>Complex sentence</u>** - it has two clauses of unequal status
     joined together by ⟹ **since** ⟹ subordinator
     since introduced the subordinate clause

c) **<u>Simple sentence</u>** - it has only subject, verb and complement
     complement is after the **<u>linking verb</u>**

                      be (is) ↵ - complement ⟹adjective phrase

d) **<u>Compound sentence</u>** - two independent clauses joined together
     by a coordinating conjunction ⟹ but

e) **<u>Complex sentence</u>** - it has three clauses:

- subordinate clause 1 began with although ⇒ conjunction
  - it contrasts with the truth statement in the main clause
  - it is an adverbial clause of exception or concessive clause

- subordinate 2 clause began with because ⇒ conjunction
  - it is an adverbial clause of reason

- main clause ⇒ I enjoyed
  - it tells the truth which is contrasted by clause 1

f) <u>**Simple sentence**</u> – it consists of
                          subject + verb + object + **adverbial**

- from a rented small premises ⇒ adverbial phrase

- it refers to the object ⇒ my business

g) <u>**Simple sentence**</u> – it consists of
                          subject + verb + object + **object complement**

- bankrupt ⇒ object complement and it refers to the <u>**object**</u>
                                    John ↵

h) <u>**Compound sentence**</u> - it is composed of three clauses, each of which is an independent clause – can stand alone.

1 - We went to Scarborough
2 - (we) came across Colin Smith
3 - (Colin Smith) was with his family on a day trip to the seaside

These short independent sentences/clauses are joined together by two suitable **conjunctions** to form a compound sentence.

i) <u>**Complex sentence**</u> – it has three clauses:

- it begins with a subordinate and an adverbial clause of time:
  'As soon as, our stores' gates were open'
- <u>**'sales hunters(shoppers) rushed in'**</u>

    independent clause ↵ - complete in itself
- (they) '<u>grabbed high quality merchandise at the lowest prices</u>'

    independent clause ↵ - complete in itself
These clauses are joined together to form this complex sentence.

j) **Compound sentence** – it has three independent clauses joined

together with **or** ⟹coordinating conjunction
These are imperative sentences (equivalent to independent clauses)

3.
   a)   Do they live in France these days?
   b)   Were you burgled while you were away on holiday?
   c)   Is London the capital city of the United Kingdom?
   d)   Does your company genuinely care about staff?
   e)   Is she a good mother and hardworking employee?
   f)   Did you walk up to the top of the hill?
   g)   Are there a lot of holiday-makers from Germany
         in the Lake District in summer?
   h)   Did you suffer many hardships during the transition between
         the old political system and the new one?
   i)   Did Doris content herself with a small flat in Chelsea?
   j)   Did the customs officer find drugs in her luggage?

4.

The prime function of a performative verb is to express explicitly
the action performed by the speaker or the writer. Here are five
examples to illustrate it:

   • Today a large number of pensioners staged a protest against the
     present government's pension policies.

   • She was nominated as best dancer. (without **as** is also correct)

   • Since he was made bankrupt, he **renounced** his former partners.

   it means to break the connection because you disapprove of them

   • I forgive you for what you have said this time.

   • He confessed to the police that he was one of the suspects.

5. Here are five sentences giving negative meaning:

   • I saw **no one** going to that shop.

- She reported **nothing** stolen.

- **Nobody** saw me running away.

- There was **nowhere** for me to sit on that train.

- They could not understand this, **neither** can I.

6. **An imperative** type sentence is constructed with the base form of the verb without a subject. This is exemplified below:
   . Stop crying.
   . Enjoy yourself.

It is used for a variety of actions and feelings such as to give an order, make a request and make a slogan (advertisement). Sometimes it sounds abrupt.

On the other hand, **an exclamative** sentence(exclamative mood) is used to express surprise, shock and similar feelings or experience. For example:

. How stupid!
. What a surprise!

Chapter 14

---

1. Suggestions are within boxes.

a) The importance of language skills in a literate society can hardly be exaggerated. People are judged on how they speak, **and** nearly all academic teaching is done by means of language. so anyone who has not achieved an average standard in literacy is likely to be seen as deficient across a wide range of skills.

Use of capital letters in correct places. A comma is needed to join main clauses. Place a comma before **and**. No comma before **who** as it is introducing identifying (restrictive) clause. It is identifying the noun **anyone** in the main clause. Full stops inserted.

b) Humour is a diffuse, fuzzy sort of thing - a matter of taste and something you do not expect to find in even the most sophisticated computer, unless it has been programmed in by human beings.

> Began with a capital letter $\Rightarrow$ H. A dash is used to add additional information. A comma is essential before **unless** $\Rightarrow$ conjunction. It is introducing a relative clause - adding information that we can leave out and the sentence will still make sense. A full stop inserted. A complex sentence.

c) Unlike space, time, **as we understand**, has a direction. There is an asymmetry between the past **(fixed)** and the future **(yet to exist)**. **Time's** arrow is whatever gives time this direction.

> Capital letters used in appropriate places. The highlighted subordinate clause is separated from the main clause by two commas for the same reason as given for b) above. A couple of parentheses are used to enclose additional information. An apostrophe is added to show possession. Full stops inserted.

d) 'It's my nature to be like I am,' she said, ' I was fated to be unhappy.'

'I believe you can learn to be happy and healthy,'
I replied.

> Capital letters used as needed. Direct speech is enclosed within the single quotation marks. Here an apostrophe is used for contraction of **it is** to become **it's**. Two paragraphs – to denote change of speaker.

e) The man, Mr Joe Bloggs, was reported present when the morning roll call was taken, though officials are not sure now whether it was he, in fact, who replied 'Present'.

> Capital letters used as necessary. The phrase –Mr Joe Bloggs has commas around it. It is giving an additional information. The main clause is 'The man was reported present'. The phrase in fact has commas around it to isolate it as it only additional information.

f) Did people really speak this way?

   Of course they did, but as with many other aspects of the language,
   the words and phrases, which people use change and change again
   as the years go by.

> Question mark needed. For the sake of clarity, it is a good idea to
> have a question sentence on a separate line. There is a comma before **which**.
> It is introducing an adding clause.

g) This woman was still unemployed. She had neither money nor
   prospects. Even so, her world was relatively good for she was
   at peace with herself. She was not eating away at her health, her
   resolve and stamina with angry self-defeating thoughts. She was
   not filling her mind with negative ideas.

   Positive thinking helped her to take great strides. She could sleep
   at night. Her stomach was better and she didn't blow her top
   like she used to. In other words, she was learning how to make
   the world a great place to be with her positive attitude. Soon
   she found a new job. A well paid job, in fact. Well done!

> Punctuated text is in two suitable paragraphs. capital letters, commas, full
> stops and apostrophe are added as required. The last paragraph ended with an
> exclamation mark instead of a full stop.

h) A week later I was thrilled to see Nancy open her eyes and gaze at
   me with loving recognition. From that day her recovery was swift.
   Although she regained her usual weight, she bore one sad scar of her
   nearly fatal illness; her legs were paralyzed.

   As both armies waited for sunrise, a tempest arose and dawn was
   darkened by dust clouds, so that men could scarce behold one another. Evil were the omens. Blood dropped like rain out of heaven,
   while jackals howled impatiently, and kites and vultures screamed
   hungrily for human flesh.

> Text separated as these are two unrelated passages. All necessary punctuation
> rules applied as required.

i) It is necessary to return to those centuries, which followed after the fall of the Roman Empire, north of the Alps, in Europe.

In the first centuries AD, the Romans crumbled under the repeated onslaughts of those tribes who were part of the great and still mysterious migration westwards from the Asian steppes. In the fifth century , one of the most infamous tribal leaders, Attila,* king of Huns, made his base in the fertile plains of the middle Danube. He gave the region the name by which it is still known to most of the world – Hungary.

> * Attila (c.406-53) Hunnish King(434/53).
> His dominion extended from Rhine to the Caspian Sea.

Chambers Dictionary of World History 1994.

The text is divided into two paragraphs. The purpose of the first paragraph is to introduce what is to follow. A footnote is added together with its source. All other punctuation marks are necessary.

J) The following members have won prizes:

- Sarah Dean First Prize - £1000 (one thousand pounds)

- Robert McDonald Second Prize - £200 (two hundred pounds)

- Natasha Robinson Third Prize - £50 (fifty pounds)

Our annual membership fee, in accordance with the cost of living index, will rise to £55 (fifty-five pounds) from £50, from 1st January, next year.

Finally, Our revenue for the year just ended amount to £550, 0000.

This exercise is all about numbers. Capital letters, dashes, commas, hyphen, etc. are placed in correct places.

Glossary   **421**

****

<u>Glossary</u>

<u>A</u>

absolute adjectives – adjectives which exist in their basic form only, e.g. ⇒ wrong.

abstract nouns – nouns that are used for concepts, which have no material existence, e.g. ⇒ anger. They describe ideas or qualities instead of something physical such as a house(it is a concrete thing).

active clause – a clause in which the action or doing of something is taken by the agent (subject), e.g. ⇒ John is writing a letter.

active participle – the **-ing** form of a verb in the continuous form, used after **be**, e.g. ⇒ I am reading.

active verb – when the subject performs the action or experiences the state or condition, e.g. ⇒ I write a letter.

active voice – same as active verb. Here is another example: she has won the first prize. She ⇒ subject and performs the action of winning. See ⇒ active verb.

adding relative clause – it is separated from the main clause by two commas. It gives some additional information about the headword,
e.g. ⇒ Frank, *__who is Elina's friend__*, is working abroad
            relative clause ↵

adjective – a word that modifies/qualifies the meaning of a noun, or pronoun, e.g. ⇒ she is **kind**.

adjective phrase – a phrase which has an adjective in it,
e.g. ⇒ she is very beautiful. In this sentence:
very beautiful ⇒adjective phrase **and** the headword ⇒<u>beautiful</u>
                          adjective ↵

adjunct (adverb) – an adverb or phrase that adds meaning to the verb in a sentence or part of a sentence or clause e.g. ⇒ he screamed loudly. Here, loudly ⇒ adverb is acting as an adjunct and adds meaning to the verb - **scream**. It shows the extent to which something happened. Thus, it adds information about manner, time or place.

adverb – the most common function of an adverb is to modify the main verb in a sentence, e.g. I can do it *easily*. easily ⇒ adverb.

adverb phrase – it can be an adverb on its own e.g. ⇒smoothly. It can also be part of a phrase, which has an adverb as its headword (see ⇒headword), e.g. very abruptly ⇒ very ⇒headword.

adverbial clause – in a complex sentence, it modifies the main clause, e.g. I will talk to you when I meet you tomorrow. An adverbial clause is joined to the main clause by the conjunction ⇒ when.

adverbial element (or phrase) – a part of a sentence which gives the least compulsory information in a sentence,

e.g. ⇒ I wrote this letter <u>in a great hurry</u>.

adverbial element ↵

agent – in an active clause/sentence, the subject is doing the action. It is known as the agent, e.g. ⇒I write it. Here, agent ⇒ I. In a passive clause, an agent comes after *by*, e.g. the letter is signed by *Anne*.

agreement (or concord) – it is a rule in accordance with the verb form which is agreed with the subject and number of the subject (singular/plural), e.g. ⇒ she sings. On the other hand, e.g. ⇒ they cry.

apostrophe – a punctuation mark, e.g. ⇒ Joan's father is a phrase in which the apostrophe is placed between Joan and s to indicate the possessive case. For other usage, see punctuation.

apposition – when in a sentence or clause, two *noun phrases* come one after the other and both refer to the same thing, then phrases are in apposition, e.g. ⇒ *Mr Brown, our director*, is retiring today.

article – there are two types of articles: *a* and *an* ⇒ indefinite article and *the* ⇒ definite article.

aspect – there are two verb aspects: progressive aspect, e.g. ⇒ I am writing and perfect aspect ⇒ I have written. These two aspects can be combined together, e.g. ⇒ she has been living in the UK.

asterisk '*' – it is a star symbol used as a punctuation mark to indicate the omission of letters, the importance of a particular word , a reference or a footnote at the bottom of the text, or elsewhere.

attributive adjective – it comes before a noun or clause, e.g. ⇒ my **new** car has arrived.

auxiliary verb – a small number of verbs such as *be, will, have* are used with ordinary verbs, such as *work*. These are divided into modal and primary auxiliaries. See ⇒ modal.

B

bare infinitive – verbs without the particle *to* e.g. ⇒ talk . Bare infinitive is the base form.

base form ,(*root form* or *stem*) – verbs as listed in a dictionary, e.g. ⇒ walk.

brackets – in British English, for writing purposes, the round brackets ( ) which are known as parentheses are used. They indicate alternatives, include abbreviations or show additional information.

C

cardinal numbers – a whole number, e.g. ⇒ 1,2,3.

classifying relative clause – it describes the head noun in the main clause by its nature or type. It does not have commas around it, e.g. ⇒ she likes John *who is very intelligent*. John ⇒ head noun.

clause – it is a group of words containing a finite verb, and any other verb complement, e.g. ⇒ he went home early tonight. See ⇒ main clause and see ⇒ independent clause.

clause elements – there are five clause elements: subject, verb, object, complement and adverbial. A clause may have some or all of these elements.

clause of manner – it tells us the way something is done or someone's behaviour, e.g. I don't work **like he does**.

clause of manner↵

collective noun – a noun that refers to a group of objects, or things or people e.g. ⇒ team, committee, government.

colon ':' – a punctuation mark. It is used for different purposes.

comma ',' – like the full stop, it is a common punctuation mark. There is a tendency to use too many or too few commas despite the fact that it is well. documented and understood.

common noun – nouns that that refer to many of the same type of things, places, objects or people, e.g. country ⇒ there many countries in the world. People ⇒ there are millions of people in the world. Common nouns are divided into abstract and concrete nouns. See ⇒ proper nouns for a comparison.

comparative clause – this is used to express comparison, e.g. Anne is less interested in eating out *than her husband*. It is introduced by the subordinators *than* or *as*. It is a subordinate clause.

comparative form of adjective – for comparing two things or people, e.g. ⇒ he is older than me. old ⇒ adjective and older ⇒ comparative form (oldest ⇒superlative form).

complement – a noun or adjective phrase that follows a linking verb, e.g. ⇒ she is the *champion*. See ⇒ copula verb and **see** ⇒linking verb.

complex sentence – in a complex sentence, one clause is a main clause, with one or more subordinate clauses, e.g. ⇒ I telephoned my wife when I arrived at Heathrow Airport. Main clause ⇒ underlined.

compound sentence – a compound sentence has at least two clauses of equal status which are joined together with a coordinating conjunction, e.g. *he lives downstairs* and *I live upstairs*.

compound word – it is composed of two or more words, e.g. mother-in-law.

concessive clause – it is a subordinate clause which begins with a conjunction (although, despite, whilst, while, much as, in spite of, even though, even if). For instance: Although we get on well, I don't want to marry her.

concord - see ⇒ agreement.

concrete noun – a tangible thing that can be seen or touched is a concrete noun, e.g. ⇒ book. These are common nouns. see also ⇒ abstract noun.

conditional clause – it is constructed when you want to talk about a possible situation and the likely outcome. It usually begins with **if, e.g.** ⇒ if she comes, she will try to take over.

conjunction – a conjunction functions as either a coordinating or subordinating conjunction, and joins clauses, e.g. ⇒ when in:
I will meet you *when* you are upstairs.

coordination of phrases – it means joining together two phrases or clauses of the same status.

coordinator – a coordinator is a coordinating conjunction, e.g. ⇒ *and, but, or*. It joins clauses of the same status.

copular verb – it links the subject with a complement. The basic linking verb is 'be'. There are only a few copular verbs. These include *be, appear, become, seem.*

countable(count) noun – it has singular, and plural forms and can be preceded by a determiner such as *the, a, an, every, many, one, two, three, four*, etc. For instance: She has a cat. She has several cats.

D

dash '-' – a punctuation mark. It is used for a variety of purposes.

declarative (sentence/statement) – its order is:
subject ⇒ verb ⇒ verb complement (if any).

declarative structure – it means the structure of a declarative sentence or statement.

defining relative clause – see ⇒ identifying relative clause.

definite article – see ⇒ article.

degree (adverb of) – a word such as *very, rather, somewhat*, quite, *pretty*. It shows the extent of quality, e.g. ⇒ she is very clever. Here, very ⇒ adverb of degree.

demonstrative pronoun – it is used to refer to a particular person, or thing, e.g. ⇒ *this* is a car. Other demonstrative pronouns are *that, these* and *those*. These are also demonstrative determiners.

dependent clause – it cannot stand alone, e.g. ⇒ *when I gave him a cup of tea*, he drank it fast.

determiner – a simple word that is placed before a noun phrase, e.g. ⇒ this.

direct object – I gave students passes. In this sentence: passes ⇒ direct object because the direct effect of the verb *gave* is on passes. In the same sentence: students ⇒ indirect object because the indirect effect/ secondary effect is on students.

direct speech – the exact words of the speaker which are enclosed within the quotation marks, e.g. ⇒ ' We were aware of your financial problems,' said the chairman. It is quoted in someone's words.

dummy subject – when the word *it* or *there* is used in the subject position and does not relate to any specific thing, e.g. ⇒ **It** appears she is late again. It

is also known as an empty subject. It is used because it is needed in the subject position.

E

ellipsis – usually three dots are used to indicate that some words are left out, e.g. ⇒ get the---out of here!

embedded prepositional phrase – prepositional phrases are embedded in the noun phrase, e.g. ⇒ you spoke to Rachel about her journey. In this sentence: [Rachel about her journey] ⇒ noun phrase   and [about her journey] ⇒ prepositional phrase.

empty subject – see ⇒ dummy subject.

empty verb – *have* is the most commonly used empty verb but there are other empty verbs, e.g. ⇒ take, give, do. We use them as: *give* an example, *have* tea. In these examples, the action is indicated by the nouns *example*, and *tea*.

exclamation mark – it is a punctuation mark represented by ! e.g. Cheers! It is a terminator.

F

finite clause – He walks to work. In this clause, the verb walk is marked for tense ⇒ present tense. When in a clause the verb is marked for tense it is called a finite clause. See ⇒ non-finite clause.

finite phrase and finite verb – a finite verb or finite phrase such as *talk, went, was going, will be* are finite verbs and finite phrases. These are marked for tenses, e.g. ⇒ he is singing a song. In this clause, the finite phrase is singing and is marked for tense ⇒ present continuous.

footnote – it is a punctuation mark. It is written below the text to give further information.

formal style – it is used in official and important situations. It often indicates a distant rather than a close relationship. It is very correct in both writing and speech.

fraction – a number which is not a whole number, e.g. ⇒ half, two-thirds, four fifths.

full stop – it is the most commonly used punctuation mark. In the USA it is called a period.

future (tense) – it is a state or action that will take place in the future, e.g. ⇒ I will come. It is formed as: auxiliary verb (will or shall) + bare infinitive verb.

future continuous(progressive)– it expresses a state or action that will continue in the future. It is constructed as ⇒ shall/will + participle –ing form, e.g.⇒ *I will be thinking of you*.

future perfect – it refers to our thinking in the future and then looking back when something will be completed at a specific point in the future, e.g. By next Friday, I will have met him in Paris. It is constructed as:
will/shall + have + past participle.

future perfect progressive – it is as future perfect, but the action. or state of something continues in the future, e.g. Next month, you will have been studying at the university one year. It is constructed as:
will/shall + have been + participle –ing form.

G

gender – in English the gender classification is: feminine ⇒ woman, masculine ⇒ man, and neuter ⇒ artefacts/things such as radio.

genitive case – it shows possession . It is a noun in its possessive form, e.g. John's car.

gerund – When a participle verb formed with *-ing* is used in a clause or a sentence as a noun, it is known as a gerund, e.g. *Dancing* is her favourite hobby. In this sentence, dancing is a gerund.

grammar – it has rules for combining words together for a meaningful communication in spoken and written language.

H

headword – it is a main noun or pronoun in a phrase, clause or sentence. For instance: a **bundle** of files. a paperback **book**. Headwords are highlighted.

hyphen '– ' – it is a punctuation mark. It is used either to join two words together or to split the word at the end of a line of print.

I

identifying relative clause – its purpose is to identify the earlier noun in the main clause, e.g. 'The young man **who is smartly dressed** is my son.'

idiom or idiomatic expression – it is a group of words. Its meaning is different from the meaning of individual words forming the idiomatic expression.

imperative mood – it is a command and an order. It can also be a polite order, e.g. *forgive me*. **go away. please take a seat.** There is no subject and the verb is in the base form.

indefinite article – see ⇒ article.

indefinite pronoun – a word which does not refer to any particular person or thing, e.g. ⇒all.

independent clause – see ⇒ main clause.

indicative mood – when we make a statement, ask a question or state a fact, e.g. ⇒ I'm here. See ⇒ moods.

indirect object – see ⇒ direct object.

indirect speech – it is not in the words of the speaker but its meaning is reported in our own words, e.g. I said she told me about her love affairs.

infinitive – it is the base form of the verb. e.g. ⇒ **go**. See ⇒ base form and bare infinitive (without the participle to-) as shown in a dictionary.

infinitive clause – it has an infinitive verb, e.g. We **walk** every evening. I wanted **to go**.   bare infinitive ↵
     to-infinitive ↵

infinitive particle – see ⇒ particle.

inflection – it means changing the ending or spelling of a word in accordance with its grammatical function, e.g. ⇒ She studies French.

The verb **'study'** is inflected to match the present tense of its subject.

informal style – the use of the English language in social circumstances, e.g. both - spoken and written communication between relatives and friends.

ing- form – when **-ing** is added to a verb and used as a participle, or gerund e.g. write⇒writing.

interjections – a minor class of word. Used for expressing feelings, e.g. ⇒ *Gosh!*

interrogative pronoun – what and which are used with nouns to ask questions, e.g. ⇒*Which* book was it?

intransitive verb – it does not take an object or complement, and it can stand alone, e.g. ⇒ I talk.

inversion – it occurs when the regular word order is changed to form a question, e.g. ⇒ Has she finished that job? In this sentence: the subject *she* has changed (inverted) place with the auxiliary verb *has*.

irregular verbs– they do not follow the pattern of adding '-ed' to form the past tense, e.g. ⇒ begin: its irregular past tense ⇒ began.

L

linking verb – see ⇒ copular verb. Linking and copular both mean the same.

M

mass noun – it is an uncountable noun. It refers to things such grass, hair, sugar, medicines. Sometimes it can be used as a countable noun, e.g. ⇒ two sugars. one hair. It is used for quantities.

main clause – any clause which can stand alone is a main clause, e.g. ⇒ I walk. It stands alone as a meaningful clause or a short sentence.

main verb – it is the finite verb in the main clause, e.g. ⇒ When the doorbell rang, I *opened* the door.

manner – it is the adverb of manner. It tells us *how* something happened, e.g. ⇒ she cried *loudly*.

modal (auxiliary verb) – these are auxiliary verbs, e.g. ⇒ can, could, may, might, etc.

modify (modifier) – it means giving further information about a word or phrase, e.g. It is a *tall* tree. 'tall' modifier is an adjective, but functioning as a modifier. It gives further information about ⇒**tree**.

moods – see ⇒ indicative, imperative and subjunctive entries.

N

negative – a phrase, clause or sentence which has a word meaning 'no', 'not' is a negative phrase, clause or sentence.. You can have a negative question as well. For instance: Didn't you shout at her? ⇐ negative interrogative sentence. I never went to Paris. ⇐ negative declarative sentence.

Glossary **431**

****

negative word – a word like never, nothing and nowhere is a negative word, e.g. ⇒ I can see nothing wrong with her idea. ⇐ negative meaning intended by the word ⇒ **nothing**.

non-finite clause – it has a to-infinitive form verb, ⇒ We asked them.

to return our camera.

noun – it is a name given to a person, place, object, etc., e.g. ⇒ John, London, book ....

noun (nominal) clause – it can act as the subject, object or the complement of the main clause, e.g. ⇒ He thought *that she was not at home*. Here, the noun clause is acting as an object.

noun phrase – it has a noun or pronoun as its headword, e.g. ⇒ I wanted John *as our leader*.

number – in grammar, the distinction between singular and plural is expressed as number, e.g. cap ⇒ singular noun and two caps(plural) number of the same object ⇒ cap.

O

object – it comes after the verb in a clause. For example:
this is Andrew. object ⇒ Andrew.

object complement – it comes after the verb in a clause, e.g. ⇒ we all paid her **our** respects.

object predicate – see ⇒ object complement.

ordinal numeral – it refers to the position of something in a series, e.g. ⇒ he was in *third* place. Some other examples: fourth, fifth, , hundredth, etc.

ordinary verb – there are thousands of ordinary verbs, such as ⇒ go, run, jump, write, etc. Auxiliary verbs are not included in ordinary verbs. See auxiliary and modal verbs.

participle – it is a non-finite verb form. It ends either with *–ing* or *-ed*.
See ⇒ present and past participle.

****

P

participle clause – it has a participle verb form in it, e.g.⇒ *Coming* to London, we were late.

particle – it is the word *to* with the base form of the verb, e.g. ⇒ to run.

particles class – it is a minor word class, e.g. ⇒ she *fell off* her bicycle on to the road.

passive – in a passive clause/sentence something is done to the subject (agent), e.g. ⇒ the report *is being typed*.

passive verb (or passive voice) – when the subject is affected by the action. The passive voice involves the use of the **auxiliary verb.** For instance, the house **is** occupied. Here is ⇒ auxiliary verb.

past continuous/progressive – it expresses what was happening at some point in time in the past, e.g. ⇒ I *was working* in London.

past participle form – Regular verbs: it ends in –**ed**. Irregular verbs: it ends in some other ways. e.g. ⇒eaten, drunk, etc. In the perfect it comes after 'have, e.g. I have *finished* it.

past perfect – it is formed with 'had' and a past participle e.g. ⇒ she *had received* my letter.

past perfect continuous/progressive – it is formed with 'had been' and an active participle, e.g. ⇒ We *had been dancing* all night. Here, *dancing* ⇒ active participle.

past simple – it is the past tense, e.g. ⇒ they *returned* home. It tells what happened or existed at a particular time (then) before the present time (now).

perfect – it expresses an action completed by the present, or a particular point in the past or future. It is constructed with 'have' with the past participle of the main verb, e.g. ⇒ *I have left* (present perfect), *I had left* (past perfect), and *I will have left* (perfect future).

perfect aspect –it is the underlined in: She *has been living* in Germany. See ⇒ aspect.

performative verb – it means the action it performs, e.g. ⇒ *I accept*. The action ⇒ accept.

person (singular and plural) – first person ⇒ **I, we**. Second person ⇒ **you**. Third person ⇒*he, she, it, they*.

personal pronoun – I, you, he, she, etc.

phrasal verb – it is a verb combined with an adverb or a preposition, e.g. ⇒ fall off, break down, etc.

phrase – a word or some words, e.g. ⇒ rubbish, a white elephant. There are five types of phrases: verb phrase, noun phrase, adjective phrase, adverb phrase, and prepositional phrase.

plural – it means more than one, e.g. ⇒ a song is the singular form but songs ⇒ the plural form of the noun.

possessive determiner – it is a possessive pronoun, when it replaces a noun, e.g. ⇒ this is *my* car.

possessive pronoun – mine, yours, ours, etc. This coat is mine. Possessive pronoun ⇒*mine*

postmodifier(postmodification) – it comes after the head noun in phrases, e.g. It is a nice **car** fitted with audio equipment.
     postmodification ↲⇒ head noun

predicate – in a clause, it is the verb element and any other elements that follow the verb, e.g. ⇒ England is the largest part of the UK. The underlined part is the predicate.

prefix – many words can be created by adding the beginning to a word, e.g. ⇒ *un*necessary. It is *un + necessary*. See ⇒ suffix.

premodifier(premodification) – an adjective (sometimes an adverb) that comes before a head noun is a premodifier. There can be several premodifiers, e.g. ⇒a **tiny shining** star. star ⇒ head noun/head word.

preposition – a class of word, e.g. ⇒ over, since, for. Also more than one word, e.g. ⇒ instead of.

prepositional idioms – it is the preposition used with an idiom, e.g. ⇒ *at heart*.

prepositional phrase – it is the preposition plus a noun or an adverb e.g. ⇒ in our school, over there.

prepositions of relationships – express a variety of relationships. Most common are time and place.

present continuous/progressive – it is the present tense that shows the action is continuous.

present participle form – it is the part of the verb which ends in *–ing*, e.g. ⇒ missing, crossing, etc.

present perfect – it indicates that the action or state was complete in the near past up to the present time, e.g. ⇒ The parcel has arrived.

present perfect progressive – an action or state in the past which continues up-to the present time, e.g. ⇒ it has been raining. It is formed as: have/has + been + active participle.

present simple – it is the present tense, e.g. ⇒ I work. It expresses a current action or state.

pronoun – a word used instead of a noun or noun phrase, e.g. ⇒ *You* are kind.

Q

Qualifier (s) – postmodifier and premodifier are qualifiers.A qualifier can come before or after a head word, e.g. ⇒ He has a corner shop near here. corner ⇒ premodifier and near here ⇒ postmodifier element.

qualify – see ⇒ modify.

question – it is a sentence for asking a question, e.g. ⇒ What's wrong with you?

Question tag – a short question at the end of a statement, e.g. ⇒ She loves him, doesn't she?

question word – these are:

    what, when, where, who, whom, which, how, whose, why.

R

reciprocal pronoun – it is used to express mutual relationships, e.g. ⇒ they love *each other*. There are only two reciprocal pronouns each other and one another.

reflexive pronoun – it refers to the subject, e.g. ⇒ They can do it *themselves*. I do it *myself*.

regular verbs – they change their forms in the past by following a set pattern of *–ed ending*, e.g. ⇒ verb 'help' its regular past tense form ⇒ 'helped'.

relative adverb – where, when and why are used in relative clauses as relative adverbs, e.g. ⇒ the house *where* I was born.

relative clause – it modifies a noun, e.g. ⇒ the salesman *who talked too much*.

relative pronoun – it links a subordinate clause to a main clause, e.g. ⇒ it is not me *who* hit first.

S

s-form of the verb – it is the inflected form of the bare infinitive. It is formed with either *s*, or *es* added, e.g. ⇒ he *runs*. Here *s* is added.

She *cries*. Here, cry is inflected by *es*.

sentence – a sentence is the largest syntactic unit which has at least one clause.

simple tense – it is without the auxiliary verb, e.g. ⇒ I go.

singular form – it means one thing only, e.g. ⇒ noun 'man' refers to only one person/man.

slang style – it is an informal way of speaking used between a specific group of people, e.g. ⇒ criminals.

split infinitive – the placing of a word or words between the *to* and the *verb* creates a split infinitive.

standard English – a form of the English language that is nationally used. Speakers of other languages learn standard English. For instance, broadcasting services use standard English.

statement – it is a declarative sentence which gives information. It is not a question.

structure - for our purpose, it means the way some words are arranged in accordance with the rules of grammar, e.g. ⇒ I went there.

style – it is a distinct way of doing something, e.g. writing or speaking in the language context. There are many styles. For instance, various styles are imposed on the use of idiomatic expressions.

subject –in a sentence, it comes before the verb, e.g. ⇒ he writes a letter. he ⇒subject/agent.

subject complement – in a clause/sentence it comes after a linking verb. e.g. ⇒she appears *calm*.

subject element – it precedes the verb in a clause. It is the agent of an active clause, e.g. ⇒ I'm writing this text. Here, I'm ⇒ **subject** or subject element. It is also the agent of this active clause.

subject position – it is the first element in a clause, e.g. ⇒ she loves you. subject ⇒ begins the clause.

subject predicate – see ⇒ subject complement

subjective pronoun – *I, you* (both singular and plural) , *he, she, it, they* and *we*. They occur in the subject position in a clause.

subjunctive mood – it indicates possibility, uncertainty, wish, etc., e.g. ⇒ she wanted a baby.

subordinate clause – it supports the main clause. See ⇒dependent clause

subordinator – in a complex sentence clauses are of unequal status. We use a subordinator (**when** …) to join two clauses of unequal status.

suffix – words can be created by adding **an ending** to a word,
e.g. ⇒ soft + *ly* = *softly*.

superlative – the form of an adjective for comparing three or more things,
e.g. ⇒ highest, tallest (adjectives).

T

taboo style – use of swear words.

tense – it is a form of the verb which indicates when the action of the verb
occurs, or the state affected by the verb, e.g.

    . I talk ⇒ present tense

    . she cried ⇒ past tense

    . We will dance tonight. ⇒ future tense
It indicates a particular period of time or a point in time.

to-infinitive – it is a verb form which is preceded by 'to', e.g. to run, to sign,
to smile.

to-infinitive clause – see ⇒ infinitive clause.

transitive verb – it cannot stand alone and it is followed by an object,
e.g. ⇒ she *rang* the <u>bell</u>.
         object ↵

U

uncountable noun – it has only one verb form. Some uncountable
nouns are only plural such as jeans, e.g. ⇒ **a pair of jeans**. On the
other hand, some uncountable nouns such as **space** are only singular,
e.g. ⇒ There **wasn't much space** in the room. When an uncountable
noun is the subject, the verb is singular, e.g. ⇒ Some *money is* in Euro
currency.

unclassified style – no restriction is imposed on the use of some idiomatic expressions.

V

verb – doing, action/state word. It is the most important part of speech, e.g. ⇒ she *loves* her children. Without the word *loves* which is a verb, the sentence will not make any sense.

verb aspect – see ⇒ aspect.

verb element – it is the focal point of a clause, e.g. ⇒ she <u>has completed</u> her assignment. In this sentence, the underlined element is the verb.

verb phrase – it is an ordinary verb, e.g. ⇒ run, have gone, etc. it may also have an auxiliary verb and other words, e.g. ⇒ will go, had gone away.

verbals – these are derived from verbs but are <u>not</u> used as verbs, e.g. ⇒ it was a *horrifying* scene.

voice – see ⇒ active verb (voice) and passive verb (voice).

vocabulary – it consists of words, e.g. all words in the English language.

W

wh-question – it is the question which begins with a question word or wh-word, e.g. ⇒what, where., etc. See⇒wh-word.

wh-word – there are nine such words: how, what, when, where, why, which, who, whom, whose.

word class – it is another name for parts of speech, e.g. ⇒ noun, adjective, etc.

XYZ

'yes/no' question – a question which can lead to a simple answer whether 'yes' or 'no', e.g. Were you present in the class at that time?

+---+
| |
| **<u>Addendum</u>** |
| |
| **<u>Word Formation</u>** |
| |
+---+

- Word formation is an important learning activity. It enables us to
  spell words correctly. Thousands of words have a base form, e.g.
  chair, book, etc. These base forms are changed to make other
  words. For instance:

  - book ⇒singular noun – base form ⇒ **<u>books</u>** ⇒plural noun

  a new word formed by adding *s* to the base form ↵

  - sad ⇒ adjective – base form ⇒ **<u>sadly</u>** ⇒ adverb

  a new word formed by adding *ly* to the base form ↵

  - direct ⇒ verb – base form ⇒ **<u>misdirect</u>** ⇒ adverb

  a new word formed by adding *mis* to the base form ↵

These examples illustrate that you can change the base form of a word by
adding something to the beginning or the end of a word to convert it into a
new word.

Some people research into word formation and have developed specific
strategies and terminology for this work. The term word formation to such
experts is an umbrella term. They apply different methods of deriving, compound words, complex words and multi-word verbs. Multi-word verbs are
mainly idiomatic or phrasal verbs whose overall meaning is different from
the meaning of the individual words they contain. For instance, **<u>drop off</u>** is a
multi-word. It is used in idiomatic expressions such as:

. Jane **dropped off** during the lecture.

This sentence has a phrasal verb (multi-word) which consists of two
individual words (verb + preposition). It means fall into a light sleep.

A multi-word may consists of a verb plus a preposition or a verb plus an adverb. It may also be a combination of: verb +adverb + preposition. In Chapter 4 (page 91), you can find some phrasal verbs which show you these combinations of multi-word formation.

They study how words can be broken down into smaller meaningful units, the origin of words, import of words into the language and some other aspects such as the spelling of words. It is all part of linguistic study.

Word formation has been introduced when the idea of inflection, prefixes, suffixes, converting adjectives to adverbs, etc. is discussed in this book. The book contains many examples of word formation. In this limited space, suffice to say that the bulk of word formation is by the **process of affixation**. This process involves prefixes and suffixes, that is fixing something in front of a word or at the end of a word. There are many recognisable forms of both prefixes and suffixes in modern English. Here are a few examples of each type of affix.

Prefixes	**word formed**	**Suffixes**	**word formed**
after-	**after**noon	-able	advis**able**
ana-	**ana**logy	-age	marri**age**
anti-	**anti**pathy	-ant	pregn**ant**
auto-	**auto**bigrophy	-craft	handi**craft**
bio-	**bio**cycle	-ee	divorc**ee**
counter-	**counter**attack	-en	gold**en**
ex-	**ex**-wife	-friendly	user-**friendly**
hand-	**hand**some	-ish	pol**ish**
il-	**il**legal	-ly	year**ly**
off-	**off**spring	-ware	hard**ware**

There are certain rules of spelling which apply to the process of affixation. For instance, if the suffix begins with a vowel, the last consonant in the base word is doubled, e.g., regret $\Rightarrow$ regret**t**able. The other methods of word formation include **acronyms**. It is not the oldest method of word formation. Nevertheless, it is used to form new words by using the first letters of the words that make up the name of something. For example:

NATO $\Rightarrow$ **N**orth **A**tlantic **T**reaty **O**rganisation.

If you are fascinated by word formation techniques: **go for it**.

a phrasal word – multi-word formation↵

****

Index

****

444 **Index**

****

Index

****

****

R

rather --- than, 209
reciprocal pronouns, 435,
see pronouns
recognisable adjective/word endings,
133
reflexive pronouns, 45-6,379
reflexive verbs, 45
regular verbs ,*see* verbs
relative adverb, 435
relative clause, 435, *see* clauses
relative pronoun, 435 *see* pronoun
reported speech, 103-4,364
rule, 1

S

s-form of the verb, 435
s-inflection, 97, *see* also s-form
of the verb
semicolon, 318,366-8
sentence, 435
sentences,
    active, 284,288-91
    complex, 284
    compound, 284, 308-12
    declarative, 284, 291-3
    exclamative, 284, 305-6
    imperative, 284 , 302-4
    interrogative, 284,295-302
    negative, 284-8
    passive, 284,288-91
    positive, 284 -7
    simple, 284, 306-8,435
several, 51, 189, 195.
shall, 67,73,106
she, 44
should, 67,73
since, 206,210,308-12
singular form, 435, *see* noun(s)
slash, 318,368-9
so, 199,201-2,206
so that, 205-6,208,210
some, 195

somebody, 51
someone, 51
something, 51
split infinitive(s), 86
split infinitive, 86- 88 ,436
standard English, 1,00436
statement, 436 *see* declarative
strong verbs, 60
subject, 40,436
subject complement, 252,436
subject element, 241,436
subject/predicate/ predicative, 253,
436
subjective pronoun, 436, *see*
pronouns
structure, 436
subjunctive mood, 63,436
subordinate clause(s,) 242, 260-80,
436
subordinator or
(subordination conjunction), 436
suffix(es), 129,358, 437, 440
superlative, 437
    adjectives, 127
    adverbs, 161-2

T

tag questions, 68-9,341,360,434
tangible, 14
'tempus', 96
tense(s), 95-118, 437 see also
individual entries
    active voice table, 115
     passive- table, 389
than, 206
that, 47,49, 50, 190-1, 195
the, 34, 180-4
their, 44, 188, 195
these, 49-51, 190-1, 195
those, 49, 51, 190-1, 195
this, 49-51,190,195
till, 206
to-infinitive, 57,85, 92,384, 437
to-infinitive maker (to), 57

448   **Index**

****